By the hard work of others, we *u. ↗ ↝u*
to the most beautiful things that have been dragged
out of darkness and into the light.
Everyone is invited to experience the light
of every age and every people.
So, let us walk hand in hand with those from every age.
Let us turn from this brief and transient time
and offer our minds and hearts to the past,
which is long and eternal.

—Seneca, *On the Shortness of Life*

THE CLASSICS CAVE
Sugar Land

THE CLASSICS CAVE
the earliest light for a brighter life
www.theclassicscave.com

ARE YOU looking for the best books ever? Or new ways to read and benefit from them? To practice what you've read? To learn and grow a little? Let the Cave be your guide!

THE CLASSICS CAVE (the Cave) is an educational* organization centered on the classics of Greek and Roman antiquity, with an emphasis on the best of ancient Greek literature.

OUR MISSION is to shine the light of the past into the present for a brighter life today.

OUR GOAL is practice—the application of ancient wisdom and ways to our contemporary lives.

WE publish books, develop and provide online content, organize and do outreach, and produce and distribute a variety of print and other media intended to entertain and educate, inspire, encourage, and cultivate.

VISIT THE CAVE online (www.theclassicscave.com) to support our mission and to access a growing catalog of engaging books and other beneficial content designed for individuals, educators, groups, and all others interested in benefiting from ancient literature.

SUPPORT THE CAVE by telling others about our work and by leaving a positive review online. You may also wish to buy a book or join The BAGL Club or the AAGS (to adopt an ancient Greek). Or sponsor the BAGL. Or partner with us by giving a donation. Thanks!

With GRATITUDE, we thank our readers, members, sponsors, donors, and all participants in Cave content—you who make the work and outreach of the Cave possible. Without you, the Cave would not exist!

*For the Cave, **education** is that happy transition from ignorance to knowledge; from foolishness to wisdom; and from mediocrity or vice to excellence or virtue, culminating in good habits and character.

In praise of Homer & his poetry

"I rank Homer among the oldest and wisest of the poets."
—Aeschines *Against Timarchus*

"Homer, as always and everywhere, should be first, like a god."
—Charles-Augustin Sainte-Beuve, *What is a Classic?*

"The verses of Homer have continued twenty-five hundred years, or more, without the loss of a syllable or letter, during which the infinite palaces, temples, castles, cities have been decayed and demolished."
—Francis Bacon, *The Advancement of Learning*

"Like the sun, which furnishes with its light the close courts . . . of London, while himself unseen by their inhabitants, Homer has supplied with the illumination of his ideas millions of minds that were never brought into direct contact with his work, and even millions more, that have hardly been aware of his existence. . . . And this universality is his alone."
—William E. Gladstone, *Studies on Homer and the Homeric Age*

"I also wish to recommend the epic poetry of Homer to you. In your fathers' estimation he was an excellent poet of such worth that [the Athenians] passed a law that every four years at the Panathenaea he alone of all the other poets should have his works recited."
—Lycurgus, *Against Leocrates*

"When young, any composition pleases which unites a little sense, some imagination, and some rhythm, in doses however small. But as we advance in life these things fall off one by one, and I suspect that we are left at last with only Homer and Virgil, and perhaps with Homer alone."—Thomas Jefferson, *Thoughts on English Prosody*

"Homer may seem divinely inspired. . . . He was the very best poet in the serious style, since he alone made his representations not only good but also dramatic."—Aristotle, *Poetics*

"As Achilles is among warriors, so Homer is beyond all comparison among poets. . . . He has given us a model and an inspiration for every branch of eloquence. Most will admit that no one has ever surpassed him in the sublimity with which he endows great themes or the propriety with which he handles the small. He is at once luxuriant and concise, sprightly and serious, remarkable at once for his fulness and his brevity, and supreme not only for poetic but for oratorical power as well." —Quintilian, *Institutes*

"In the age which preceded or introduced the first formations of Human Society . . . we may dimly discern an almost mythical personage, who . . . may be called the first Apostle of Civilization. . . . He was to do such great things, and to live in the mouths of a hundred generations and a thousand tribes. . . . At length an Athenian Prince took upon him the task of gathering together the scattered fragments of a genius which had not aspired to immortality, of reducing them to writing, and of fitting them to be the text-book of ancient education. Henceforth, [Homer] . . . was submitted . . . to a sort of literary canonization, and was invested with the office of forming the young mind of Greece to noble thoughts and bold deeds. To be read in Homer soon became the education of a gentleman."
                    —John Henry Newman, *The Idea of a University*

"When Aristodemus was asked who he admired for wisdom, he told Socrates: 'In epic poetry Homer comes first.'" —Xenophon, *Memorabilia*

"[They say that] Homer has been the educator of Greece, and that for the education and government of humans, we should take him up and learn from him, and that we should build up our entire lives with the assistance of this poet." —Socrates in Plato's *Republic*

"Where did godlike Homer obtain honor and glory if not from useful teaching in tactics, virtues, and the arming of men?"
                    —Aristophanes, *Frogs*

"Hesiod and Homer . . . are the ones who taught the Greeks the

descent of the gods, and gave the gods their names, and determined their spheres and functions, and described their outward forms."
—Herodotus, *Histories*

"I have heard a man say who is skillful at closely examining the mind and meaning of a poet, all Homer's poetry is a commendation of virtue. . . . Homer practically shouts it aloud in these passages, saying, 'You must care for virtue, men . . .'"
—Basil the Great, *How to Benefit from Reading Greek Literature*

"In his *Miscellaneous History*, Favorinus says that Anaxagoras was the first to maintain that Homer in his poems treats of virtue and justice."
—Diogenes Laertius, *Lives and Opinions of Eminent Philosophers*

"[Homer] teaches more clearly, and better than Chrysippus and Crantor, what is honorable, what is shameful, what is profitable, and what is not so. . . . Excellent Homer . . . animated the manly mind to martial achievements with [his] verses."
—Horace, *Epistle* and *The Art of Poetry*

"Everything Homer wrote is both beneficial and useful, [so] it would be a vast undertaking to go through everything he has said about virtue and vice. . . . Both [Homer and Socrates] spoke about the same things . . . human virtue and vice, and things done poorly, and things done well, and truth and deceit, and how many have only opinions while the wise have true knowledge. . . . Homer is a marvelous and truly divine herald of virtue."
—Dio Chrysostom, *Discourses*

"The grammarians describe . . . the rules of poetry out of the poems of Homer." —Thomas Hobbes, *Leviathan*

"Homer's book is a delightful treasure. All that he has touched has turned to gold. . . . Everywhere he entertains and never grows tired. A happy warmth animates his speeches. . . . Love his writings with a sincere love." —Nicholas Boileau-Despreaux, *The Art of Poetry*

"To one only . . . has it been given to draw characters, by the strength of his own individual hand, in lines of such force and vigor, that they have become . . . the common inheritance of civilized man. That one is Homer. . . . We may . . . find an admirable school of polity . . . in the writings of Homer. . . . There is an inner Homeric world, . . . a world of religion and ethics, of civil policy, of history and ethnology, of manners and arts."
—William E. Gladstone, *Studies on Homer and the Homeric Age*

"This is the age of Homer, the golden age of poetry. Poetry has now attained its perfection: it has attained the point which it cannot pass."
—Thomas Love Peacock, *The Four Ages of Poetry*

"[May] Homer's works be your study and delight. Read them by day, and meditate [on them] by night."
—Alexander Pope, *An Essay on Criticism*

"Wisdom among the gentiles began with the Muse defined by Homer in a golden passage of the *Odyssey* . . . It is Homer's privilege to be, of all the sublime, that is, the heroic poets, the first in the order of merit as well as in that of age."
—Giambattista Vico, *The New Science*

"Homer surpassed all the poets whom he encountered, each in his own area of expertise." —Philostratus, *On Heroes*

"Homer was the most ancient and greatest of all poets."
—Diodorus Siculus, *Library*

"We're going to translate [for] you part of a Greek novel, . . . the best novel that was ever written, Cyril, The *Odyssey* [of Homer]."
—Julian, in *Julian Home* by Frederic W. Farrar

"Homer himself is eternally interesting. . . . The epic form . . . has attained, in the poems of Homer, an unmatched, an immortal success."
—Matthew Arnold, *On the Modern Element in Literature*

THE BEST OF
HOMER'S *ILIAD*

THE BEST OF
HOMER'S *ILIAD*

The Best Parts in Translation
with
a Narrative Summary of the Rest

selected, introduced, and edited by
The Classics Cave

CAVE BEST OF SERIES
the best of the classics for today

THE CLASSICS CAVE
Sugar Land

The Best of Homer's *Iliad*:
The Best Parts in Translation with a Narrative Summary of the Rest

ISBN 978-1-943915-00-2

Published in the United States by
The Classics Cave
P.O. Box 19038
Sugar Land, TX 77496
contact@theclassicscave.com
www.theclassicscave.com

The Classics Cave (the Cave) is an educational organization centered on the classics of Greek and Roman antiquity, with an emphasis on the best of ancient Greek literature. Our mission is to shine the light of the past into the present for a brighter life today. Our goal is practice—the application of ancient wisdom and ways to our contemporary lives. We publish books, develop and provide online content, organize and do outreach, and produce and distribute a variety of print and other media intended to entertain and educate, inspire, encourage, and cultivate.

   Visit the Cave online (www.theclassicscave.com) to support our mission and to access a growing catalog of engaging books and other beneficial content designed for individuals, educators, groups, and all others interested in benefiting from ancient literature.

For the one entering this great work . . .
Pause for a moment before its door.

Such is the holy gift the Muses give to human beings.
—Hesiod, *Theogony*

CONTENTS

POINTS OF WISDOM & WAYS OF PRACTICE

OTHER MATTERS OF INTEREST
RELATED TO HOMER'S *ILIAD*

CAVE BEST OF SERIES
INTRODUCTION
the best of the classics for today

H AVE YOU EVER considered how many excellent works of ancient Greek and Latin literature there are to read? Think of all the significant works of poetry and prose—of all the epics, tragedies, comedies, histories, philosophies, orations, biographies, and more!

The problem, of course, is in the approach. How should you read them all? It is The Classics Cave's goal to offer a possible solution— and so the Cave Best of Series, which presents the best of an author, title, or group of authors.

Take the author, title, or group you have in hand. Of the available versions of the work, the Cave Best of Series version is unique for a few reasons. One, it is much shorter than most renditions of the work—oftentimes the number of pages totals anywhere from one-third to one-half of other versions.* Consequently, if you are pressed for time or do not know how many hours you would like to invest in reading the work, then the Cave Best of Series version may be for you.

That is not to say you will not get the whole work—the whole story or discourse or whatever the work centers on. Rather, you will get it in two forms—another unique feature of the Cave Best of Series presentation of a work. Whereas most versions offer either the whole or parts of a work (without any significant explanation of what happens in between each part), the Cave Best of Series version gives you the best or most significant parts in translation, along with a narrative summary of the rest that will tell you exactly what is going on in between. This means you will get the full content, feel, and experience of the work without missing out on anything essential.

And that's important. Unlike study guide versions that offer summary outlines alone, you will have extensive passages and narrative summaries of the whole work that will allow you to judge for yourself what is happening, what characters are central, what themes are significant, what the arguments are and whether they succeed or not, and the like—all depending on the work itself.

This is what the Cave Best of Series offers: the whole work in translated and narrative summary form, making for a relatively quick read that will let you come to terms with the work by yourself.

Not only that but there is also an information-packed introduction that is meant to draw the reader into and answer the most significant questions about the author and the work. Why should we care about *this* author and *this* work? What are the essential facts we should know? What are the work's most important ideas and themes? There is always a full exploration of these points that references the work itself as well as any pertinent scholarship.

Toward the end, there is a section presenting a "Plan of Life" (or something similar), "Points of Wisdom," and "Ways of Practice" related to the author. The latter "Ways" consist of workbook or journal-like prompts and exercises intended to motivate the reader to feel, think, and act in beneficial ways according to the author's "Points of Wisdom" (just as ancient readers or auditors would).

Finally, there is a unique section called, "Other Matters of Interest Related to [the Author]." It offers additional information about the author, whether a summary of the work, a cast of characters found therein, maps, a glossary of relevant Greek terms, suggestions for further reading, and so on.

In the end, when you read the work as presented in the Cave Best of Series, you will be entertained, educated, and, we at The Classics Cave hope, motivated to practice—to act in an intentional, specific manner toward a better life. With this in mind, welcome to the . . .

Cave Best of Series
the best of the classics for today

---

* Even so, whole, or mostly whole, works are sometimes included in the Cave Best of Series if the work is particularly short.

INTRODUCTION

[They say that] *Homer has been the educator of Greece, and that for the education and government of humans, we should take him up and learn from him, and that we should build up our entire lives with the assistance of this poet.* —Socrates, reporting the view of "Homer enthusiasts"

L ET'S FACE IT. Homer has fallen on hard times. Very few read the *Iliad* or the *Odyssey* anymore. When most people hear the name Homer, they think of Homer Simpson—the same yellow cartoon character that invades the screen upon doing a simple image search for "Homer." For the online Urban Dictionary, *this* Homer is synonymous with an "American Bonehead." *D'oh.*

Others may recall the nineteenth century American painter Winslow Homer, who is famous for his landscapes. It's possible diehard baseball fans will mistake the word for a homerun. *There it goes . . . it's flying . . . a homer over the right field fence.* A small number may remember their childhood hometown of Homer, New York, named after the poet. Others may have been to Homer, Alaska, christened for the late nineteenth century gold seeker Homer Pennock. It's now the halibut fishing capital of the world, and, according to the city's website, it is "quickly becoming known as the Eco and Adventure tourism capital of Alaska."

But Homer, the ancient poet of the *Iliad* and the *Odyssey*?

Sure, most have heard of (or even read about) Odysseus' renowned adventures, including the man-eating Cyclops and the stunningly beautiful but deceptive Sirens. Or of Helen's legendary beauty. Or of the Trojan Horse that brought down a whole city. Or of the broader Trojan War—thanks to Brad Pitt in Wolfgang Petersen's epic film *Troy*, or the far more recent Netflix-BBC version, *Troy: Fall of a City*. But fewer and fewer people know the full story of the *Iliad* and the *Odyssey*, let alone anything about Homer.

It is the goal of The Classics Cave's rendition of Homer's *Iliad* to change that. If only a little. And if only beginning with *you.*

Not only is Homer exciting literature but there's so much to con-
sider while reading his poems. There's epic anger and longing love.
There's suffering as thick as mud and lust as liquid as Homer's
ubiquitous wine. There's everything that makes us human and eve-
rything that matters most to us. Most of all, there's the mad quest
for happiness, for the good and noble life. But more on that in a
moment (see The Big Themes and Ideas of the *Iliad*). First—

WHY SHOULD WE CARE ABOUT HOMER?

Go back a few thousand years and Homer was the best thing on
television, the hottest new album, or the summer blockbuster. The
great Cambridge classics scholar Moses Finley once claimed that "if
a Greek owned any books—that is, papyrus rolls—he was almost
as likely to own the *Iliad* and the *Odyssey* as anything from the rest
of Greek literature."[1] Homer was the thing to have, the thing to
know about, and the thing to love.

The first reason we should care about Homer, then, is because
millions of others deeply cared about him for well over a thousand
years.

Everyone who was anyone in ancient Greece name-dropped
Homer in their own works. To give a handful, there was the epini-
cian poet Pindar; the earliest historians Herodotus, Thucydides,
and Xenophon; the encyclopedic philosopher Aristotle; and the or-
ators Isocrates, Aeschines, and Demosthenes. Plato, perhaps Eu-
rope's greatest philosopher of all, dropped his name the most,
though, citing Homer over fifty times in his dialogues and letters.
Later Greek authors, such as the geographer Strabo, the essayist
and biographer Plutarch, and the Stoic philosopher Epictetus, did
the same.

Although we don't literally see Homer's name in other Greek lit-
erature, we may nevertheless easily spot his spirit and influence.
Take the Spartan Tyrtaeus' seventh century BC notions of courage; or
Sappho of Mytilene's conception of great poetry early in the next cen-
tury (she, by the way, positively compared herself to Homer); or Si-
monides' pessimism regarding the flux of life late in the same

century; or the tragic content of Aeschylus, Sophocles, and Euripides during what has been called the Golden Age of Athens in the fifth century BC. A few anonymous authors even wrote humorous Homeric-style epics pitting frogs against mice, or cats against the same mortal enemy. In the latter, a mouse army gathers against a cat after the cat kills their intrepid mouse hero, Trixos. Regretfully, we don't know how the story ends as we only have a few fragmentary passages. Still, it goes to show how much the ancient world appreciated and imitated Homer.

To give a specific example regarding how adored Homer was, there was the philosopher Socrates (fifth century BC), who was, we may confidently assert, addicted to the poet throughout his life thanks to the immense pleasure he felt in hearing or reading Homer's emotionally powerful poems. In Plato's *Republic*, Socrates readily admits that "a certain love and respect for Homer possessed me from the time I was a child to now."[2] Did you hear that? Homer's poetry *owned* Socrates; it had him by the head and heart!

Observing Homer's rather flatline status now, at least the appearance thereof, it is hard to believe that anyone, let alone someone with the creative and revolutionary mind of Socrates, could have been addicted to him. But Socrates wasn't the only one utterly enamored with Homer. No, the poet was incredibly important to everyone in the ancient world. For centuries ancient Greeks read and listened to him, memorized his lines, and used his poetry to make arguments. In short, Homer's *Iliad* and *Odyssey* influenced their feelings, thinking, speech, and behavior, and so the way they navigated and endured life. There was a passage of Homer for everything—healthcare, warfare, politics, business, education, rhetoric, culture, and every other aspect of public and private life.

This is the second reason we should care about Homer. More than anyone else, Homer formed the Greek mind, shaped Greek sensibilities, inspired Greek culture, and encouraged Greek behavior. It was common for ancient Greeks to spend years studying the poet and, therefore, to be profoundly influenced by him. Diogenes Laertius reports that Menedemus, one of Socrates' students, "applied himself to the study of Homer."[3] He wasn't the only one. We know that others memorized large portions of Homer's *Iliad* and *Odyssey* in order to improve themselves. The Athenian Niceratus, the son of Nicias, for example, told Socrates that he was happy that his "father was careful to see me develop into a good man." By good, we should understand noble and brave. Describing how this development came about, he revealed that, "As a means to this end, he had me learn every word of Homer." He did so, apparently, by listening to the recitation of Homer's poems "nearly every day," as Xenophon reports. Yet more. As Socrates explains, Niceratus not only learned the literal words of the poem but their "deeper sense," that is, what they really meant.[4] Similarly, the fifth century BC epinician poet Pindar recommended the memorization of and adherence to Homer's wisdom. "And among the sayings of Homer, treat this one with care and observe it."[5]

Given Greece's leading educators at the time, this appreciation of Homer only makes sense. For the wealthy and those with influence—men like Niceratus' father, Nicias—these teachers were the sophists, a group of educator-philosophers that dominated Greek learning during the fifth century BC. Interestingly, Plato (through Glaucon) labels Homer himself a sophist in the *Republic*.[6]

According to Werner Jaeger, the author of the landmark history of Greek education, *Paideia: The Ideals of Greek Culture*, the "sophists regarded Homer as an encyclopedia of human wisdom . . . a mine of prudential wisdom for the conduct of life."[7] In this way, ancient Greeks looked upon Homer's works as ancient Indians did the similarly encyclopedic *Mahabharata* or ancient Hebrews the Old Testament (the *Tanakh*). Socrates, for example, reports that "some men claim that Homer and the other poets know all human arts and skills—everything having to do with human virtue and vice." He later goes on to say that there are certain "Homer enthusiasts" who "declare that Homer has been the educator of Greece, and that for the education and government of humans, we should take him up and learn from him, and that we should build up our entire lives with the assistance of this poet."[8]

The point is that Homer was Greece's chief educator and coach. The first century AD Stoic philosopher Heraclitus recognized

Homer's influence at every time and on every aspect of life: "From the very earliest infancy, young children are nursed in their learning by Homer . . . it may be said that the same limit is set to both Homer and life."[9] The Roman orator and educator Quintilian put it this way: "As Achilles is among warriors, so Homer is beyond all comparison among poets. . . . He has given us a model and an inspiration for every branch of eloquence."[10]

Recent assessments of Homer's influence have reached similar conclusions. In his classic work on Greek religion, Walter Burkert explains that "to be a Greek was to be educated, and the foundation of all education was Homer."[11] In a short book describing his own academic interests and life, the influential Bernard Knox observes that since the Greeks had no authoritative religious text, they would oftentimes appeal to Homer and the other poets "on questions of conduct and belief."[12] In his own work, Cambridge archeologist Anthony Snodgrass concurs, noting that "there was one huge sphere of action where Homer was widely held to be an infallible guide, and that was good conduct. Not only poets, but politicians, teachers, and thinkers were happy to inculcate a code of behavior that was derived from Homer." Again, Snodgrass reveals that "we know of relatively late compilations which actually spelled out in detail how Homer could be used as a guide for every sphere of life."[13]

The last observation leads us to the third reason why we should care about Homer. Imitating the ancients and the many who lived after them in the Medieval (both Latin and Greek-Byzantine), Renaissance, and early modern world, we can learn much from Homer about how to live and flourish today. I heartily agree with the University of Chicago's James Redfield, who admits, "I find much truth in the Homeric way of seeing the world."[14] In my mind, the truth in the Homeric way is the raw material that may be utilized by us to think about and practice the good life. Not only did Homer help ancient men and women live better lives but if we let him, he can show us the way, too.[15] Along with independent scholar and writer Adam Nicholson, we can accept Homer as "the most truly reliable voice I had ever known," and as "a guidebook to life," even as "a kind of scripture"—in short, as "a source of wisdom" (about which Nicholson at one point admits that, after encountering Homer anew in midlife, he "felt like asking, 'Why has no one told me about this before?'").[16]

Some may find this suggestion absurd—that we can learn much from Homer about how to live and flourish today. That's fine. The truth is that not everyone appreciated Homer in the ancient world. This was particularly true for some during the early centuries of the Christian Church. Theophilus, for instance, the second century bishop of Antioch (in present-day Turkey), questioned the point or profit of Homer, who, he claimed, "deceived many."[17] About the same time, Justin Martyr suggested that Homer's "Odysseus made a virtue of vice."[18] And, perhaps most horrible of all for aspiring orators, St. Augustine, the outstanding Christian theologian and bishop of Hippo, judged Homer dull—this despite the fact that Homer was frequently and positively referenced in ancient Greek and Latin textbooks of composition and rhetoric (for instance, in his *Exercises*, Aelius Theon [first century AD] explains that "we praise Homer first because of his ability to attribute the right words to each of the characters he introduces").[19]

But let's not forget that the first Christians were not only following their own theological tradition but also the example of earlier Greek critics. For instance, the sixth century BC poet and philosopher Xenophanes criticized Homer for "attributing to the gods all things that are shameful and a reproach among mankind: theft, adultery, and mutual deception."[20] A bit later the enigmatic philosopher Heraclitus declared that "Homer deserved to be chased out of the assembly and beaten with rods."[21] And recall that Socrates (or Plato through him), though he loved and learned from him, felt he had to give up the pleasure of Homer for something better—that is, philosophy. In fact, in an early instance of European censorship and editing for the political common good, Socrates wanted to cut out parts of Homer or get rid of him all together. No matter how enjoyable he was, Socrates felt this would be better for everyone. Even though he admitted that "Homer was the best of the poets," he concluded that a truly healthy city could not admit him or similar poetry within its walls. "For if the city gives itself over to the sweet and salty Muse in lyric songs or epic poetry," he warned, "then pleasure and pain will rule your city instead of custom and the law and . . . the best possible deliberations."[22] So it was that his was a call for the sober clear-mindedness of water over the intoxicating euphoria of wine—a call for sanity in place of addiction.

Fortunately—as we've already noted—everyone's view was not negative. Some early Christian theologians, for example, used Homer's tales as grist for the mill of delivering moral lessons. Take the significant fourth century bishop of Caesarea, St. Basil the Great, who is counted among the chief teachers for both Roman Catholic and Orthodox Christians. In contrast to Justin Martyr, who saw nothing but vice in Odysseus (the chief hero of Homer's *Odyssey*), Basil approvingly reveals, "I myself have heard a man, who is skillful at closely examining the mind and meaning of a poet, say that all Homer's poetry is a commendation of virtue. And with Homer, everything apart from what is incidental leads to this end." He goes on to explore how Odysseus was, in his interaction with Nausicaa and the Phaeacians, an encouragement toward virtue.[23]

This idea—that "all Homer's poetry is a commendation of virtue"—was nothing new. In his work on Basil, Oxford classics professor N.G. Wilson concludes that, in his claim about Homer and virtue, Basil was likely referencing Horace (first century BC) or Dio Chrysostom (first century AD).[24] We see, for instance, a strong admiration for the moral side of Homer's poems in Horace's second epistle. There he explains to the Roman politician Lollius that he has been going over the "writer of the Trojan War [Homer], who teaches more clearly, and better than [the Stoic] Chrysippus and [the Platonist] Crantor, what is honorable, what is shameful, what is profitable, and what is not so."[25] As for Dio Chrysostom, he asserts in one discourse that "since everything Homer wrote is both beneficial and useful, it would be a vast undertaking to go through everything he has said about virtue and vice." In another discourse comparing Homer and Socrates, Dio explains that "both were devoted to and spoke about the same things . . . human virtue and vice, and things done poorly, and things done well, and truth and deceit, and how the many have only opinions while the wise have true knowledge." Finally, he cites Alexander the Great's view of Homer with approbation, that "Homer is a marvelous and truly divine herald of virtue."[26]

Before moving on, we should briefly note that the "Homer is about virtue" thesis is one that had deep roots. In his third century AD *Lives and Opinions of Eminent Philosophers*, Diogenes Laertius reports that "Favorinus in his *Miscellaneous History* says that Anaxagoras [fifth century BC] was the first to maintain that Homer treats of virtue and justice in his poems."[27] And recall Socrates' report that "some men claim that Homer and the other poets know all human arts and skills—everything having to do with human virtue and vice."

The big question, of course, is this: why did it matter so much to the ancients that Homer was singing or writing about virtue? It did for the same reason that certain literature matters to us today. Considering the many reasons why we read, somewhere toward the top of the list is that we read for know-how and wisdom. Most importantly, we read to know how best to live. It was this "how best to live" that ancient Greeks were interested in. They wanted to have the best, to do the best, and to be the best.

To understand this, we need to take a brief detour into the land of language. The Greek word for "best," *aristos*, is etymologically related to the word for "virtue" or "excellence," *aretē*, which is, in turn, related to *aretaō*, meaning "to thrive, to prosper" and "to flourish." To complete the circle and to answer the question, then, the Greeks devoured Homer to find out how to flourish as human beings, to thrive and prosper. All that to say they wanted to be virtuous or the best, to be outstanding.

But we should understand that the Greek term *aretē* shifted significantly in meaning during the millennium following Homer (roughly from c. 700 BC to 300 AD).[28] During that time, we see *aretē* in non-animate things as well as animals, human beings, and gods. As for humans, it could mean anything from valor, courage, success, and merit, to moral or ethical goodness having to do with the perfection of the soul (such as wisdom, courage, moderation, and justice). So, when we read that "Homer is all about *aretē*," we must keep in mind what the one making the claim would have meant by *aretē*. Regardless, each believed Homer was a profitable guide to virtue, to excellence.

In general, and for one reason or another, Homer was looked on favorably by those in the later ancient world. Among the many Romans who adored Homer, Virgil was perhaps his greatest admirer, writing his own epic poem, the *Aeneid*, in the manner of the poet. Well over a millennium after Homer's poems were first written down, the Neo-Platonic philosopher Proclus (fifth century AD), who wrote a commentary on them, declared that Homer's epic cycle was a "compendium of 'useful literary knowledge.'"[29]

A thousand years later, Homer continued to shape Greek (and Byzantine Roman) thinking and life down to the end of the Byzantine Empire, when its capital, Constantinople, fell to Ottoman Turk canons in 1453.[30] And even though Homer's pull lessened during the western Middle Ages, the desire and admiration for his poetry strongly returned during the Renaissance and the following centuries. For instance, in his 1605 work *The Advancement of Learning*, the scientist and philosopher Francis Bacon remarks on the staying power of Homer's epics relative to seemingly far more durable human creations: "The verses of Homer have continued twenty-five hundred years, or more, without the loss of a syllable or letter, during which the infinite palaces, temples, castles, cities have been decayed and demolished." In *The Art of Poetry* (1674), Nicholas Boileau-Despreaux declares "Homer's book . . . a delightful treasure," advising his readers to "love his writings with a sincere love." A century and a half later, Thomas Love Peacock judges Homer and his age "the golden age of poetry" in his *The Four Ages of Poetry* (1820). Finally, in his *Thoughts on English Prosody*, Thomas Jefferson similarly recognizes Homer's ongoing power to please:

> When young, any composition pleases which unites a little sense, some imagination, and some rhythm, in doses however small. But as we advance in life these things fall off one by one, and I suspect that we are left at last with only Homer and Virgil, and perhaps with Homer alone.

The title page of George Chapman's 1616 translation of the

"whole of Homer" suggests that Homer was the "prince of poets." As prince, he went on to oversee, as it were—through the influence of the Romans—the flourishing of European literature. As a later commentator wrote, without Homer "there would be neither an *Aeneid*, [Dante's] *Divine Comedy*, [Milton's] *Paradise Lost*, nor the comic epics of Ariosto or Pope or Byron."[31] During the last five-hundred years, Homer has universally inspired admiration in Europe.[32]

Homer was important to many until recently when there was a sharp decline in interest some fifty to one hundred years ago. Writing just after World War II, W.H. Auden judged that "the days when classical studies were the core of higher learning have now passed."[33] Homer included. For several reasons, George Chapman's prince has been buried under a mound of other authors, concerns, approaches, and ways of thinking about life.

But let me say it again: The Classics Cave hopes to change that.

If nothing else, we should care about Homer because his poems are the earliest Greek literature we possess. Consequently, they most clearly reveal the earliest feelings, thoughts, and behavior of this dynamic people that profoundly influenced the Romans, who, in turn, influenced every other European kingdom and nation-state. And whether for good or ill—doubtlessly both, though on balance for good—Europe went on to influence American culture and thus, directly or indirectly, the culture of most peoples.

These early Homeric Greek "first words," and the feelings, thoughts, and actions or behavior they reveal, are somewhat like those we have, however well-formed or not, when we first wake up in the morning—the feelings and thoughts that guide the rest of the day. To leave off with them—to forget them—would be like forgetting why we are doing whatever we are doing *right now* on *this* day. Have you ever had that feeling? Well, the same can happen to all of us, collectively. Why are we here? Why do we feel as we do? Why are we thinking *this* among all possible thoughts? Why are we doing *this*? Behaving *this* way? Reading Homer will help us remember our first feelings and thoughts, and how we first behaved. And perhaps if we carefully look at the beginning, we will feel a bit more comfortable with who we are now, and we'll know how to better trudge forward in the minutes and hours to come in this long human day.[34]

What were we doing? Oh yeah, *that*. So with Homer in hand—Homer the adored, Homer the culture-creator, Homer the life-guide, and Homer manifesting some of our first words, feelings, thoughts, and behavior—let's confidently move ahead, knowing we are engaged with someone whose work truly matters.

BASIC FACTS ABOUT HOMER

Who was Homer? In the ancient world, Homer was the divine "adorner of warrior heroes, the godly Homer."[35] At least that is what one epigram we have claims. Alongside Hesiod, he was "the most inspired of poets."[36] More specifically, for most ancients, Homer was known as the sole creator or *maker* of several long epic poems that brought to life and glorified many heroes among the ancient Greeks.[37]

In more recent times, however, and for good reason, scholars have doubted that one man alone was responsible for these poems. Rather, in one way or another, they have suggested that the epic poems are the evolved result of a long process through time. Consequently, various answers have been given to the *who was Homer* question. Of them, two stand out. What follows simplifies each thesis considerably.

One is that no one man called Homer ever existed. Rather, following the nature of oral poetry—with its basic themes, type scenes, and formulaic phrases combined like Legos or the colorful shapes in that old video game Tetris—, the epic poems were created or composed by countless bards over hundreds of years and just as many performances before live audiences. Some have called this the creation-by-committee approach. Bard A would recite a version of the poem following the usual poetic conventions and restrictions, yet putting it together in his own way to suit the audience listening to him. Bard B would do the same with another crowd, as would bards C, D, and E. When they all got together, as it were, for their annual bard convention in Chios (or when they met over the years and ensuing centuries), they would discuss their performances over cups of wine—what they sang and how they sang it. Their conversation about certain points of difference may have gone something like this: *What terms do you use to describe ships? How do they work— metrically, rhythmically? You regularly call Diomedes* that*? Is Achilles' anger the major theme for you? Oh, so that's how you describe Hector's death. Are the gods always* makar *(blessed) in your recitation? And what about arming or sacrifice—how do you depict them?* And ultimately— or so goes this view of Homer and Homeric poems in a nutshell, and all-too simplistically—the committee-originated poems were written down by some scribe once the Greeks had access to a suitable alphabet.

The other major view is that the poet who gave final shape to these epic poems *was* Homer himself—or, at least, a bard who came to be called Homer. Cambridge classics scholar G.S. Kirk shares this view when he writes that "Homer was an individual singer who came near the end of a long tradition of heroic poetry; he presumably acquired a repertory of songs from other singers and reproduced them in his own manner."[38] In this manner, this one poet was responsible for the poems in a way that the scribe of the committee-originated poems was not.[39] Though not creating them *ex nihilo*, from nothing, he was nevertheless the creative force behind the poems, a creativity that can be detected throughout.

What are Homer's major works? The sixth century AD Byzantine Hesychius of Miletus tells us that Homer's "undisputed poems are the *Iliad* and the *Odyssey*." Modern scholars all tend to agree. Therefore, we may safely say that Homer's most important works are the *Iliad* and the *Odyssey*. The one narrates a portion of the tenth year of the Trojan War. The other tells of the hero Odysseus and his travels home to Ithaca after the same war.

Were any other poems attributed to Homer? If we were to time travel back a few thousand years and ask the ancient Greeks this question, many would tell us that Homer composed the *Homeric Hymns*, some thirty-plus poems meant to glorify one god or goddess or another—Dionysus, Demeter, Hera, Zeus, Helios the Sun, and Earth, the mother of all, among others. Despite this ancient testimony, however, modern scholars deny Homeric authorship, dating the hymns to the few centuries (seventh century BC and on) after the *Iliad* and the *Odyssey* were written down. Otherwise, one life of Homer tells us that the poet composed a series of "fun poems" for a group of boys he was teaching in Chios: the *Cercopes*, the *Heptapaktike*, the *Epikichlides*, and some truly entertaining ones, the *Battle of Frogs* and the *Battle of Starlings*. The *Margites*, a comic narrative poem, fits in with these fun poems. Still others attribute the whole epic cycle to him, those poems narrating the events surrounding the Trojan War.[40] Today, as we have noted, the *Iliad* and the *Odyssey* alone are ascribed to Homer.

When were Homer's epics written down? Most contemporary scholars argue that, utilizing a modified version of the Phoenician alphabet, Homer or a scribe probably wrote the epics down sometime toward the end of the eighth century BC.[41]

What time does Homer represent? Without entering the academic battlefield that is this question, Homer's epics represent the world and values of not only the end of the eighth century BC, when the poems were written down, but also the three or four (or more) centuries before, including the Greek Dark Age and the earlier late-Mycenaean period. The reason why this is the case mirrors the long evolution of the *Iliad* and the *Odyssey*. When the poems were first recited—possibly as long ago as the very late-Mycenaean Age, let's say—they had certain features and reflected certain cultural elements and artifacts that were carried through time to recitations during the Greek Dark Age (c. 1100-776 BC) and onward into the Archaic period (776-479 BC). The result was that the poems came to represent the time when the scribe or final poet wrote them down, as well as the long centuries before. Consequently, relative to the first feelings, thoughts, words, and behavior mentioned in the previous section, the *Iliad* represents some of our first words and the like from as far back as three thousand years ago.

THE TROJAN WAR AND THE TWO BATTLING ARMIES

The Trojan War. The Trojan War was fought by the Achaeans (the

Greeks) against the Trojans and their allies in order to restore stolen goods and gain revenge. The major thing stolen was Helen, the former wife of Menelaus, the ruler of the Spartans. Sometime before the war, the Trojan man Paris (also known as Alexander) had seduced and taken Helen from Menelaus. Paris was the son of the Trojan king, Priam, and the brother of Hector. Paris took Helen in response to Aphrodite's promise to reward him the most beautiful woman in the world—which happened to be Helen.

Aphrodite's own promise came because of a beauty contest between the three goddesses Hera, Athena, and Aphrodite. Thanks to the goddess Strife, the three were at odds with one another. Why? Because Strife, the quarrel-loving goddess, had tossed an apple inscribed with "For the most beautiful" onto the banquet table at Thetis and Peleus' wedding on Mount Olympus. When Hera, Athena, and Aphrodite went to grab the apple, assuming the *obvious*, they ended up fighting over who was the most beautiful. And Strife smiled. When they couldn't agree, they chose Paris to judge between them. He chose Aphrodite, who in turn rewarded him with Helen.

When Paris stole Helen, the Achaeans gathered and sailed to Troy, in present-day north-western Turkey, where they waged a long war to retrieve her. Through the deception of the Trojan horse, Troy finally fell in the tenth year (after the action of the *Iliad*). After the Achaeans killed all the men and divvied up the wealth, women, and children of the fallen city, they returned to their various lands and homes. The latter "returns" (*nostoi*) form the content of other epic poems, including the *Odyssey*, which centers on the return of the hero Odysseus to his home in Ithaca.

The events of the Trojan war—what led up to it, the war itself, and its aftermath, including the so-called returns—are told in the Trojan epic cycle. The *Iliad* and the *Odyssey* are two of the eight Trojan epics that once existed in the ancient world. Unfortunately, the other six are only preserved in fragments or short ancient summaries.

The Achaeans. The Achaeans were an allied group of Greek men, who were out to retrieve Helen from the Trojans. They were led by Agamemnon, the ruler of Mycenae. That said, the Achaean army was a coalition of the willing, as it were, and the not so willing. Odysseus, for example, did not at first wish to go and feigned insanity to avoid it. The Achaeans were an alliance of many independent realms, territories, and households from the north and south, east and west of Greece, including many Greek islands.

Aside from naming them the "Achaeans," Homer also frequently calls the Greeks "Argives" and "Danaans." On one occasion, he terms them the "Panhellenes," and later the "Hellenes," which is similar to the ancient Greek name for Greece, *Hellas*.

If we take Homer's Catalogue of Ships denoting the Achaean army found in the second book of the *Iliad* seriously, then there were "29 contingents, 44 leaders, 175 named towns or other localities, 1,186 ships, and . . . about 100,000 men" on the Achaean side.[42] For many reasons, however, including the doubtful logistics of feeding such an army, we cannot take this description literally.

That pointed out, there are a few basic ways to picture the Achaean army—geographically and in terms of leadership. If we look at a map, they were generally from what we call Greece today and the western half of the Aegean Sea. "Generally," because there were a few eastern Achaean contingents, such as the one from the island of Rhodes, which was historically an Achaean colony, as well as one Trojan ally further west. But if we draw a line through the middle of the Aegean Sea, down from the modern Greek regional capitals of Xanthi or Komotini (near the ancient city of Ismarus in the land of the Cicones), then the Achaeans were from the western half of the map, and the Trojans were from the eastern half (see "The Warring Sides of the Trojan War" map in "Other Matters of Interest Related to Homer and the *Iliad*").

Otherwise, we may view the Achaeans through the most significant leaders as they appear in the *Iliad* itself. If we look down at them from the sky, as an eagle might, then we can see each leader's ships and camp lined up facing the Trojans in the following manner, from left to right. First there is Telamonian Ajax, the ruler of the Salaminians, on the far left. Next comes Idomeneus of Crete, with his righthand man Meriones. They neighbor the camps of (in order) Menelaus of Sparta, Agamemnon of Mycenae, and Nestor of Pylos, the father of Antilochus. In the center are three camps, those of Odysseus of Ithaca, Eurypylus of the Northern Greeks, and Diomedes, the ruler of the Argives. Moving on to the right, there is the lesser Ajax, the son of Oileus and ruler of the Locrians. Then there is the camp of Meges, the leader of men from several western islands, Dulichium included, followed by the camp of Menestheus, the Athenian commander, and the camp of Podarces and Protesilaus of the northern Thessalian contingents. Achilles, the leader of the Myrmidons, and his cherished friend, Patroclus, hold down the far right.

The Trojans and the Trojan allies. Although from the standpoint of the *Iliad*, the Trojans are the enemy of the Achaean Greeks, we should not think of them as non-Greek—not as they would have been if Homer had presented a more historically accurate enemy from a kingdom neighboring Hittite Anatolia. Rather, as Moses Finley writes in *The World of Odysseus*, "the Trojans are as Greek and as heroic in deeds and values as their opponents in every respect."[43]

At the center of the Trojan alliance was the city of Troy (Ilios, or the Latinized version, Ilium), ruled by the aging king, Priam, and his wife, Hecuba. Their son Hector was the most significant Trojan leader, the "best of the Trojans." In Homer, he is oftentimes offset by his comrade in arms and co-commander, Polydamas. Other important Trojans are Pandarus, who shoots Menelaus with an arrow; Aeneas, the son of Anchises and Aphrodite; and the elder counselor to Priam, Antenor, whose many sons appear throughout the *Iliad*. As for the allies, Homer most frequently refers to Zeus' son Sarpedon, the ruler of the Lycians, and his dear friend and partner Glaucus.

Of the twenty-seven Trojan leaders named in the Catalogue of Trojans in the second book of the *Iliad*, seventeen are killed in the course of the *Iliad* compared with a much smaller count for the Achaeans. If you were an Achaean, therefore, you had about a sixty-five percent chance of surviving the *Iliad's* violence, as one out of every three warriors on the Achaean side perished. On the other side, the odds were almost exactly reversed for the worse. Roughly two out of every three men died.

With this, if from nothing else, we see that Homer favored the Achaeans. But when it comes to the major combatants of the war, the matter is not always so clear. Take Hector, for example. In many ways, it is the Trojan Hector who tugs at our minds and hearts as we read the *Iliad*. It is his yearning for glory and his desire to avoid shame that drives him to leave his wife, Andromache, in order to fight while she remains behind, out of her mind with grief.

Nevertheless, the *Iliad* is about the Achaean hero Achilles and his overwhelming anger that wreaks havoc on the Achaean army. It is to that anger, then, and to the other major themes and ideas of Homer's *Iliad* that we must now turn.

THE BIG THEMES AND IDEAS OF THE *ILIAD*

Anger. The first book of the *Iliad* begins with what amounts to a fireworks finale of anger. Chryses, the priest of Apollo, is angry at Agamemnon for refusing to return his daughter, Chryseis, to him for a generous ransom. Following this refusal, when Chryses prays to Apollo for revenge, the god becomes furious at Agamemnon. As a result, he casts a deadly plague onto the Achaeans. Nine days go by. When the seer Calchas reveals that Agamemnon's refusal to return Chryseis is the reason for the plague, Agamemnon is livid— "his heart was black with raging passion, and his eyes flashed fire." He's even angrier when Achilles tells him to return the girl to her father. *Why*, he asks, *should he lose his honor-prize without compensation?* When Agamemnon finally threatens to take Achilles' honor-prize, Briseis, to make up for his own loss, Achilles is irate. It is this anger, the famous "wrath of Achilles," that is at the center of the *Iliad*.

> Wrath! Sing, goddess, about the destructive wrath of Achilles, the son of Peleus—the anger that caused so much pain and suffering among the Achaeans.[44]

But what is the significance of anger in the *Iliad*? Stated simply, anger is a form of desire. Rather than being a desire *for* something clearly and directly, however, it is more directly and clearly *against* something. As such, anger (*cholos*) or wrath (*mēnis*) is always the direct negative expression of an indirect positive desire for something in Homer. Negatively, anger-desire is an aversion; it communicates what it does not want—what it does not wish to happen, past, present, or future. Positively, it expresses what it wants. As such, it serves to defend a person's portion, what he or she has in terms of wealth, power, status, reputation, honor, and other desired things of life.

In Achilles' case, the positive desire is to retain the girl Briseis, his honor-prize, and, therefore, to maintain his honor before others, the sense that he is somebody. When he later speaks with his mother, Thetis, Achilles complains that Agamemnon has dishonored him by taking the girl. "The wide-ruling son of Atreus has dishonored me since by force he has robbed me of my honor-prize [Briseis]."[45] Doing so, Agamemnon has treated him like a coward (*deilos*) and a nobody (*outidanos*).[46] From his own words, then, we know that Achilles' anger-desire is largely about shame avoidance, dodging the shame of being judged a coward, of losing honor before all the other men. Conversely, or positively, it is about his great desire to be counted somebody important, and so to be honored.

The same is true for Agamemnon's anger over losing Chryseis. He too must have something to make up for his lost honor and thus status. Speaking to Achilles, he says,

> What—will you keep your own honor-prize while I sit here without one? I tell you what, have the Achaeans hand over something that is pleasing to me, an honor-prize that is suitable to my status and worth just as much as the girl is. But if they refuse to offer it up, I'll come myself and seize one with my own mighty hands! I'll come for your prize or that of Telamonian Ajax or Odysseus! And once I take it, I'll carry it off! Then we'll see who's angry!

Yes, anger-desire must protect Agamemnon's honor and status. The problem with anger, however, is that it has serious negative consequences. Not only does Achilles'—and Agamemnon's—anger disrupt the unity of the Achaean army, but it is responsible for the deaths of many Achaean men, including Achilles' dear friend Patroclus.

Homer explains that "his anger sent many strong souls—the breath-like phantoms of men—down to the dark hall of Hades."[47]

Interestingly, Achilles later wishes that this kind of anger, and the strife it spawns, would disappear from the face of the earth:

> May strife utterly perish from among both the gods and men, and anger that incites a wise man to be savagely angry—an anger that drips like very sweet honey and expands like smoke in the breast of a man, growing ever larger. Even so has the lord of men Agamemnon now provoked me to anger.[48]

Admittedly, he is wildly out of his mind with sorrow when he wishes that anger would disappear, and strife. Nevertheless, his prayer reveals something true: anger leads to strife; and strife often means the loss of loved ones, as it does in the *Iliad*, when he loses Patroclus. After the fact, Achilles knows that if he could somehow go back in time and cause the former anger (and strife) to disappear, then the latter man would reappear.

Alas, given Homer's competitive world, it isn't possible for anger to just vanish. It is too important of an emotional driver for desired things like honor and a defender against undesired things like shame. For without wisdom, skill, and courage, on the one hand, and anger, black-hearted revenge, and violent strife on the other, how would one seek honor and avoid shame?

Shame. Shame avoidance is one of the great motivators in the *Iliad*, in which shame (*aidōs*) is the belittling and denigration of one's reputation and status (what others say about one, and one's consequent standing among them), and so the erosion of one's ability to satisfy desire. Like anger, shame avoidance is actually a desire—the desire for honor and a positive reputation, the desire to be called "good."

Generally speaking, Homer terms the heroes of the *Iliad* "good" (*agathos* or *esthlos*)—that is, good and noble men, brave and strong. The last thing any hero wants a reputation for is cowardice (*kakotēs*). In fact, a man will go so far as to declare he would rather be dead than be revealed a coward. This is so because the coward (*deilos*) is known as a bad man (*kakos*)—he is weak (*analkis*) and ugly (*aischros*).[49]

According to Odysseus, it is the coward who retreats from battle. However afraid the good or noble man may be, he cannot flee from a fight. Speaking to himself amid "the throng of men," Odysseus says, "I know that only cowards run off from a fight, and that those who are the best in battle feel a great need to make a mighty stand, whether he hits and drops his man or the other hits and drops him."[50] Another time, the hero Diomedes chastises Odysseus for speeding away from battle toward the ships. (In his defense, all the Achaean heroes are fleeing thanks to the sound of Zeus' thunder, which signifies a shift in the god's favor toward the Trojans.) Diomedes calls out, "God-born son of Laertes, much-able Odysseus, why are you running off with your back turned like a coward? May some man not plant a spear in your back while you flee!"[51]

For Homeric Greeks, the bad man or coward deserves nothing and has no leading role to play in the assembly or on the battlefield. For this reason, the good and brave man must stand up for what is his own in a fight. Simply put, he must *be a man*. "O friends, be men!" Nestor calls out to the Achaeans. "And drum up in your spirits a sense of shame and self-respect before other men . . . I implore you to be ready and make a mighty stand, and not turn back in panicked flight."[52]

The "sense of shame," here, signifies the desire to avoid shame. Similarly, when Hector gives the reason for the need to make a stand in the last moments of his life, it is all about avoiding shame and maintaining his sense of honor. Oh, and winning glory.

Honor and glory (reputation). Hector is standing alone before Troy, and Achilles, the best of the Achaeans, is barreling straight for him, full of rage over Patroclus' death at Hector's hands. The obvious thing for Hector to do would be to flee into the city. (Many of us would do so, anyway!) In fact, Hector considers this option. But as any other Homeric hero knows, he knows that behaving in such a manner is what a shameful coward would do. Not only that but "some cowardly man" would blame him, he fears, for his recklessness in leading the Trojan army to destruction.

So it is that Hector ends up standing his ground to face Achilles in the hope that he will win the glory-boast (*euchos*). "It would be better," he says, "to encounter each other quickly in combat to see which one of us the Olympian will grant the glory-boast."[53] And when he finally comes to know that he has likely been beaten, that "the gods have lured me to my death," he says to himself, "now my fate has come! Let me not then die ingloriously and without a struggle, but let me first do some great thing that men to come will hear about!"[54]

Achilles similarly chooses glory (*kleos*) over life. When in Book 9 the embassy comes from Agamemnon to seek reconciliation with him, Achilles explains that his mother revealed two possible fates for the course of his life. One, he could stay home in Phthia and have a long life without glory. Or, two, he could go to Troy and win everlasting glory on the battlefield before the city's walls.

> My goddess mother, the silver-footed Thetis, tells me that there are two possible fates carrying me toward the fulfillment of death. If I stay here and fight nearby the city of the Trojans, then I give up my return home, but my glory will never die. But if I return home to the land I love, then I give up my noble glory, yet my life will be very long.[55]

For Achilles, the choice is obvious. Good men, brave and noble men, choose glory. That's why Achilles is so upset when Agamemnon dishonors him by seizing Briseis, his honor-prize. Agamemnon has shamed him by treating him like a bad man, a cowardly nobody, the very opposite of a good and brave man. In short, he's sullied his honor (*timē*) and reputation (*kleos*)—everything Achilles came to Troy to obtain. Whereas Hector employs violence to win glory against Achilles in his last battle, Achilles employs wrath or anger against Agamemnon to restore his own honor. Either way, both men are competing to maintain their reputation, which amounts to their status held among the other men and, therefore, their ability to obtain what they desire.

Competition in word and deed; being the best. During the embassy to Achilles, Phoenix reminds his charge of why his father sent him with Achilles to Troy in the first place. He explains that before coming to Troy, Achilles was "a silly child and knew nothing yet of distressing war nor of assemblies in which men stand out from others"—and consequently win honor, glory, and a reputation. "For this reason," Phoenix goes on, "[Peleus] sent me with you to instruct you in all these matters, to be a speaker of words and a doer of deeds."[56] Some time later, Nestor recalls that "Old Peleus enjoined his child Achilles to always be the best and to stand out among other men."[57] The command to "be the best and to stand out" was a directive to practice excellence or virtue (*aretē*).

We learn two important points about Homer's world from Phoenix's and Nestor's statements. One, the goal of all behavior for Homeric men is to be preeminent, to stand out from others, to be the best or to possess excellence. This in turn leads to honor and glory and the kind of reputation one would want, to be known for being the best. Two, the means by which a man is the best and stands out from others are various competitions. Phoenix mentions battle and speaking in the assembly. If we round these out with athletic competitions such as chariot racing, boxing, foot racing, wrestling, and the like, then we will understand the major arenas in which men competed for and won a reputation in Homer's world.

That said, standing out or being the best isn't always up to a human being's efforts alone. Rather, to a large extent, being great is up to Fate and the gods.

Fate and the gods (and good fortune). To the point, it is Fate and the gods that determine whether a human being will live or die, be great or not, remembered or not, and so have the kind of honor, glory, and reputation that all Homeric heroes desire.

What is Fate in Homer? Simply put, Fate is that which apportions the world, giving each god and man his portion (the Greek is *moira*, portion, whereas *Moira* is Fate, or portion personified).[58] After his death at the hands of Achilles, Hector's mother Hecuba acknowledges that "mighty Fate" spun this particular end for him "at his birth, when his mother bore him."[59] Similarly, Zeus recognizes that his mortal son Sarpedon "is fated to be struck dead by Patroclus."[60] And such is his end.

It is not always possible to distinguish the apportioning action of Fate from the determining action of the gods. Rather, they seem to act in tandem. Patroclus, for instance, explains to Hector that "Zeus, the son of Cronus, and Apollo have readily given you victory over me." He goes on to add, "Destructive Fate and the son of Leto [Apollo] have killed me"—these along with the humans who struck him down.[61] Elsewhere, the god Ares allows that "it may be my fate to be struck with the bolt of Zeus and lie low in blood and dust among the dead"—an admission revealing that fate (or Fate) somehow operates through the gods.[62]

If Fate is the divine apportioner, then Fate through the gods ultimately determines who lives or dies, has strength or doesn't, wins or loses, obtains glory or doesn't, and who gets what in terms of various good or bad things. As for the latter, which is to say good or bad fortune, Achilles tells Priam that the gods plan sorrows for humans and that Zeus has two large jars on the golden floor of his house from which he dispenses good and bad things to human beings.

> For while the gods plan sorrow upon sorrow for wretched mortals, they live without any sorrow or grief. . . . On the floor of Zeus' house, there are two jars from which he gives gifts. The one is filled with evil and the other with good. To whomever Zeus, who delights in thunder, mixes and gives out both, that man will meet now with good and now with evil fortune. But for the man who only receives evil gifts—ah, that man will suffer shameful treatment. Evil poverty and hunger will drive him back and forth over the earth, and neither the gods nor men will honor him.

Achilles goes on to catalogue a variety of goods, "glorious gifts," that his own father, Peleus, received "from the moment of his birth," that is, thanks to Fate. Among other goods, "he ruled over the Myrmidons, surpassing all other men in happiness and wealth." Achilles also acknowledges the fact that Priam was "once happy" in that he "surpassed the rulers of all the lands surrounding [his] own" in "wealth and number of offspring."[63]

Zeus and the other gods are similarly responsible for strength, victory, and glory. For instance, when Nestor persuades Diomedes to retreat, he shouts,

Son of Tydeus, turn your horses in flight! Don't you see that Zeus isn't giving
you strength? No, he's giving glory to Hector today. Tomorrow, if he wills it,
he'll grant us glory. Whatever the case, no man, however brave he is, may
thwart the will and purpose of Zeus, for he is stronger than all men are.[64]

After battling him in single combat, Hector tells Telamonian Ajax
that they should "stop the fighting and battle-strife for today." He
clarifies the point by promising that "in the days to come we'll fight
again and let some god decide who is better, giving victory to one
side or another."[65]

Whoever wins in the *Iliad* is happy—at least for the moment. We
see this most clearly when a hero is busy slaughtering the enemy and
thereby winning a glory report.

The glory report (traditionally called an *aristeia*[66]). In Book 11 of the
Iliad, Hector realizes a change of fortune in his favor after the Trojan
man Coōn wounds Agamemnon. Calling out to his men, command-
ing them to "be men, friends, and remember the strength and valor
by which you rush into the fight," he tells them that Zeus "has now
granted me the glory-boast (*euchos*)." Accordingly, he urges them to
"drive your chariots straight at the strong Danaans, so that you may
raise up an even greater glory-boast." Homer in turn asks the
Muses—their knowledge is implied—to reveal which men Hector
was able to slay first and last "now that Zeus granted him glory (*ku-
dos*)."[67] What follows is a list of men, some nine in all, killed by Hec-
tor. And, Homer says, Hector would have slain more if Odysseus
had not stepped up to Diomedes to remind him of what a shameful
dishonor it would be if they allowed Hector to take the ships.

In a way that is perhaps hard for contemporary readers to under-
stand, the whole *Iliad* is a glory report for Achilles. It is the story—
however tragic—of Achilles heroically employing anger in order to
avoid shame and restore his honor and reputation. As said before, the
unfortunate aspect of this strategy is that it ends up leading to a great
deal of suffering—so much, in fact, that Homer tells us it is impossible
to count it all.

But this is normal in the pursuit of one's portion and glory that
confer status and the ability to satisfy desire. One man's victory

means another man's death. One man's satisfaction means another man's dissatisfaction—or suffering.

Suffering. In the first few lines of the *Iliad*, Homer asks the Muse to sing about "the destructive wrath of Achilles . . . that caused so much pain and suffering among the Achaeans." Next to glory reporting, which the poet frequently engages in, Homer seems to relish recounting how it is that various men suffer in the *Iliad*. For example, one of the distinctive features of the poem is the way Homer describes the oftentimes very violent and gruesome battle deaths. Eyeballs pop out. Brains smashed to mush. Blood gushing from gaping wounds, the ground soaked with a man's life.

There are a few reasons for these graphic descriptions of suffering. One, the suffering of one man serves to glorify another. When Hector slays a man in battle, and the man dies a truly horrific death, then Hector himself stands out. He is superior to that man. Frequently, the victorious warrior stands over the loser on the ground glory-boasting. Though ultimately an empty boast since Diomedes lives, Lycaon's glory-boast to Diomedes is typical: "You're hit! I hit you through the belly! And I don't think you'll be standing for very long. No, you've granted me a great glory-boast!"—which is to say, *I won and you didn't; therefore, I'm better than you and other men are.*

Two, a man must suffer to accomplish anything great and therefore stand out among others. The truth is Achilles and his men are bored when Achilles withdraws from the battle. But the boredom is worth it. So too is Patroclus' death in the end. The simple fact is that the price of glory is oftentimes suffering. Indeed, the whole Trojan War that is fought to avoid the shame of losing Helen and to restore Menelaus' honor and glory is ten long years of suffering hell. Or so declares Nestor in the *Odyssey*.

Endurance. But that's to be expected—suffering is the norm in Homer's world. According to one scholar, Homer's epic poems are full of "sleep-depriving anxiety, hellish war, debilitating injury, grizzly death, worming sorrow, gnawing homesickness, deplorable betrayal, and tunic-wetting fear."[68] The logical question that follows, then, is what to do about all the suffering. The answer: to get to the other side of a situation involving suffering, one must learn to endure.

It's a must. Even the gods must endure. When Aphrodite goes off crying to her mother, Dione, after Diomedes wounds her, the blood-like ichor flowing from the wound on her delicate hand, her mother matter-of-factly tells her she must endure the suffering. "Endure, my child, and bear all your troubling distress."[69] In Homer's *Odyssey*, the point is made again and again relative to humans. To give one example, the Phaeacian princess Nausicaa admonishes Odysseus to put up with whatever suffering Zeus has given him.

> Since Olympian Zeus himself dispenses fortune and happiness to men, to both the good and the bad as he wills, whether he be brave or a coward, noble or base—so I believe that surely he has given misfortune to you. Regardless, you must endure it either way.[70]

Fortunately, humans come well-equipped to handle suffering. As Apollo explains to the gods in the last book of the *Iliad*, "the Fates put an enduring spirit into men."[71] Utilizing this natural ability to endure, then, men and women can get to the other side and, let's hope, arrive at something better—preferably happiness.

Happiness. In Homer, happiness is rather straight-forward: it is the satisfaction of desire. The good, happy life is full of the experience and satisfaction of things desired—from the desire for life itself and the avoidance of death, to the satisfaction of desire for things like good food, a warm bath, sex, and various forms of entertainment. Other desiderata include the desire to be part of a household that will help a man secure all these good things and defend the ones he already has. But let's be honest. If you're a Homeric hero, you want the best of all things—the best women, the best seat in the feasting hall, the best cuts of meat, and the choicest wine. And you want power over others, the ability to harness their collective strength and marshal them for your own purposes. For this, you need to stand out among men. Accordingly, you require status, one built on the firm foundation of a solid reputation. Consequently, you desire honor and glory, which both confer the kind of reputation you hope for. In the end, therefore, we see that to be an honorable and glorious man, the kind who avoids shame, is to be a happy man.

This fact explains why Achilles is so angry. In attacking him, in seizing his honor-prize, Briseis, Agamemnon has stolen Achilles' happiness from him by slighting his honor and making of him a no-body. So in the end, the *Iliad* is really about happiness. Yes, it is an epic poem about Achilles' anger or wrath. But seen for what it truly is, his anger is a rearguard action to defend his happiness. And that's why we feel sympathy for Achilles. We understand the hero because we can all relate to his urgent and profound desire to be happy.

This only makes sense. According to Aristotle's fourth century BC treatise the *Nicomachean Ethics*, happiness is what every human desires and the ultimate thing that every human shoots for.[72] The big question is how we should aim for happiness. Is anger-fueled competition in warfare, the assembly, and athletic competition the best means by which to seek the good life? Is it happy-making for one group of men to attack another group and sack their city in order to get wealthy and obtain glory?

If we listen closely to Homer, perhaps it's not.[73] But that possibility is far beyond the scope of this brief introduction to the *Iliad*. For now, it is enough to know that such competition for happiness was the norm in Homer's world.

LET'S GO!

The Achaeans sailed to Troy in what would have probably been relatively small ships—at least compared to later Greek triremes. When there was wind, they hoisted sails and utilized wind power to help them on their way. Otherwise, they rowed using long oars. The Trojans and Trojan allies, by contrast, simply marched out from the city, or they came to Troy on foot, or, perhaps, they arrived riding on horseback or speeding along in war chariots.

The Classics Cave invites you to come to the battlefield before Troy. Join the Achaean heroes in their shelters by the ships, or the Trojan women and older men atop the walls of Troy, or the Trojan warriors and their allies sitting by their thousands of fires flickering beneath an ancient night sky. Sense Achilles' anger at Agamemnon. Know Hera's frustration with Zeus. Feel Dolon's fear as he weeps before his captors, Odysseus and Diomedes, begging for his life. Taste the sweat streaming down a warrior's face as he fights—and perhaps the spattered blood of the man he dropped to the ground with his spear. Hear Andromache as she cries out for Hector. Sink down with Helen who feels shame at all she's done. Cry with Briseis when she learns of a loved one's death. Whatever you do, join the others in this great tale of human suffering and, just possibly, some measure of redemption and happiness.

However you come, get ready to learn something about the way ancient Greeks felt, thought, spoke, and behaved thousands of years ago. Doing so, you'll learn more about our own lives today.

Note: As you read along, observe that you will always know where you are in *The Best of Homer's* Iliad in a few ways. First, the very top of the righthand page will let you know what book you are in, along with the book's title—say, Book 15 • THE BATTLE AT THE SHIPS. Second, you will notice line numbers for both translated and summarized passages. Translated passages have an overall block number, for example, 101-187 (as appears in Book 1), which signifies lines 101 through 187 (that is, lines of the poem). Translated passages are also numbered every ten lines, indicated by bracketed numbers such as [70]. Narrative summary passages (in *italics*) are likewise assigned a block number, say 43-100 (as appears for the narrative summary passage that comes before the aforementioned passage in Book 1). The only exception to this system of block numbering is beginning passages, which are not numbered. The reason for this is that all beginning passages start with line one. The ending line number may be determined by looking at the first narrative summary passage and subtracting one. For instance, if that number is 43-100, as in the example above, then the translated beginning passage's range would be lines 1-42.

NOTES

[1] Moses Finley, *The World of Odysseus* (New York: The New York Review of Books), 12. See also Raffaella Cribiore, *Gymnastics of the Mind: Greek Education in Hellenistic and Roman Egypt* (Princeton: Princeton University Press, 2001), 194 ff.
[2] For Socrates' admission and what he has to say about Homer, see Plato, *Republic* 10.595b-c. For Socrates, Homer was "the beginning of the poetic tribe" and "the first teacher and beginner of all these beauties of tragedy." Still, he level-headedly asserts that "we must not honor a man above truth, but, as I say, speak our minds." More recently, but similarly relative to addiction, Adam Nicholson has explained that "Homer-love feels like a disease" (*Why Homer Matters*, 32).

³ See Diogenes Laertius, *Lives and Opinions of Eminent Philosophers* 2.133.

⁴ See Xenophon, *Symposium* 3.5-6. Socrates goes on to explain that Niceratus "overlooked nothing valuable or worthwhile in the poems."

⁵ See Pindar, *Pythian* 4.277-278.

⁶ See Plato, *Republic* 10.596d. In this case, the label was no compliment. In Plato's *Theaetetus* 152e ff., Socrates calls Homer and his sophist allies the philosophers of flux or becoming. Since Plato preferred being to becoming, this assessment was tantamount to saying that the sophists didn't know what they were talking about.

⁷ Werner Jaeger, *Paideia: The Ideals of Greek Culture*, vol. 1, trans. Gilbert Highet (New York: Oxford University Press, 1945), 296.

⁸ See Plato, *Republic* 10.598d-e and 606e. In this case, the Greek words for virtue (*aretē*) and vice (*kakia*) may also be given as "excellence" and "mediocrity" or "success" and "failure."

⁹ Heraclitus, *Homeric Problems* 1.5-7. Cited in Richard Hunter, "Homer and Greek Literature," in *The Cambridge Companion to Homer* (Cambridge: Cambridge University Press, 2004), 235.

¹⁰ Quintilian, *Institutes* 10.2.

¹¹ Walter Burkert, *Greek Religion*, trans. John Raffan (Cambridge: Harvard University Press, 1985), 120.

¹² Bernard Knox, *The Oldest Dead White European Males and Other Reflections on the Classics* (New York: W.W. Norton and Company, 1993), 94.

¹³ Anthony Snodgrass, *Homer and the Artists: Text and Picture in Early Greek Art.* (Cambridge: Cambridge University Press, 1998), 2, 4, 6.

¹⁴ James M. Redfield, *Nature and Culture in the Iliad: The Tragedy of Hector*. Expanded edition. (Durham: Duke University Press, 1994), xv.

¹⁵ For how this may be the case, see *The Wisdom & Way of Homer: Pocket Edition* and *Homer Workbook & Journal* (Sugar Land: The Classics Cave, 2021).

¹⁶ See Adam Nicholson, *Why Homer Matters* (New York: Picador, 2014), 11, 32. For Nicholson, this "scripture" is "for me, an ancient book, full of urgent imperatives and ancient meanings . . . to be puzzled out" (32). Similar to Nicholson, though in different terms, for William E. Gladstone, the long-time, on-again-off-again nineteenth century prime minister of Great Britain, "Homer was," as Richard Jenkins explains in *The Victorians and Ancient Greece* (1980), "quite literally, a sacred book." This conclusion fit well with the general Victorian view that "Homer had been the Bible of the Greeks." Indeed, Homer (and other Greeks) was a "preparation for the gospel," whose "religion contained memories of God's revelation to primitive man" (202-204).

¹⁷ See Theophilus of Antioch, *To Autolycus* 3.1-2.

¹⁸ See Justin Martyr, *Discourse to the Greeks* 1.

¹⁹ For St. Augustine's response, see Cathy Gere, *The Tomb of Agamemnon: Mycenae and the Search for a Hero* (London: Profile Books, 2007), 5.

²⁰ Xenophanes, fragment 11, in Kathleen Freeman, *Ancilla to the Pre-Socratic*

Philosophers: A Complete Translation of the Fragments in Diels (Cambridge: Harvard University Press, 1948).

[21] Reported by Diogenes Laertius, *Lives* 9.1.

[22] Plato, *Republic* 10.607a.

[23] See Basil the Great (here slightly modified) in The Classics Cave's *The Best of Basil the Great on Reading Literature and Education* (2021), 54. Commenting on the scene when Odysseus, naked, is introduced to the beautiful Phaeacian princess, Nausicaa, Basil observes that "Homer portrays Odysseus as adorned with virtue instead of clothing" (54). Therefore, he concludes, there was no shame in being seen naked. What other moral points or comparisons does Basil find in Homer? Elsewhere, to give a few examples, in his *Letter* 147 to Aburgius, he compares the unsettling plight of the prefect Maximus to Odysseus' own, "who had great wealth, but returned [from the Trojan War and his adventures] stripped of everything." In *Letter* 148 to Trajan, he mentions "the *Iliad* of misfortune in which Maximus is involved."

[24] *Saint Basil on Literature*, ed. N.G. Wilson (London: Gerald Duckworth & Co., 1975), 52. For the whole of Basil's text, see his short work, *How to Benefit from Reading Greek Literature*, found in The Classics Cave's *The Best of Basil the Great on Reading Literature and Education* (Sugar Land: The Classics Cave, 2021).

[25] Horace, *Letter* 2.

[26] Dio Chrysostom, *On Homer* 53.11 (or 36.11); *On Homer and Socrates* 54.9 (or 38.9); *On Kingship* 2.6.

[27] Diogenes Laertius, *Lives* 2.11.

[28] To understand how the Greek understanding of *aretē* shifted during this time, see *Aretē: Excellence or Virtue—What the Ancient Greeks Thought and Said about Aretē* (Sugar Land: The Classics Cave, 2021).

[29] For Proclus, see Caroline Alexander, *The War that Killed Achilles: The True Story of the Iliad* (London: Faber and Faber, 2010), 13.

[30] For the influence, see, for instance, N.G. Wilson, *Scholars of Byzantium* (London: Gerald Duckworth & Co., 1996).

[31] W.H. Auden, ed., *The Portable Greek Reader* (London: Penguin Books, 1977), 10.

[32] This was particularly true during the late nineteenth and early twentieth centuries. See, for instance, "Homer and the Edwardians," in R.M. Ogilvie, *Latin and Greek: A History of the Influence of the Classics on English Life from 1600 to 1918* (London: Routledge & Kegan Paul, 1964).

[33] W.H. Auden, ed., *The Portable Greek Reader*, 3.

[34] It goes without saying that other examples of early world literature are also vitally important to the project of knowing who we are as humans and how we are joined together as a human family. Not only is there the literature of Greece and Rome but there is that hailing from ancient China, India, and the Near East, as well as (though recorded much later) the great variety of Native American and early European literature, Aboriginal storytelling, and the rich narrative tradition originating with the many peoples of Africa.

35 See *The Contest of Homer and Hesiod* 1, in *Homeric Hymns, Homeric Apocrypha, Lives of Homer*, ed. and trans. Martin L. West (Cambridge: Harvard University Press, 2003), 319.

36 Ibid., 18, 353.

37 The English words *poet* and *poem* are derived from the Greek verb *poieō*, "to make." Accordingly, one life of Homer tells us that Homer "made [*poieō*] the *Odyssey* . . . having already made the *Iliad*."

38 G.S. Kirk, "The Search for the Real Homer," in *Homer*, ed. Ian McAuslan and Peter Walcott (Oxford: Oxford University Press, 1998), 39.

39 The sixth century AD Byzantine Hesychius of Miletus had this to say about the making and writing down of one of Homer's poems: "He did not write the *Iliad* all at once or in sequence, as it has been put together: he wrote each rhapsody and performed it as he went around from town to town to make a living, and left it there, and subsequently the poem was put together by various people, above all by Pisistratus, the Athenian tyrant [sixth century AD]." See "From Hesychius of Miletus: Index of Famous Authors," in *Homeric Hymns, Homeric Apocrypha, Lives of Homer*, ed. and trans. Martin L. West (Cambridge: Harvard University Press, 2003), 429. Hesychius' report reflects the two major positions scholars have historically taken since the late eighteenth century (and the analysis of Friedrich Wolf) regarding the fundamental unity (the Unitarians) or lack of unity (the Analysts) of Homer's poems. The poems were either composed "all at once or in sequence," or they were "put together by various people" over time. The debate shifted emphasis in the early twentieth century with Milman Parry's observations regarding the oral composition of the poems (though similar ideas may be traced back to the nineteenth century).

40 Poems in the Epic Cycle include, among others, the *Cypria*, the *Aethiopis*, the *Little Iliad*, and the *Nostoi* or *Returns*.

41 We should nevertheless note that there are some who argue for a later date, suggesting the latter part of the sixth century BC in keeping with the above remark (among other considerations) of Hesychius of Miletus that "the poem was put together by various people, above all by Pisistratus, the Athenian tyrant."

42 For the numbers, see Malcolm M. Willcock, *A Companion to the* Iliad (Chicago: The University of Chicago Press, 1976), 22-23.

43 Moses Finley, *The World of Odysseus*, 38.

44 Homer, *Iliad* 1.1-2.

45 Ibid., 1.355-356.

46 See ibid., 1.293-294, where Achilles interrupts Agamemnon and observes, "The men will call me a coward and a nobody if I give in to you!" Though he ultimately allows Agamemnon to take Briseis, this one line lets us know what Achilles' anger is really about.

47 Ibid., 1.3-4.

48 Ibid., 18.107-111.

49 *Kakos* oftentimes simply means a "coward" or a "cowardly man." The *kakos*

man is the opposite of the *agathos*, the brave and good man.

[50] See ibid., 11.401-410.

[51] Ibid., 8.93-95.

[52] Ibid., 15.661-666.

[53] Ibid., 22.129-130.

[54] Ibid., 22.304-305.

[55] Ibid., 9.410-415. Related to *kleō* (to tell of, make famous, celebrate), *kleos* also signifies one's reputation, what one is reputed for—that is, the (typically good) things one is known for, what others say about one.

[56] Ibid., 9.440-443.

[57] Ibid., 11.783-784.

[58] The goddess of destiny, Aisa, or one's appointed lot or destiny, also shows up in the *Iliad*. As for the three goddesses of fate, the *Klōthes* or Spinners, they do not. In the *Odyssey*, however, Homer mentions them relative to Odysseus: "When he gets home he will suffer whatever fate that the grievous Spinners spun out for him with their flaxen thread when he came to be on the day his mother gave birth to him" (7.196-198). In Hesiod's *Theogony*, a work slightly later than the *Iliad*, Themis (with Zeus) produces "the Fates (*Moirai*) to whom Zeus the counselor offered the greatest honor. These are Klotho, Lachesis, and Atropos, the ones who grant mortal human beings their portions of good and evil" (905-907).

[59] Ibid., 24.209-210.

[60] Ibid., 16.434.

[61] Ibid., 16.844-845, 849-850.

[62] Ibid., 15.117-118. Interestingly, it also reveals that the gods are somehow fated.

[63] Ibid., 24.525-546.

[64] Ibid., 9.139-144.

[65] Ibid., 7.290-292.

[66] For instance, the orator Dio Chrysostom (c. 40-112 AD) calls such a glory report "the telling . . . of the excellence or excellent deeds (*aristeia*) of Hector" (*Oration* 11.83).

[67] See ibid., 11.284-290 and 11.299-304.

[68] Tim J. Young, *A Hero's Wish: What Homer Believed about Happiness and the Good Life* (Sugar Land: EuZōn Media, 2015), 246.

[69] *Iliad* 5.382.

[70] *Odyssey* 6.188-190.

[71] *Iliad* 24.49.

[72] For more on what the Greeks believed about happiness, see *Happiness: What the Ancient Greeks Thought and Said about Happiness* (Sugar Land: The Classics Cave, 2025).

[73] For more, see Caroline Alexander, *The War that Killed Achilles: The True Story of the Iliad* (Faber and Faber, 2010). Tim J. Young also explores Homer's possible pacifist leanings in *A Hero's Wish: What Homer Believed about Happiness and the Good Life* (see Chapter 12, "Must We? An Apparent Shift").

THE *ILIAD*
TRANSLATED AND SUMMARIZED PASSAGES

BOOK 1

ANGER AND FRUSTRATION
ACHILLES & AGAMEMNON, ZEUS & HERA

IN BRIEF: *Wrath! Agamemnon refuses to return the battle captive Chryseis to her father Chryses, the priest of Apollo. His refusal causes Apollo, now angry, to cast a plague upon the Achaeans. When Achilles calls on Agamemnon to return the girl in order to appease the god's wrath, Agamemnon agrees. Yet in recompense for his loss, and fuming, he demands Achilles' own honor-prize, Briseis, for himself. In response, Achilles moves to slay him in anger. Although Athena prevents the murder, the goddess doesn't stop Achilles from calling on his divine mother, Thetis, for revenge. Thetis talks to Zeus, who promises to restore her son's honor. To this end, the god will help the Trojans against the Achaeans—all contrary to his wife Hera's ardent war objectives. And now Hera is troubled—frustrated! Nevertheless, she can do nothing about it, nothing against Zeus' power and plans. Knowing this, her wise son Hephaestus advises Hera to be gentle with her husband and obey him. And that's what happens. And so it is that the divine feast goes on.*

WRATH! SING, GODDESS, about the destructive wrath of Achilles, the son of Peleus—the anger that caused so much pain and suffering among the Achaeans. Who could possibly measure it all?

His anger sent many strong souls—the breath-like phantoms of men—down to the dark halls of Hades, while above, their fallen bodies became food for wild dogs and scavenging birds.

In this way Zeus' plan advanced to the very end.

Sing from the exact moment when the lord of men Agamemnon and godlike Achilles stood apart quarrelling with each other. Reveal the god that urged them forward, face to mighty face, in strife and disputation.

Ah—it was Apollo, the son of Leto and Zeus. He was angry with lord Agamemnon. [10] So he fired a wicked plague down upon the army, and the men were dying a violent death all because Agamemnon refused to honor Apollo's priest Chryses.

Now Chryses had come to the Achaean ships to free his daughter. He brought with him a whole load of treasure for ransom and carried in his right hand the golden scepter of far-shooting Apollo. Standing there, he begged the Achaeans to release his prized daughter, but most of all, he entreated the two sons of Atreus, Agamemnon and Menelaus, the army's commanders.

"Sons of Atreus and all you other well-greaved Achaeans," he called out, "may the gods who dwell upon Olympus allow you to sack the great city of Priam. And later, may you safely come to your homes. [20] In return, all I ask is that you release my dear child — that you accept this ransom for her out of respect for Zeus' son Apollo, who strikes from afar."

Hearing this, all the Achaeans shouted and clapped their hands in approval, giving their assent to Chryses. They wished to respect the priest of Apollo and accept his shining payment.

But not the son of Atreus! No, the proposal didn't please Agamemnon at all. Instead, he wickedly sent off Chryses by means of this cruel speech:

"Old man," he said, "don't let me find you hanging around our ships. Hear me when I command you to never come to our camp again. If you do, the god's golden scepter will not protect you. Listen to me. I will not let her go! No, your prized daughter will grow old in [30] my house at Argos far away from her own home. There she will busy herself by working the loom and by visiting my bed. So go! And if you wish to return home safely, alive and well, then do not any longer provoke me to anger."

That's what lord Agamemnon said. And hearing him, the old man feared the leader and obeyed his command.

Chryses walked off and silently ambled along the shore of the loud and roaring sea, quietly praying to lord Apollo, whom fair-haired Leto bore. "Hear me," he cried, "god of the silver bow, you who protect the port city of Chryse and holy Cilla, and you who

mightily rule Tenedos. Hear me Sminthian god! If I have ever
pleased you in building up a temple [40] or in offering the burnt
thighbones of great bulls or goats wrapped in layers of fat, then
may the Danaans pay for my tears with your deadly arrows tipped
with disease and suffering!"

*43-100 Hearing Chryses' prayer, a furious Apollo steps down from Olym-
pus and fires his arrows upon the Achaeans. He rains death upon them,
beginning with the mules and swift dogs first, before hitting the men. All
day long the pyres of the dead crackle and burn, reducing the remains to
bones and ash.*

*Nine days pass by. On the tenth, Achilles calls together the assembly
of men, spurred on by Zeus' wife, Hera. Standing in the middle of the
gathering, he wonders aloud why Apollo is so angry with the Achaeans.
He asks if some seer, priest, or reader of dreams will rise to explain.*

*Calchas, the son of Thestor, and the best of those who read the flight
patterns of birds, stands to give the reason for Apollo's wrath. But first, he
makes Achilles promise to defend him against Agamemnon, who is, he ob-
serves, the most powerful ruler among the Achaeans. Once the son of Pel-
eus agrees to this defense, Calchas explains that the god is not angry
because of a broken vow or a missed sacrifice. Rather, he's upset with Ag-
amemnon for not honoring his priest Chryses. And so he will go on angrily
destroying the army with disease until Agamemnon restores Chryses'
daughter without expecting anything in return. Lastly, Calchas adds that
when the Achaean leader sends her home, he must include the offering of
a hecatomb if he hopes to appease Apollo's wrath.*

101-187 With these words Calchas sat down, and the hero Aga-
memnon, the wide-ruling son of Atreus, stood up annoyed. His
heart was black with raging passion, and his eyes flashed fire as he
scowled at the seer.

Uttering words that foretold evil, he started off by shouting,
"Prophet of miserable shame! You've never yet spoken a useful
word for me—one that's agreeable. No! Instead, you like to spout
off ugly words, those fit for a coward. Nor have you ever accom-
plished a noble word for me. And now you come haranguing me in

the assembly of the Danaans, [110] asserting that the far-shooting god is raining down his arrows all because I do not wish to accept the shining ransom for the maiden girl, Chryses' daughter.

"But since I desire to keep her in my house, why should I return her? For I prefer Chryseis to my own wedded wife, Clytemnestra. Indeed, her body's form is in no way inferior to my wife's in shape and size. Moreover, she's smart and she works well upon the loom and at other tasks. Even so, I'll give her up if that's best. I'd rather the men be safe than suffer destruction. Just prepare for me another honor-prize so that I'm not the only man among the Argives without one. That wouldn't be right—[120] not when you all witness my honor-prize going off to another man and place."

After Agamemnon had spoken, godlike Achilles said in response, "Most glorious son of Atreus, of all men a super-lover of everything valued and esteemed! Tell me how the great-hearted Achaeans will now deliver up for you an honor-prize. Nothing at all remains from the great haul of goods we brought back with us after sacking and pillaging city after city along the plain. It's all been divvied up and distributed—the gold and silver, and all the women, children, and other property. It wouldn't be right to call everyone together again to make a collection of their prizes. Instead, you should give the girl up to the god. And if Zeus ever lets us sack the well-fortified city of Troy, we'll make up for your loss by repaying you three and four times over from all the plunder."

[130] In reply, lord Agamemnon said to him, "You won't deceive me like that, Achilles. Even though you're a good and noble man, you'll not slip by me, nor will you win me over. What—will you keep your own honor-prize while I sit here without one? I tell you what, have the Achaeans hand over something that is pleasing to me, an honor-prize that is suitable to my status and worth just as much as the girl is. But if they refuse to offer it up, I'll come myself and seize one with my own mighty hands! I'll come for your prize or that of Telamonian Ajax or Odysseus! And once I take it, I'll carry it off! Then we'll see who's angry!

[140] "But let's consider this matter again later on. For now, let's drag a black ship down into the sea and find a crew for her. Drive

a hecatomb of cattle onboard along with the beautiful girl, Chryseis. And may one of the leading men serve as captain—Ajax or Idomeneus or godlike Odysseus, or you, son of Peleus, most fearful of all men. Go and offer sacrifice to Apollo, the one who works from afar, so that you might appease him for us."

Looking grimly at Agamemnon, swift-footed Achilles said to him, "I can't believe it! Now you've thrown a mantle of shame upon your shoulders! You're always scheming and plotting, greedy for gain! [150] But think about it—why would any of the Achaeans now do your bidding? Why would any man march for you or fight against the mighty foe? I didn't come to Troy because *I* had a problem with the Trojans. *I* have no quarrel with them. They didn't raid *my* cattle or *my* horses. Nor did they waste *my* fields by cutting down the harvests on the rich plains of Phthia. Why would they? There's a vast distance between my land and theirs that's all filled up with shadow-casting mountains and the roaring sea. But *you*— you great shameless one! Even though no one else had a problem with the Trojans, we followed you here to make you happy, to delight *you,* hoping to win back from them Menelaus' honor and the same for your whole family—you dog-faced bitch! [160] Yet now you turn away and won't trouble yourself with this one inconvenient fact.

"More! Now you threaten to come up to me and strip me of the honor-prize I fought and suffered for—the very one that the sons of the Achaeans awarded me when we divided the plunder. You should already know that whenever we divvy up the goods, I never have an honor-prize that is equal to yours. No! When the Achaeans sack a Trojan city, I'm there managing much of the furious battle. But when the time comes for dividing the loot, you get the biggest honor-prize of all, and I get very little, taking back to my ship's hold just a few things of value, even though I'm bone-tired with fighting.

"Fine. I'll go to Phthia since that is by far the better thing for me to do. [170] I'll return home in my curved ships. That way I'll no longer pile up riches and more for you while I myself have no honor."

The lord of men Agamemnon answered him by saying, "Run away if you want! I'm not begging you to stay. There are others who will honor me—most of all Zeus the counselor. Anyway, of all the lords raised up by Zeus, you are the most distasteful to me—hateful even. I give you this simple reason: strife is always pleasing to you, and wars and battles. So what if you are super-heroically strong! Some god gave you that power anyway. Go home, then, with your ships and your comrades in arms. [180] Go and rule over the Myrmidons. I've already put you and your anger out of mind!

"But I promise you this. After I send Chryseis to her father at Apollo's bidding, I myself will come to your shelter and take from you your own girl with the beautiful face. I'll seize your honor-prize, Briseis, so that you will know how much better and braver I am than you. And when that happens, another man will hesitate to declare himself my equal or liken himself to me."

188-225 Hearing this, Achilles feels the pain of being shamed by another man. Part of him wants to draw his sword and murder the son of Atreus. The other part thinks it may be better to check his rising anger. Finally, just as he is pulling out the long bronze blade to slay him, Athena appears and commands him to stop and fight Agamemnon with words alone. Knowing he must obey the goddess no matter how angry he feels, he agrees, thrusting the sword back into its scabbard.

After Athena flies off to Olympus, the young Achaean hero turns against the older man and rails on him, beginning with: You dog-faced drunkard, you who possess the courage of a prancing deer!

226-231 "You never venture out to fight with the men of the army, nor do you dare to join the best of the Achaeans in an ambush. No—you shun these tasks just as you shun death itself! You'd rather go around seizing [230] gifts from the man who has the courage to speak against you. You people-eating king! Ha! When in fact you rule a bunch of worthless nobodies!"

232-274 Saying this, Achilles vows to stop fighting for Agamemnon. He goes on to predict that Agamemnon will one day regret his refusal to honor "the best of the Achaeans" when Hector eventually destroys his army and Achilles is already far away. Then the hero sits down.

Nestor, the old and long-time ruler of Pylos, stands to speak. He explains that Agamemnon and Achilles are doing exactly what Priam, the lord of Troy, and his sons would like for them to do. They'd rejoice to see you quarrel! he says. Before going on, Nestor explains why the Achaeans should listen to him. He came from and fought alongside a better and stronger generation of men, he asserts. And they, as great as they were, nevertheless listened to him. Getting back to the Achaeans, he advises them to obey his words. Turning to Agamemnon and Achilles, he says . . .

275-284 "Even though you are a good man and strong, Agamemnon, you should not carry off the girl from Achilles. The reason is simple—the sons of the Achaeans awarded her in front of everyone.

"And you, son of Peleus, you should not wish to strive with a king, your force against his. Let me tell you something. Sceptered kings do not have just any ordinary honor from Zeus. Not at all. Rather, Zeus has given them glory. [280] So even if you are strong and have a goddess for your mother, Agamemnon is better and stronger than you since he rules over far more men."

Turning to Agamemnon, Nestor finished, "And you, son of Atreus, check your wrath. I implore you to let go of your anger against this man, who is a towering wall for the Achaeans against all the evils of war."

285-291 *Hearing Nestor's counsel, Agamemnon agrees that he has spoken well. Still, he must not let Achilles usurp his power as he surely wishes to do.*

292-296 But godlike Achilles interrupted him. "The men will call me a coward and a worthless nobody if I give in to you! Order other people around—not me! I won't obey you!"

297-351 *Still, Achilles agrees to give up Briseis to the chief leader. But, he declares, I won't hand over any of my other possessions to you! And if you try to take anything else, my spear will soon be reddened by your dark blood!*

Finishing their verbal scuffle, they break up the assembly. Achilles returns to his own camp with his dear friend Patroclus, the son of

Menoetius, and Agamemnon prepares the ship with the hecatomb and Chryseis. He appoints Odysseus of many counsels to serve as its captain.

When the ship sails off, Agamemnon orders the men of the army to purify themselves in the sea's salty water. He offers many sacrifices nearby. All along, however, he doesn't forget his quarrel with Achilles and his promised threat. Consequently, he sends Talthybius and Eurybates to retrieve Briseis. The henchmen go, and with Patroclus' help, Achilles willingly hands her over while swearing before the blessed gods and other men that he will never fight for Agamemnon again—a man, he charges, who is mad with rage.

After Briseis unwillingly walks away, the young hero sits by the gray and limitless sea and mournfully raises his hands in prayer to his immortal mother, Thetis.

352-356 "Mother," he cried, "you brought me into this world doomed to live a brief life. Surely, therefore, Zeus, who thunders from Olympus, owes me honor. Yet now he has given me very little. And the wide-ruling son of Atreus has dishonored me since by force he has robbed me of my honor-prize."

357-412 *Hearing her weeping son, Thetis rises from the depths of the sea and asks him to reveal what's wrong. Even though she already knows, Achilles explains. They went to Thebes, he says, sacked it and carried off all the plunder. After, when the Achaeans divided the loot, Agamemnon got Chryseis. But when Apollo's priest, her father, came to fetch Chryseis with an aptly large ransom, Agamemnon refused to give her back because it didn't please him. At least that's what he said! So he told the old man to buzz off. This disrespect infuriated the priest. As a result, Chryses prayed to Apollo for revenge, for the restoration of his own honor. The god delivered by sending the plague on us. So when Calchas told us why Apollo was so angry, I was the first to stand and recommend giving the girl back. It was the only way to appease the god, I said. But Agamemnon didn't see it that way! Not exactly. Rather, he said that he would take my girl to make up for his loss.*

After Achilles recounts what happened, he begs his mother to go to Olympus to enlist the help of Zeus in regaining his honor. Remind him,

he says, of what you did to free him when Hera, Poseidon, and Athena
bound him that time—how you called the hundred-hander, Briareus, to
the rescue. Remind him of how all the blessed gods feared him then.

413-430 Thetis wept and answered him, "Dear son! My heart aches
because I gave birth to you. If only you could have remained un-
harmed by your ships without all these tears! For I know that your
allotted time will be short anyway. Out of all men, you will be mis-
erable and die early. Therefore, it was for a wretched fate that I bore
you in my great home.

[420] "Nevertheless, I will go to the snowy heights of Olympus
and report your story to Zeus, who delights in thunder, if indeed
he will listen to me. Meanwhile, stay here and stoke your wrath
against the Achaeans. Let them feel it. And hold back from the fight
until Zeus returns from feasting with the Ethiopians. He only left
yesterday, traveling toward Oceanus with the other gods. But he'll
be back in twelve days. Then I will go to his bronze-floored house,
clasp his knees in supplication, and I imagine I'll be able to win him
over for you."

Saying this, she left Achilles who was still furious at the loss of
the well-dressed girl Briseis—angry that Agamemnon and his men
were able [430] to wrest her away from him by force against his will.

431-502 *While Achilles prays to his mother, Odysseus and the other*
Achaeans sail to Chryse in order to return Chryseis to her father.

When they come to the port city, the old man rejoices to see his daugh-
ter. Straightaway, Chryses asks Apollo to stop striking the Achaeans with
his deadly arrows. The god hears the prayer and is appeased by the
Achaean sacrifice. The following morning, they sail back to Troy.

Twelve days go by, and the immortal gods return to Olympus after
feasting with the Ethiopians. Remembering Achilles' request, Thetis rises
from under the sea and goes to the ridges of the mountain to talk with
Zeus.

503-516 "Father Zeus, if among the immortals I ever did anything
for you in word or deed, hear my prayer and honor my son, whose

life will be cut short anyway. The lord of men Agamemnon has dishonored him by seizing his honor-prize and keeping her. Make up for this lost honor and pay my son back, Olympian lord of counsel. Grant might to the Trojans, and victory that follows from such might, until the Achaeans [510] pay back my son and increase his honor."

That's what Thetis said. And Zeus, the son of Cronus, just sat there in silence for a moment, not saying a word.

Finally, Thetis grabbed his knees and begged him a second time. "Nod your head," she implored, "and promise to do what I ask. Or, if you wish, deny my request since you fear nothing and can refuse if you want. If you do, though, I'll know how much I'm honored among the gods—the very least!"

517-539 *Frustrated, Zeus explains his hesitation. It is his wife, Hera. The whole business will cause them to fight. She will accuse him of aiding the Trojans again, and then she will tell everybody. Still, he will do it. He nods his head in favor of Thetis' request—the most solemn sign Zeus can offer to indicate his deepest intentions.*

After they plan together, Thetis flies back to the sea and plunges into its depths, and Zeus walks down from the ridges of Olympus to his great house. When he arrives, the gods stand up and nod out of respect for him. The respect doesn't last, though. When he sits down, it is to a full measure of Hera's indignation—for she has just seen Thetis leave the mountain and dive into the sea.

540-550 "You cunning sneak!" she tore into him. "Which of the gods have you been talking to now? You are always negotiating and secretly making agreements behind my back! You never tell me what you intend to do!"

The father of men and gods replied, "Hera! You mustn't expect to know the substance of every conversation I have. Even though you are my wife, my judgments will be hard for you to bear. When it is appropriate for you to listen, then no one will know before you do—neither god nor man. But when I intend to keep a matter to myself, [550] then you must not pry or ask questions."

551-564 *Feigning astonishment, Hera denies any such nosiness and vows to abide by whatever Zeus has planned. Still, she is worried that he has pledged honor to Achilles by allowing harm to come to the Achaeans. Zeus admits it—she has guessed the plan. So what? As for Hera, the cloud-gatherer orders her to be quiet.*

565-611 "Sit down, hold your tongue, and obey my words. For if I lay my invincible hands on you, none of the Olympian gods will be able to help you."

So he spoke, and the cow-eyed queen Hera was afraid and sat down. Silently, she forced herself to obey, bending her dear heart to his will. [570] Still, all the heavenly gods in Zeus' house were upset. They felt troubled, frustrated.

That was until Hephaestus, famous for his art, attempted to talk to and pacify his mother, white-armed Hera. "It will be intolerable," he said, "if you two start quarrelling like this over mortals. It will cause a brawl among the gods. And if that happens, there won't be any pleasure at all in the noble feast—not if inferior matters such as mortal human beings get the better of us. Here's what I advise, mother, though you already know it yourself. Turn on your charm and show our dear father Zeus some affection." Hephaestus paused and turned to the other gods. "Otherwise the father may have to school all of us with violence, and the feast will be ruined. [580] Think of it! What if the one who loudly thunders and flashes lightning strikes so hard that we go flying from our seats? He can do it, too, for he is by far the best of the gods. But if you lay hold of him with soft and conciliatory words, then the Olympian will be appeased, and at once he will be gracious to us."

When Hephaestus was done speaking, he jumped up from his chair and put a two-handled cup into his dear mother's right hand. Then he spoke to her, saying, "Endure, mother. Hold yourself up through all your troubles. Because you are dear to me, I don't want to see you beaten before my eyes. I would help you, but there's no chance of making a stand against Zeus. Don't you remember? [590] Once before when I was trying to help you, he seized me by the foot and hurled me from the heavenly threshold. All day long, from morning until evening, I was falling—falling until at sunset I eventually came to the ground upon the island of Lemnos. There I lay in pain with very little life in me until the Sintian men came along and took care of me."

That's what Hephaestus said, and the white-armed goddess Hera smiled. And smiling, she took the two-handled cup in hand from her child.

At this, Hephaestus drew sweet nectar from the mixing bowl and served it around to all the other gods, moving from left to right as he did so. And the blessed gods busted out with unstoppable laughter [600] when they saw him rushing around all out of breath, up and down the great hall of Zeus' house.

So it was that they feasted all day long until the sun set. Every god had a full share of the spread—no god's hunger went unsatisfied. Apollo played his beautiful lyre, and the Muses sang to one another with their lovely voices.

But when the sun's glorious light had faded, they went home to bed, each to his own abode that was skillfully built by the glorious smith Hephaestus, the one with two disabled feet but an understanding heart and mind. And Zeus himself, the Olympian lord of thunder and lightning, crawled into bed [610] where he usually slept when sweet sleep came upon him. There he stepped up and slept next to Hera of the golden throne.

BOOK 2

TO BATTLE MEN!
THE CATALOGUE OF THE BEST

IN BRIEF: *Carrying out his plan to honor Achilles, Zeus sends a dream to Agamemnon. Waking up, Agamemnon calls the men together to test them. Do you want to go home? he asks. We do! they respond—all but for Odysseus and Nestor. They shouldn't go home until each has a Trojan wife to avenge Helen! After feasting, the multitude assembles by the ships like— as Homer has it—flies around a pail of milk. The poet catalogues the Achaean ships and leaders, offering an extended glory report. He lists various Achaean bests before panning over to the Trojans to do the same.*

ZEUS COULDN'T SLEEP. While all the other gods and chariot-fighting men slumbered through the night, sweet sleep didn't take hold of the god. Instead, he anxiously thought about how to honor Achilles and destroy many of the men nearby the Achaean ships.

5-169 Zeus eventually hits upon a plan. He sends a destructive dream to Agamemnon in the likeness of Nestor. The Nestor-dream encourages Agamemnon to call the men together to fight, assuring him of Zeus' compassionate care. Moreover, thanks to Hera's persuasion, the gods are now united on the most significant point, he declares. After nine long years of war, the Achaeans will finally sack Troy. Hearing this, Agamemnon is thrilled. Poor man. He is clueless about the death and destruction that Zeus has in store for him and his army.

When daylight comes, Agamemnon gathers the elders together to tell them about the dream. Afterward, all the lesser men join them in assembly. Surrounded by the chaotic, swarming army, Agamemnon decides to test his men and their willingness to fight. He calls out, Who wants to flee?

Who wants to go home? Then he claims that Zeus has shamefully tricked them all—that despite nine years of toilsome combat they will never sack Troy! The men fail the test. Barely waiting to hear him finish, they swivel in the sand and loudly and wildly run off toward their ships where they eagerly prepare to return home.

The problem: an Achaean retreat is not what Fate has ordained. Hera notices the army's flight and orders Athena to do something about it. Obeying the command, the bright-eyed goddess flies down from Olympus and gently speaks to Odysseus, who, says Homer, is like Zeus in counsel.

170-267 So far, Odysseus had not yet touched his black well-benched ship in order to go since he felt distressed in his heart and spirit.

Bright-eyed Athena approached him. Standing near him she said, "God-born son of Laertes, much-able Odysseus—are you too going to jump into your many-benched ship in order to flee to your dear home and the land of your fathers? Are you really going to surrender the glory-boast, Argive Helen, to Priam and the Trojans? Think about it. Many Achaeans have died here at Troy, far from their own homes. No, you can't just run away. So here's what I command. Make your way through the army of the Achaeans. [180] Speak gently to them, to each man, and restrain them. And don't let them drag their rolling ships down to the sea."

That's what the goddess said. Knowing it was her voice, Odysseus threw off his cloak from around his shoulders and set off running. Behind him his herald Eurybates, who was also from Ithaca, picked up the covering.

Odysseus jogged straight up to Agamemnon and asked him for his scepter—the same imperishable staff he had inherited from his fathers. Agamemnon gave it to him. Then, with the scepter in his right hand, Odysseus went among the ships of the bronze-clad Achaeans. Whenever he met one of the chief leaders, one of those outstanding men, he stood by him and spoke to him gently in order to prevent his departure. [190] "God-possessed man," he said, "it's not fitting for you to be frightened like a coward. Rather, you should remain where you are and order your men to stay as well. Don't you know that Agamemnon was testing us? Soon he'll hammer the sons of the Achaeans. Don't you remember what he said this morning in the first council? But don't let this happen — don't let him and his anger harm the Achaeans! For great is the spirit of a god-nourished ruler. Their honor is from Zeus, and Zeus the counselor loves them."

But when Odysseus came across any common man of the people who was shouting, he struck him with his staff and upbraided him with words, saying, [200] "God-possessed man, sit still and listen to the words of other men who are better and braver than you. You are feeble and without strength — you are unwarlike! Therefore, you don't count either in battle or in counsel. We cannot all be kings here. No, the rule of many is no good. One man must be the ruler; one man must hold the scepter from the son of scheming Cronus and the right to pronounce what is customary so that he may deliberate for all the men."

Like a lord Odysseus managed the army. The people hurried back to the assembly again from their ships and shelters with a sound that thundered like big waves crashing along [210] the shore when the sea is roaring. Finally, they all took their seats in the assembly and were quiet. But Thersites of measureless speech went on wagging his unbridled tongue. In his mind he knew many disorderly words, all of them inappropriate, with which to strive and quarrel with the chief leaders. He didn't really care about what he said. His only goal was to get the Argives laughing.

The thing about Thersites was that he was truly ugly. In fact, he was the ugliest man that came to Troy. His legs bowed out, and his feet were crippled so that he had to hobble along, and his two shoulders were rounded, causing him to hunch over. But that's not all. His head ran up to a point that grew nothing but stubble. [220] Of all the leading men, Achilles and Odysseus hated him most of all because he always ranted on at them in the attempt to school them.

Now, however, despite the shame the other Achaeans felt at his inappropriate lecturing, Thersites was rebuking godlike Agamemnon. With a shrill voice he shouted at the ruler and schooled him with these words:

"Son of Atreus, what's wrong now? What more do you want? Your shelter is filled with bronze things and plenty of women, for whenever we sack a city, we give you the very first pick. Do you want more gold? Do you want to seize the gold ransom that some [230] horse-taming Trojan man will bring from Ilium in exchange for his son—even though I or another man took him hostage in the first place? Or do you want yet another young woman to mingle with in love? Whatever you want, it's not fitting that the first man— the captain!—lead the sons of the Achaeans into harm.

"O weaklings! Cowards worthy of reproof! Women of the Achaean land—Achaean men no more! Let us sail home in our ships and leave this fellow here at Troy to cherish his honor-prizes all by himself. Then he will discover whether we Achaeans were of any service to him or not. Even though Achilles is a much better man than he is, Agamemnon [240] has dishonored him, for he has seized and kept his honor-prize. Still, Achilles is not all that angry. Rather, he let the girl go. Otherwise, this would now be your last outrage, son of Atreus!"

That's how Thersites schooled Agamemnon, the shepherd of men. But godlike Odysseus went up to him at once, and full of anger, he rebuked him sternly. "Stop the rapid flow of words from your mouth, Thersites! You shouldn't strive and quarrel with the leading men when you are all alone and have no one to back you. For I declare that among all the men who ventured to Troy with the two sons of Atreus, there is no baser mortal than you. [250] So don't speak about the leading men like this. And don't censure them in the hope that you'll make it home. We don't yet know how things will turn out—whether the sons of the Achaeans will return home well and with success, or not. Regardless, how dare you reproach Agamemnon because the Danaan heroes have awarded him so much! How dare you taunt and harangue him! But I'll tell you this, and I'll make sure it happens: if I catch you again talking like a fool, then I will either give up my head [260] or the fact that I am Telemachus' father, or I will take you, strip you naked of all your clothes, and shamefully whip you out of the assembly until you go blubbering back to the ships."

That's what Odysseus said. And to make sure Thersites heard, he beat him with the scepter upon his back and shoulders until the misshapen man dropped to the ground weeping, and bloody welts rose from his back.

268-336 *Thersites sits down to the sound of the other men applauding Odysseus for shutting his mouth. Though distressed at his suffering, they all nevertheless laugh at the weeping man. Odysseus, the sacker of cities, however, isn't finished with them. He turns to the crowd of men and chastises them for wanting to go home. Still, he understands, he says. They've been away for nine years. Any man in his right mind would want to be home with his wife. All the same, it would be shameful to go home with nothing to show for all their labor. He bids them to endure, reminding them of Calchas' prophecy that is bound to come true—that in the tenth year they would take Troy. The Achaean army cheers in agreement. Then old Nestor stands to speak.*

337-381 "Shame on you!" he called out. "You're debating like a bunch of cute little infants—like children who couldn't care less for warlike deeds!

"Where now are all the promises we made and the oaths? [340] Should we toss into the fire all our plans and drink-offerings of unmixed wine and all those handshakes we shook to prove our trustworthiness? Wherever they are, let me tell you that we're wasting our time with all these words. Talking will get us nowhere. Stand, therefore, son of Atreus, and lead the Argives into battle.

"As for those few who secretly plot to go home even before we know whether Zeus has spoken falsely or not, let them rot in Hades! [350] For when we Argives set sail for Troy, the mighty son of Cronus promised that we would bring death and destruction to the Trojans. And to back his promise, he showed us favorable signs by flashing lightning on our right. Therefore, may none of us speed home until each man has first taken and slept with the wife of some Trojan man in order to pay the Trojans back for all the pain and suffering we've had to endure to get Helen back. Still, if any man is in such a hurry to go home again, let him just touch his hand to his black well-benched ship, and very soon he'll find his home in his destined death, long before all the others."

[360] Turning to the ruler Agamemnon, Nestor said, "You should be mindful and listen to what I say. Do not disregard the word I speak to you. Separate the men according to their tribes and clans so that all the brothers and cousins may aid their clan, and the clansmen may help the tribe. If you do this, and if the Achaeans obey you, you'll find out who the cowards and the brave men are from among the leaders and all the ordinary men. Consequently, you will learn whether it is the will of the gods that causes you to fail to take the city or the cowardice of your men and their thoughtlessness and ignorance of warfare."

Answering him, lord Agamemnon said, [370] "Nestor, you have once again outdone the sons of the Achaeans in counsel. Hear me father Zeus, Athena, and Apollo—if only there were ten such counselors among the Achaeans! If there were, then lord Priam's city would quickly fall into our hands, as we would conquer and sack it. But instead, aegis-bearing Zeus, the son of Cronus, gives me over to suffering and pain, introducing me to useless strife and quarrels. For Achilles and I are fighting about this girl with heated words. And I admit it, I was the first to be angry. Even so, if we can join together in counsel and be united, [380] then the Trojans won't be able to delay their evil demise for even the smallest amount of time. Now, therefore, go and get your morning meal so that we may join together with the Trojans in the war god Ares' work!"

382-441 *The men shout their agreement and leave to prepare. Agamemnon and the other chief men—Nestor, Idomeneus, the two Ajaxes, Diomedes, Odysseus, and Menelaus—sacrifice a bull to Zeus for success, that Hector and the many Trojans may bite the dust. They feast and are all satisfied, setting aside the desire for food and drink. Nestor bids Agamemnon to call the army to battle. He does.*

442-454 At once, Agamemnon sent clear-voiced heralds to call the long-haired Achaeans to battle. So they called them, and the army gathered together. Those allied with Agamemnon, the chief leaders raised by Zeus, rushed around separating the men, and bright-eyed Athena, who holds the much-honored and ageless aegis . . . , [450] dashed everywhere, darting furiously among the men of the Achaeans, urging them forward to fight and putting courage into the heart of each man so that he might wage war and battle without ceasing. As a result, war became sweeter to them than returning home in their hollow ships.

455-483 From their shelters and ships, the men march out onto the plain surrounding the river Scamander. They advance like a swarming flock of birds and gather as flies do around a pail of milk. And with the morning sun shining upon their bronze armor, shields, and spears, they appear like a blazing fire pouring across the grass of the plain. As for the leaders, they direct the army as a goatherd does a herd of goats. And among them all, Agamemnon stands out like a bull does among all the cows. Finally, the poet asks the Muses for a glory report, one revealing who all the Achaean leaders are, and who is the best.

484-493 You Muses who live upon the ridges of Olympus, now tell me something great. I ask you because you are goddesses, who witness all things as they happen, whereas we humans hear and know nothing but the rumor and report of things. So I ask you, who were the leaders and rulers of the Danaans? As for the many, the men of the army, I could not name each one of them even if I had ten mouths, [490] and my voice never failed, and my heart were made of bronze. I could only do it if the Muses of Olympus, the daughters of aegis-bearing Zeus, put them into my mind, all those men who came to Ilium. Nevertheless, I will proclaim the names of the leading men of the ships, along with the number of their ships.

494-759 Beginning with the Boeotians in central Greece and finishing with the Magnesians of Thessaly and covering all of Greece of the allied Achaean army, from south to north, east to west, and all the islands in the sea, Homer recounts the catalogue of ships. It is the greatest glory report of the Iliad. Through him, the Muses declare who came from which land or island, who came with whom, the number of ships, and what their land

*was like—what flocks it held, what cities and citadels, and what estates
there were with fields of grain, vines, and orchards. Homer ends by asking
the Muses to reveal the best of the Achaeans.*

760-779 So these were the leaders and rulers of the Danaans. But
tell me, Muse, who was the best among them, whether man or
horse, among those that followed the sons of Atreus?

Of the horses, those of the son of Pheres were by far the best.
They were as fast as birds, the same age and color, and perfectly
matched in height. Apollo of the silver bow had bred them in Pe-
reira—both of them mares and dreadful as Ares in battle.

Of men, Telamonian Ajax was the best as long as Achilles per-
sisted in his wrath and anger—for Achilles was much better and
braver than Ajax, [770] and his horses were better too. As it was,
however, Achilles had withdrawn from among the leaders and
fighting men. Thanks to his anger aimed at the shepherd of men
Agamemnon, he was hiding out among his curved seagoing ships.
And his men passed their time upon the seashore throwing discs
and spears, and in archery. Their horses, meanwhile, stood nearby
grazing upon lotus-clover and wild celery. As for the chariots, they
were well-covered in each man's shelter. But the charioteers and
other men, even though they longed for their leader, who was dear
to Ares, wandered throughout the army without going out to fight.

780-810 *From their assembly held by Priam's great door, the Trojans wit-
ness the Achaeans marching out to fight. The latter men sweep the plain
below like a wildfire caused by Zeus' thunder and lightning. In the voice
of his son Polites, the messenger goddess Iris reveals the vast size of the
Achaean army to lord Priam, chastising the king for talking rather than
acting. Then she turns and orders Hector to lead the Trojans and their
allies out against the invading host. The Trojan allies are from many lands
and speak many languages. Obeying her, he does. And so the Trojan army
loudly marches out to battle, the footmen together with the chariot fighters.*

811-818 Now there is a high mound before the city . . . called by
men Thorn-hill, whereas the gods know it as Myrine's mound, that

of the bounding Amazon. It was here that the Trojans and their allies split into the various divisions of men along with their leaders. As for the Trojans themselves, Priam's son, great Hector of the gleaming helmet, led them out. Following him were a great number of men. Among them were the very best of those armed men who longed to fight with a spear.

819-875 *Homer finishes the Trojan glory report by revealing the other Trojan and allied divisions, along with the most significant leaders. Aeneas, for example, the son of Anchises and Aphrodite, leads the Dardanians. To cite a few more of the many named by Homer, there are the archer Pandarus, Adrastus and Amphius (the sons of Merops, who was the best at the art of divination), Asius, Hippothous, Acamas, and Nastes. The latter man is the leader of the Carians "of barbarian speech." He marches into the fight armed like a maiden girl with gold—gold that fails to protect the fool, Homer reveals. And lastly, the men of Lycia march out.*

876-877 There were Sarpedon and the blameless man Glaucus. They were the leaders of the Lycians, up from the land of distant Lycia, by the whirling Xanthus.

BOOK 3

THE BATTLE FOR HELEN
PARIS, MENELAUS & THE CHIEF ACHAEANS

IN BRIEF: *The armies line up. Hector schools Paris (Alexander) for shrinking back before Menelaus. In response, Paris suggests single combat with Menelaus. The winner will take Helen and all her wealth. Both sides agree to the proposal, performing pre-combat rites and swearing oaths. Meanwhile, from atop the walls of Troy, Helen introduces Priam to the big actors of the Achaean cast, including Agamemnon, Odysseus, Telamonian Ajax, and Idomeneus. Finally, the two step forward to fight. After throwing spears, Menelaus dashes forward to take hold of Paris. But just as he's dragging him off, Aphrodite spirits Paris away to make love with Helen. Agamemnon assumes the Achaeans have won and will therefore recover Helen, her possessions, and a revenge-penalty to top it off. How wrong he is!*

1-14 The Achaean and Trojan armies march toward each other — the Trojans come on loudly like birds, while the Achaeans kick up a great cloud of dust.

W HEN THEY CAME close to one another, Alexander stepped forward to serve as champion on the Trojan side. He wore the skin of a panther over his shoulders, had his bow and sword, and brandished two spears topped with bronze. With these deadly weapons he challenged the best of the Argives to meet him [20] face to face in grim battle.

Now when Menelaus, dear to Ares, observed Alexander like this going out before the throng of men with long strides, he was as glad as a lion that comes upon the fallen carcass of some goat or horned stag and devours it at once, even though a pack of dogs and shepherd boys attack him to drive him off. In this way, Menelaus was glad when he saw Alexander with his own eyes. Now he would take revenge! Now he would make the offending man pay! Clad in armor, he at once jumped down from his chariot.

[30] But when godlike Alexander noticed Menelaus appear among the men fighting out front, his dear heart was panic-stricken. He therefore fell back to his comrades among the larger body of men and avoided death. As one who leaps back—startled, trembling, and pale—when he suddenly comes upon a deadly snake on a winding mountain trail, even so did Alexander disappear into the throng of Trojan warriors, terror-stricken at the sight of the son of Atreus.

Seeing this, Hector schooled his brother with words meant to shame him. "Unhappy Paris, your form is the finest, you who are crazy for women, but you're a cheat, a deceiver! [40] I wish that you had never been born or that you had at least died unwed. That would have been far better than for you to be an outrage and for others to look at us from beneath raised brows. Will the longhaired Achaeans not laugh aloud at us? Won't they say and make known that we have a champion who is fine looking but not strong or courageous?

"Did you not, strong as you are, get your comrades together and sail across the sea to a land of strangers? There you carried off a beautiful woman who was already married to a warrior and the daughter-in-law of warriors. [50] Don't you see all the misery this has caused? Look at your father, your city, and all the people! It's a source of shame and dejection to you, but to your enemies, a source of delight! And how can you now turn away from Menelaus, dear to Ares? Shouldn't you fight him to learn what kind of warrior he is—the man whose wife you have stolen? Where will your lyre and music making be then? And your good looks and love making? Where will all the fine things be when you're lying face down in the dust? Let me tell you this. The Trojans are very fearful people. Otherwise, they would have stoned you for all the evil you've done them!"

Godlike Alexander answered him, "Hector, you upbraid me as you should and not beyond what is right—[60] though your heart is always as hard as the axe a shipwright uses to cut wood for his ship, just like the mind in your breast is fearless. Still, do not reproach me for the lovely gifts of golden Aphrodite. The glorious gifts of the gods are not to be thrown away, whatever they give, even though no man would readily choose these.

"Now, if you wish for me to battle and fight Menelaus, then have the Trojans and Achaeans sit down. [70] I will join with Menelaus, dear to Ares, in the middle, and I will fight him for Helen and all her wealth. And the victorious man, the stronger one, will seize the woman and all her possessions and carry them off to his house. But let the rest swear oaths of friendship and trust according to which the Trojans will remain where they are while the others will go home to Argos, the land of grazing horses, and Achaea, the land of beautiful women."

76-153 *They carry out this plan. The Achaeans and the Trojans swear to oaths of friendship and trust with each other. Everyone is pleased with this move because, for now at least, the fighting has stopped. Otherwise, Homer transitions to Helen's loom where she is weaving a great purple tapestry embroidered with scenes of war. The messenger goddess Iris appears to her in the form of her sister-in-law Laodice and calls her to watch Paris and Menelaus' fight from atop the walls. She explains the agreement—how Helen will go with the man who wins. Finally, the goddess puts "sweet longing" in Helen's heart for Menelaus, her former husband. As a result of Iris' visit, Helen goes with two handmaidens to the top of the wall at the Scaean gates. There she encounters Priam and other aged men, who are too old to fight but still speak influentially in the Trojan assembly.*

154-202 When the elders saw Helen coming toward the tower on the wall, they whispered quietly to one another, "No one can blame or resent the Trojans or the well-greaved Achaeans for suffering so many pains for so long for the sake of this woman, who appears like an immortal goddess. Nevertheless, as beautiful as she is, let them take her and sail home on the ships, [160] or she will cause misery for us and our children after us."

That's what the old men said. But Priam called Helen to him and said, "Dear child, take your seat in front of me so that you may see your former husband, your kinsmen by marriage, and all those men who are dear to you. To me, you are not responsible for all this. Rather, it is the gods who are to blame, not you. The gods have brought about this terrible war with the Achaeans, a war that is responsible for much crying and many tears. Anyway, tell me the name of the huge man there—the Achaean man who is noble and great. I've seen men taller by a head, but not one so fine looking [170] and majestic. He looks like one of the chief men."

And Helen, a goddess among women, exchanged these words with him. "Father of my husband, dear and respected in my eyes, I wish that I had chosen death rather than coming here with your son—far from my bridal chamber, my friends, my darling daughter, and all my childhood companions. But it was not to be, and so I melt within lamenting over what has happened.

"Still, I will tell you what you wish to know. The hero you ask about is wide-ruling Agamemnon, the son of Atreus, both a good and noble king and a strong and mighty spearman. [180] He was a brother-in-law to me—I who am a dog-eyed, shameless bitch."

That's what Helen said. And the old man marveled at him and said, "Blessed son of Atreus, offspring of Fate and prosperous-by-god! I see that many Achaeans are subject to you. When I was in Phrygia, I saw many horsemen, the people of Otreus and Mygdon, who were camping upon the banks of the Sangrius. I was their ally with them when the Amazons, peers of men, came up against them. [190] But even they were not so many in number as the Achaeans."

Next the old man looked down at Odysseus and asked, "Tell me, who is that other man, shorter by a head than Agamemnon but broader across the chest and shoulders? There's his battle gear and armor set down on the ground, the much-nourishing earth, and there he is going through the lines of men as if he were some great woolly ram ordering his ewes."

And Zeus-born Helen answered, [200] "He is Odysseus, the son of Laertes and a man of many counsels. He was born in rugged Ithaca and excels in all manner of tricks, stratagems, and subtle cunning."

203-224 Wise Antenor confirms Odysseus' traits with a story relating the time Menelaus and Odysseus came on an embassy to Troy. Odysseus pretended to be a dumb fool, but when he spoke, he was a marvel to hear and behold.

225-233 The old man Priam next spotted Ajax and inquired, "Who is that other Achaean man, good, noble, and huge, the one with the broad shoulders who is standing out above the Argives by a head?"

And Helen with the flowing robes answered him, "That's huge Ajax, the wall of the Achaeans—their bulwark. [230] And the man on the other side of him standing among the Cretans is Idomeneus—the one that looks like a god. The leaders of the Cretans are gathered around him. I know him because Menelaus, dear to Ares, would often receive him as a guest in our house whenever he came visiting from Crete."

234-345 Helen tells Priam that she can see many others. But among all the men, she cannot see her two brothers, Castor and Polydeuces. And so, she speculates about why they are not present. Homer explains that it is because they are already dead.

Eventually Priam goes down to the battlefield with Antenor by his side. In the meantime, the Achaeans and Trojans are preparing for the great sacrifice and oath-taking. Finally, with Agamemnon acting as the chief spokesman offering the prayers, and Priam standing nearby, they sacrifice and swear oaths to abide by the outcome of the single combat between Menelaus and Paris. Whoever wins will keep Helen. If Menelaus triumphs, the Trojans will furthermore pay a penalty. If not, the Achaeans will stay and force them to pay. After cutting the lambs' throats and pouring out wine in libation, Agamemnon prays that whoever breaks the oath will have his brain likewise poured out and dashed upon the ground—along with his children's brains.

At this, and just before the beginning of the battle, Priam explains he cannot bear to witness his son fighting Menelaus. So he returns to the city.

Menelaus and Paris step forward. Odysseus and Hector cast lots to see who will first throw his spear. Paris will. The men sit down in ranks while Paris arms. Finally, Menelaus and Paris step between the two armies to fight.

346-354 Alexander threw first and struck the round shield of the son of Atreus, but the spear did not pierce it, for the shield turned its point.

[350] The son of Atreus Menelaus made the next move, praying to father Zeus as he did so. "Lord Zeus, grant that this man who first did me harm would pay the penalty. May I overpower and subdue godlike Alexander with my hands so that among men to come a man may shrink from doing harm to his host, to the man who shows a guest affection and offers him friendship."

355-454 *Menelaus throws. But even though the spear finds his enemy's shield and breastplate, Paris dodges aside at the last moment to avoid death. Observing this and blaming Zeus for the missed opportunity to get revenge, Menelaus dashes at Paris and grabs him by the helmet that is fastened by a strap around his neck. He drags Paris away toward the Achaeans.*

Homer tells us that Menelaus would have won much glory except for Aphrodite's saving action: she frees Paris and transports him home to Troy.

After this, Aphrodite beckons Helen to Paris' house from atop the wall. Not wanting to go because she feels ashamed, Helen nevertheless walks off to meet him for fear of Aphrodite's anger. There, she upbraids Paris, commanding him to go out and challenge Menelaus again—like a real man, she says. Paris refuses, declaring that Menelaus beat him with the help of Athena. Instead, burning with sweet desire, greater even than the desire he felt for her when he first made love to her on the isle of Cranae just after taking her from Menelaus, he calls Helen to bed.

Meanwhile, like a wild beast of prey, Menelaus is searching for Paris. But no one can find him, not even his own men who have come to hate him like black death.

455-461 Then standing among all the men, the lord of men Agamemnon spoke to them, saying, "Hear me you Trojans, Dardanians, and all your allies. The result is obvious—Menelaus has clearly won. He's the victor. Therefore, give back Helen with all her property, and make up for Menelaus' lost honor as is appropriate, [460] so that men to come will know about it."

That's what the son of Atreus said, and the Achaeans applauded him.

BOOK 4

THE GODS IN COUNCIL
AGAMEMNON & THE ARMY

IN BRIEF: *The gods in council on Mount Olympus consider what to do with the Achaeans and Trojans. Athena is furious with Zeus. Hera and Zeus are at odds. They eventually agree that Troy will fall. This means the Trojans must break the oath they swore before Menelaus and Paris battled. At the prompting of Athena, therefore, Pandarus shoots Menelaus with an arrow. Agamemnon is angry at this, and so he stirs his men to action. The armies clash and many men die.*

NOW THE GODS were sitting with Zeus in council upon the golden floor, while queenly Hebe poured out nectar for them to drink. And with the golden cups they acknowledged one another while looking down upon the city of Troy.

Right away, the son of Cronus tried to irritate Hera, speaking to her maliciously with barbed words. "Menelaus has two goddesses on his side, Argive Hera and Athena the defender. But what do they do? Here's what—they sit apart taking their [10] pleasure while looking on from afar, while laughter-loving Aphrodite is always rushing to Paris' side to defend him and ward off the fates of death. Just now she did it again. She saved him right when he thought he would die for sure.

"Regardless, the victory clearly belongs to Menelaus, so we must consider what to do. How should we move things forward? We could either urge them on to destructive war again, to the dread sound of battle, or we could separate them in friendship. If the latter option is pleasing to you and a welcome development, then Menelaus can lead Argive Helen home again and Priam's city can go on being inhabited."

[20] That's what Zeus said. And sitting side by side, Athena and Hera whispered to each other, planning harm for the Trojans. Athena was furious with her father Zeus with a wild anger that had seized her. Nevertheless, she was silent and said nothing. Hera, however, could no longer hold in her anger, so she confronted him.

"Dread son of Cronus, what are you suggesting? What a word you have spoken! I've worked hard to topple and flatten the city of Priam and his Trojans. I've urged my horses all over the land and have sweated to gather an army for one purpose alone—to harm Priam and his sons. So do it. Separate them in friendship and let Priam's city stand. But if you do, you should know that not all the other gods will approve of you or applaud you."

[30] Cloud-gathering Zeus suddenly felt very disturbed and said, "Crazy goddess, what harm have Priam and his sons done to you that you so intensely desire to flatten the well-built city of Ilium? What, do you also want to go through its gates and long walls in order to eat Priam raw along with his children and the other Trojans? Will *that* appease your anger? Do as you wish, then. I don't want this to be a reason for us to quarrel in days to come. But let me tell you something else you better store in your heart. [40] When in the future I eagerly desire to sack a city and flatten it—one of my own choosing, where there are men who are dear to you—then don't try to hinder me in my anger, but allow me to destroy it. You must let me do this in exchange for what I'm doing now—I'm giving in to you even though I don't want to. Of all inhabited cities under the sun and the stars, there was no other that I honored in my heart like Ilium, with Priam and his people. For my altar never lacked an abundance of the equally shared feast—neither wine libations nor the smoky savor of burning fat that is the honor-prize due to us gods."

[50] In return cow-eyed queenly Hera said, "My own three favorite cities are Argos, Sparta, and Mycenae with the wide streets. Utterly destroy them whenever they inflame the hatred of your heart. I won't make a stand or think it is too much. Anyway, even if I burn with envy and don't want you to flatten them, it won't matter since you are much stronger than I am. Still, I won't have my

own work wasted! I'm a god like you, born from the same family line. I am the oldest daughter of scheming Cronus—[60] famous because I am your wife and because you rule over all the other immortals. So let's give and take from each other. Whatever we decide, the rest of the immortal gods will follow our lead. Tell Athena, then, to quickly go into the dread battle between the Trojans and Achaeans. Have her arrange it so that the Trojans violate the oath first."

73-219 Like a falling star, Athena eagerly rushes down from the peaks of Olympus in the form of the man Laodocus, the son of Antenor, and she approaches Pandarus of Zeleia, the son of Lycaon. Speaking to him, she advises Pandarus to shoot Menelaus with an arrow and reminds him of all the glory and gifts he will receive in turn. Vowing a hecatomb of lambs to Apollo, the wolf-born, he does so, and the arrow flies toward the Achaean leader. The blessed gods, Athena foremost among them, deflect the arrow, even as a mother would swat a fly away from a sweetly sleeping child. Nevertheless, the arrow hits Menelaus, and his blood flows.

Agamemnon shudders at all the blood. He's afraid the wound is mortal and his brother will die. If that happens, the army will wish to leave, the expedition will be a failure, and they will have to leave Helen as "a glory-boast" to the Trojans. Agamemnon says he would rather die than hear someone recount such a failure.

Menelaus tells Agamemnon not to worry; the wound isn't mortal. They call Machaon, the son of Asclepius, to take care of it. He comes and does so, extracting the arrow and sprinkling healing herbs on the wound, even as the centaur Cheiron once taught his father to do.

220-225 While Machaon was taking care of Menelaus, good at the battle cry, the lines of Trojan warriors marched forward as the Achaeans rearmed and felt once again a lust for battle. And suddenly, it was as though godlike Agamemnon was a new man—he was no longer cowering or unwilling to fight but was rapidly moving into battle that confers glory on men.

226-233 What was Agamemnon's goal? Leaving his chariot and horses behind, he ranges through the ranks of the army, stirring them on to battle by promising victory and revenge.

234-239 "Argives! Don't give up yet! Don't drop your shield—your battle courage! For father Zeus will not support liars or falsehoods! The Trojans swore, and yet they were the first to violate their oaths. Therefore, I say that vultures will peck at their soft flesh and devour it, and we will carry off their dear wives and infant children when we sack their city!"

240-256 *Agamemnon angrily schools the archers, who hang back from battle. Then he comes to the Cretans, to Idomeneus and Meriones. Rejoicing at their battle readiness and that Idomeneus was out front leading while Meriones was pushing the men from behind, he explains why the Cretan leader should be eager to fight for him.*

257-264 "Idomeneus, above all the Danaans with swift horses, I honor you during battle and in other matters and at other times, as well as during the feast when [260] the best of the Argives mix the shining wine for the chief men. Although the other long-haired Achaeans drink their allotted portions, your cup is always full just like mine. You always drink as much as you desire. Even so, urge yourself on to battle! Be the warrior you've boasted yourself to be!"

265-438 *Idomeneus heartily agrees. So Agamemnon passes on to the two Ajaxes, who are arming with a mass of men. He praises them before striding off to old Nestor, who is organizing and directing his footmen and charioteers, explaining how the latter should fight. Hearing this, Agamemnon rejoices, wishing Nestor was still as strong as he used to be. Nestor agrees, acknowledging his lost youth. Next, Agamemnon comes to Menestheus, the son of Peteos, who is surrounded by his men, the Athenians. Then he sees Odysseus. Homer tells us their men hadn't yet heard the call to battle. Even so, Agamemnon rousts Menestheus and Odysseus for always hearing the call to eat—the invitation to devour roasted meat and drink wine. They should therefore stand among the foremost of the warriors, he says, and join in blazing battle. When Odysseus hotly denies this judgment, Agamemnon gently rescinds it. He then moves on to Diomedes, asking him why he is hanging back and not fighting like his father, Tydeus. Diomedes takes his speech to heart. But not his comrade Sthenelus, the son of Capaneus. He claims they are better than their fathers. Diomedes hushes his friend and tells him to focus on the battle at hand.*

They all do. The two armies march toward each other and clash violently.

439-451 The Trojans were roused by Ares, and the Achaeans by bright-eyed Athena, [440] Terror, Fear, and Strife, who is always hungry. Strife is man-slaying Ares' sister and comrade. She starts small and grows bigger and taller until her head is sky-high and her feet drag along the earth. Strife lobbed distressful contention between them, and when it came among them, it increased their lamentation. And when the men met one another, shield clashed with shield and spear with spear in the rage of battle, [450] . . . and the earth flowed with blood.

452-456 *The sound of battle is enormous, like that of a torrential flood thundering down a mountainside.*

457-461 Antilochus first killed one of the armed Trojans, a noble man fighting out front, Echepolus, the son of Thalysius. He hit him on that part of the helmet where the horsehair rises up and shakes. [460] Then he drove the spear down through the helmet and between his eyes, and the point passed through the bone as the dark gloom of death covered him.

462-542 *After Echepolus falls, the two sides fight ferociously for his body. Telamonian Ajax strikes next, killing Simoisius, the son of Anthemion. Homer explains that Simoisius will never pay back his parents for his rearing. After this, Antiphus, the son of Priam, strikes one of Odysseus' comrades Leucus, even though he hoped to hit Ajax. Angry, Odysseus steps forward to throw at the Trojans. He hits Priam's bastard son Democoon with a throw that enters one side of his head and punches out the other. With this, Hector and the foremost Trojans fall back, and the Achaeans advance.*

Observing this, Apollo calls down to the Trojans from Mount Pergamos. Fight! he urges. Don't give ground to the Achaeans! Their flesh is not made of stone or iron! Now is the time when Achilles is not with them! Athena likewise rouses the Achaeans.

Many die by stone, spear, and sword—Diores, the son of Amarynceus, and Peiros, the son of Imbrasus, among them.

543-544 That day, many Trojans and Achaeans lay stretched out side by side, their faces in the dust.

BOOK 5

THE RAGING RIVER DIOMEDES
AGAINST MEN & GODS

IN BRIEF: *Before withdrawing with Ares from the fight to sit on the banks of the Scamander, Athena assists Diomedes in order to give him glory. The Achaean leaders dominate the Trojans. Diomedes slaughters many and rages over the Trojan army like a swollen winter river. After Pandarus shoots Diomedes with an arrow, and Athena heals him, he fights like a lion. Pandarus wonders if he is a god or a man. Diomedes goes on fighting, slaughtering numerous men, including, eventually, Pandarus himself, who fights from Aeneas' chariot. Next, he slams Aeneas to the ground with a giant stone. Near to death, Aeneas is saved by his mother, Aphrodite. Diomedes' comrade Sthenelus rides away with Aeneas' horses. Finally, Diomedes goes up against the gods Aphrodite, Apollo, and Ares. He wounds Aphrodite, who zips off to her loving mother and the gentle reproach of Zeus. Apollo warns him off. And with the help of Athena, he drives a spear into Ares's stomach. Meanwhile, led on by Hector, the Trojans face the Achaeans, and Agamemnon inspires his men to fight. Zeus scolds his son Ares, who whines to him after being wounded. Paieon heals him.*

A ND NOW, ONCE again, Pallas Athena gave courage and battle might to the son of Tydeus, Diomedes, so that he would stand out among all the Argives and be elevated upon the wings of noble glory. Therefore, she made a stream of fire flare from his shield and burst from his helmet like the star that shines most brilliantly in summer after its bath in the streaming waters of Oceanus. It was with a fire like this, brilliant upon his head and shoulders, that she sent him rushing into the thickest of the fight.

Now among the Trojans, there was a certain rich and blameless man, [10] a priest of Hephaestus, and his name was Dares. He had two sons, Phegeus and Idaeus, both skilled in all the arts of war. These two came forward from the crowd of Trojans and went up against Diomedes, who fought on foot upon the ground, while they battled from their rolling chariot. When they were close to him, Phegeus took aim and cast first, but the spear whizzed over Diomedes' left shoulder without hitting him. Diomedes was next. He threw. And with success! The bronze spear sped until it slammed into Phegeus' chest right between the nipples. The force of the throw was so hard that it blasted him from his chariot.

[20] Observing Diomedes' might, Idaeus didn't hope or dare to stand over his brother's body to guard it. Instead, he jumped down from the beautiful chariot and took off. If he hadn't, he would have surely shared his brother's fate that day. Not only that, but Hephaestus saved him by wrapping him in a cloud of darkness so that his old father wouldn't be totally overwhelmed with grief. Even so, the son of Tydeus drove off with the chariot and horses and ordered his followers to take them to the ships. The great-hearted Trojans were horrified when they saw the two sons of Dares—one of them in flight and shunning battle and the other lying dead by his chariot.

Bright-eyed Athena, therefore, [30] took the war god by the hand and said, "Ares, Ares! You miserable bane of mortals and bloodstained stormer of cities! Should we not allow the Trojans and Achaeans to do battle in order to see which side father Zeus will grant glory? Let's fall back and dodge Zeus' anger."

Finishing her speech, she led raging Ares away from the fight, and they sat down upon the steep banks of the Scamander. And the Danaans drove the Trojans back, and each one of their leaders killed his man.

38-83 Homer pans across the field of battle where we witness the Achaean leaders dominating the Trojans, each one dropping one of the enemy men. Agamemnon spears a fleeing man called Odius. Idomeneus kills and strips Phaestus. Menelaus drives a spear through Scamandrius' back. Meriones slays Phereclus. Meges drops Pedaeus. And Eurypylus completely severs Hypsenor's arm so that he meets his fate in death.

84-94 So it was that all the leading men labored in mighty combat. As for the son of Tydeus, Diomedes, . . . he rushed across the plain like a late winter river swollen by rain and snow—one that smashes into the retaining barricade piled high with earth and breaks it up with its surging flow. This earthen mound is meant to defend against attack, but it doesn't hold back the flooding river, [90] nor do the stone walls of the luxuriant vineyard restrain the river's sudden coming when the heavy rain of Zeus falls in torrents. Rather, before its torrential surge, the many beautiful and strong works of men collapse. Just like this, then, were the dense battle lines of the Trojans driven in rout by the son of Tydeus. Despite their numbers, they couldn't hold him back.

95-273 *Just then, Pandarus, the son of Lycaon, sees Diomedes battle raging. (Recall, Pandarus is the Trojan man who shot Menelaus with an arrow after Aphrodite saved Paris.) Straightaway, he fires an arrow that punches into Diomedes' shoulder. Ecstatic, Pandarus boasts that Diomedes will soon be dead. But the wound isn't fatal. Instead, Diomedes' comrade Sthenelus removes the arrow while the hero prays to Athena for revenge. Healing the wound, she saves him from death, giving Diomedes the courage and might of his father. She also gives him the power to perceive the presence of the gods in battle, and permission to fight Aphrodite.*

If Diomedes was a raging river before, Homer tells us he's now like a furious lion in a sheepfold! Hunting for Pandarus along the way, he slaughters many Trojan men—Astynous, Hypeiron, Abas, Polyidus, Xanthus, Thoon, Echemmon, and Chromius. Observing him battle raging among the Trojans, Aeneas, the son of Anchises and Aphrodite, finds Pandarus and urgently speaks to him about Diomedes. Pandarus says he's already wounded him with an arrow, and that he doesn't know if he's a god or a man. He laments the uselessness of his bow, having only wounded Menelaus and Diomedes, and wishes he had followed his father's advice to ride into battle mounted upon a chariot. Aeneas quiets him and orders him into his own chariot. They turn and go after battle-raging Diomedes.

Seeing this, Sthenelus warns Diomedes and advises him to flee. The latter balks at this suggestion, proposing rather that they should capture Aeneas' horses, the best of all horses beneath the sun, he says, which were

Zeus' present to Tros, the father of Ganymede. If they do, they'll win noble glory.

274-317 That's how Diomedes and Sthenelus spoke to each other. And as they were talking, Pandarus and Aeneas quickly came near to them, driving the swift horses.

Nearing them, Pandarus, the son of Lycaon, spoke first. "Ah, great and mighty son of noble Tydeus—I see that my arrow failed to drop you to the ground. I'll try now with my spear." [280] Saying this, he poised his spear as he spoke and hurled it. Humming through the air, it struck the son of Tydeus' shield, the bronze point piercing it and passing on until it reached Diomedes' breastplate.

The son of Lycaon shouted out and said, "You're hit! I hit you through the belly! And I don't think you'll be standing for very long. No, you've granted me a great glory-boast!"

Yet without alarm, powerful Diomedes said, "You've missed! You didn't hit me! And I predict that by the end of this one of you will glut Ares with his blood!" [290] Saying this, Diomedes hurled his spear, and Athena guided it up in an arch and straight down into Pandarus' nose just below his eye. The bronze spearhead sliced through his cheek and crashed through his white teeth until it cut through his tongue and exited his chin. His armor rattled around him as he fell from the chariot to the ground. The horses jumped with fear. It was right then that Pandarus let go of his battle might and life.

Aeneas sprang from the chariot armed with his shield and long spear. He was afraid that the Achaeans would carry off the corpse. Therefore, he stood over it as a proud and strong lion. [300] And with his shield and spear before him and a battle cry on his lips, he resolved to kill the first man that dared to face him. But the son of Tydeus picked up a mighty stone so huge and great that it would now take two men to lift it. With this he struck Aeneas on the hip, and the jagged stone crushed him there, breaking the sinews and tearing away all the flesh. The hero fell to his knees, struggling to prop himself up with his hands on [310] the ground. Then the darkness of night fell upon his eyes.

And now the lord of men Aeneas would have perished if not for his mother, the daughter of Zeus, Aphrodite, who had conceived him with Anchises when he was out herding cattle. Quickly noticing his plight, she threw her two white arms around the body of her dear son and protected him by covering him with a fold of her own radiant robe. If not for this, some Danaan would have speared and killed him.

318-333 *While Aphrodite spirits Aeneas away from the fight, Diomedes' comrade Sthenelus takes off with Aeneas' horses and chariot. As for Diomedes, he goes in pursuit of Aphrodite. He knows she's weak in battle. She's no Athena or Enyo, sacker of cities.*

334-352 When, after a long chase, Diomedes caught up with Aphrodite, the great-hearted son of Tydeus flew at her and thrust his spear into the flesh of her delicate hand. The point tore through the ambrosial robe, which the Graces had woven for her, and pierced the skin between her wrist and the palm of her hand. Following this wounding, the immortal blood, [340] or ichor that flows in the veins of the blessed gods, came pouring from the wound—for the gods do not eat bread nor do they drink wine; therefore, they have no blood such as mortal men do, and so they are called immortals.

Feeling the wound, Aphrodite screamed aloud and let her son fall. But Phoebus Apollo caught him in his arms and hid him in a cloud of darkness so that no man among the Danaans would spear and kill him.

Then Diomedes, good at the battle cry, cried out to Aphrodite, "Run off, daughter of Zeus, from the fight and the battle-strife! Is it not enough for you to deceive feeble-minded women? [350] But if you frequently enter the battle and know the fight, then I think you'll shudder to learn about it from the inside."

This is what Diomedes said, and the goddess felt ill and flew off suffering dreadfully.

353-369 *With the horses and chariot of Ares and the help of Iris, Aphrodite speeds to the abode of the gods.*

370-384 Aphrodite flung herself onto the lap of her mother, Dione, who threw her arms around her and caressed her, saying, "Dear child, which of the false heavenly ones has been treating you this way as though you've openly been doing evil?"

And laughter-loving Aphrodite answered, "The son of Tydeus, proud Diomedes, wounded me because I was caring for my dear son, Aeneas, whom I love most of all. I was carrying him from the battle, for the war is no longer one between the Trojans and the Achaeans alone; [380] rather, the Danaans have now begun fighting with the immortals."

Then the heavenly goddess Dione replied to her, "Endure, my child, and bear all your troubling distress. For many of us who have our homes on Olympus endure pain from men when, on their account, we fight with one another and cause one another to suffer pains."

385-427 *Dione goes on to catalogue these pains. Ares, she says, put up with Otus and Ephialtes, and Hera and Hades both endured Heracles. And now, she goes on, you suffer thanks to your siding with Aeneas against Athena and Diomedes. After explaining this, Dione heals her daughter while Hera and Athena make fun of Aphrodite and laugh at her, and Zeus scolds her for joining in the fray.*

428-430 "Not to you, my child, are granted warlike deeds. But attend to your own lovely matrimonial duties [430] and leave all this fighting business to swift Ares and Athena."

431-439 *Down on the battlefield, Diomedes keeps up his battle rage by repeatedly rushing Apollo who is hiding Aeneas. Upon the fourth advance, Apollo warns him off.*

440-442 "Consider what I have to say, son of Tydeus, and fall back. You shouldn't think of yourself as equal to the gods. You're not. The immortal gods and men who walk the earth are not the same kind of tribe or being."

443-527 *Diomedes obeys and backs off. Apollo then spirits Aeneas away to be healed by Leto and Artemis. Afterward, Apollo encourages Ares to enter the battle to help the Trojans. He does. And urged on by Ares, Sarpedon turns to Hector and challenges him to do more than he is doing. The challenge works! Hector spurs the Trojans on to fight, and so they line up with renewed vigor against the Achaeans. Finally, Aeneas rejoins his comrades. On the opposite side of the battle, the Achaean leaders inspire their own men to fight.*

528-532 And the son of Atreus ranged among the throng of men and called out, "Be men, friends! Have a brave heart! [530] And feel shame before one another when you're fighting. More men live when there's such shame. But when men shamelessly flee, there's neither glory nor strength to avert danger."

533-849 *Saying this, Agamemnon throws and kills Deicoon, the son of Pergasus. Aeneas does likewise, slaying two Achaeans, Crethon and Orsilochus. In response, Menelaus comes out against Aeneas. The latter withdraws when Antilochus, the son of Nestor, joins the Achaean leader. Menelaus kills Pylaemenes, and Antilochus kills Mydon. Seeing them at work, Hector rushes forward. Diomedes falls back, noticing Ares by his side. Hector slays Menesthes and Anchialus. In response, Telamonian Ajax drops Amphius, the son of Selagus.*

Eventually, the son of Heracles, Tlepolemus, and the son of Zeus, Sarpedon, face each other, first trading insults and vowing to win glory from each other's death. They both cast at the same moment. Tlepolemus' spear flies and wounds Sarpedon's leg; Sarpedon's spear punches through Tlepolemus' neck, killing him. The Achaeans haul their comrade's corpse from the battlefield while Sarpedon's friends do the same for him, helping him to safety. For a moment, Odysseus considers running after Sarpedon to see if he can kill him. Instead, he turns to cutting down Sarpedon's Lycian men—seven total.

Observing Odysseus at work, Hector joins in the fray to knock the Achaeans back. Homer offers a glory report for Hector and Ares. "Who, then, was the first and who last to be slain by bronze-tipped Ares and Hector, the son of Priam? They were . . ." One man dies, then two, three, four,

*five, and six men—Teuthras, Orestes, Trechus, Oenomaus, Helenus, and
Oresbius. About this time, Hera notices what's happening and suggests to
Athena that they join in battle against Ares and the Trojans. Zeus nods
his permission, and they go.*

*Hera first shames the Argives into fighting with greater force. Athena
then makes fun of Diomedes, who is now holding back thanks to his wound
and because he thought Ares was fighting alongside Hector. But now with
Athena by his side, they go to attack Ares. The goddess is wearing the cap
of Hades that makes her invisible.*

850-863 As soon as they were nearby, Ares thrust his bronze spear
at Diomedes, hoping to take his life away, but Athena caught it in
her hand and hurled it backwards. Diomedes then turned toward
Ares and cast his spear. Pallas Athena took hold of it and drove the
spear into the depths of Ares' stomach. There Diomedes wounded
him. He tore his fair flesh and drew the spear out again, and Ares
roared [860] as loudly as nine or ten thousand warriors when they
join in the battle strife of the war god. Hearing him, the Achaeans
and Trojans were struck with panic, so terrible was the insatiable
war god's mighty roar.

864-887 *In pain, and like a dark cloud, Ares speeds off to Olympus where
he complains to Zeus about Diomedes and Athena.*

888-909 Cloud-gathering Zeus looked angrily at him and said,
"Don't come by me to sit and whine, you fickle god who says one
thing but does another. [890] Of all the gods who live on Olympus,
I hate you most because strife is the only thing you care about, and
strife's battles and fights. You have the intolerably stubborn spirit
of your mother, Hera—and it is all I can do to dominate and control
her with words alone. I imagine she's behind your suffering too.
Still, I won't let you remain in pain. No, you are my own offspring,
and it was by me that your mother conceived you. If, however, you
had been the son of any other god, I would have tossed you down
from Olympus so that you would have fallen lower than the Ti-
tans."

That's what Zeus said. He then asked Paieon to heal Ares, [900] and so Paieon sprinkled pain-killing herbs upon his wound and cured him, for Ares was not made like a mortal. . . . Then Hebe washed him and clothed him in beautiful clothing, and he took his seat by his father, Zeus, exulting in his glory.

Now that they had stopped Ares' slaughter, Ares the bane of mortals, Argive Hera and Athena the defender returned to great Zeus' house.

BOOK 6

HECTOR RETURNS TO THE CITY
DIOMEDES & GLAUCUS, HECTOR & ANDROMACHE

IN BRIEF: *The battle continues. The Trojan warrior Helenus encourages Hector to return to Troy in order to propitiate Athena. While Hector is making his way inside the city walls, Diomedes encounters Glaucus, and they realize they are guest-friends. Within Troy, Hector commands his mother, Hecuba, to offer Athena a gift. She does, but the goddess refuses to be appeased. Otherwise, Hector rebukes Paris for lounging around with Helen. He must fight! he admonishes. Thereafter, he meets up with Andromache and Astyanax atop the Scaean gates. His wife tearfully begs him not to go out again. He must fight, he counters. He holds his son and prays for him. Finally, Hector returns with Paris to the battle.*

N OW THAT ALL the gods had returned to Olympus, the Trojans and the Achaeans carried on in dread battle, and the fight raged in every direction over the plain as they hurled their bronze-tipped spears straight at one another, battling between the river Simois and the streams of the Xanthus.

5-66 Telamonian Ajax bursts forward and strikes down Acamas, the best of the Thracians. Other Achaeans make their kills. Diomedes strikes down Axylus and Calesius; Euryalus kills Dresus, Opheltius, Aesepus, Pedasus, and Melanthius; Polypoetes slays Astyalus; Odysseus drops Pidytes; Antilochus lays low Ablerus; Agamemnon and Leitus kill Elatus and Phylacus, respectively. In the distance, Menelaus captures Adrastus, who successfully begs to be spared for a ransom. Agamemnon comes along, however, and refuses to let him to live. The reason is straightforward—harm must be done to those who have done harm. All Trojan males must perish, he declares, even those still in their mother's womb. Homer comments that this was the appropriate counsel. As a result, Menelaus roughly shoves Adrastus to the ground, and Agamemnon slays him. Meanwhile, Nestor shouts out that the Achaeans should kill now and strip the fallen bodies later.

67-72 "My dear friends, Danaan heroes, Ares' helpers! May no man drop back and remain behind to collect the armor of all the fallen enemy men so that he can carry off most of the spoils when he returns to the ships. Not now! [70] Now's the time to kill men! Afterward, you can leisurely strip the dead littering the plain."

Nestor's words encouraged the battle might and spirit of each man.

73-118 *With Nestor's inspiration, the Achaeans nearly drive the Trojans back. But Helenus, the son of Priam and the best reader of birds, admonishes Aeneas and Hector to fire up the Trojans before they fearfully flee and weakly retreat behind Troy's walls into the arms of their women. The responsibility is theirs, he asserts, because Aeneas and Hector are the best in battle and deliberation.*

After they rouse the men, Helenus advises Hector to return to Troy in order to have the women appease Athena in her temple with the gift of a fine robe. The hope is that Athena will hold back Diomedes, who has become a greater source of trouble than Achilles ever was.

Hector goes out to the men and shouts, "Be men, friends! Put in mind your courageous strength to serve as a shield rushing into battle! I'm going to Ilium to tell the old men and our wives to pray to the gods and vow hecatombs in their honor." Upon saying this, Hector turns toward Troy.

119-129 Then Glaucus, the son of Hippolochus, and Diomedes, the son of Tydeus, [120] went into the open space between the two armies, eager to fight. When they were close to each other, Diomedes, good at the battle cry, was the first to speak. "Who are you, brave one, among mortal men? I have never seen you in battle, where men win glory, until now. But now you step out from the battle lines and courageously face my spear. Unhappy are those children of men who encounter my battle might! If, however, you are one of the immortals and have come down from heaven, I will not fight you."

130-140 *To justify his position, Diomedes tells Glaucus the story of Ly-curgus, the son of Dryas, who engaged in strife with the gods by abusing the nurses who were caring for the young god Dionysus. The gods "who live at their ease" were angry with him for this and struck him blind. Con-sequently, Lycurgus ended up dying early because of all the divine hatred for him.*

141-151 "Therefore, I will not fight with the blessed gods. But if you are of mortal men, and you eat the fruit of the earth, then come and try to kill me and so meet with a swift destruction."

The glorious son of Hippolochus answered him, "Great-spirited son of Tydeus, why do you ask me about my lineage? Men come and go as the leaves do year after year upon the trees. The wind sheds the autumn leaves upon the ground, but when the spring re-turns, the forest buds again with fresh ones. The generations of mankind are like this. The new generation springs up as the old is passing away. [150] If, then, you wish to learn of my descent, it is known by many."

152-206 *Glaucus offers a detailed report of his lineage, telling his family's story from Sisyphus, the craftiest of all men, to beautiful Bellerophon, Glau-cus' own grandfather—who, thanks to Proteus' wife, Anteia, was made by Proteus (through the king of Lycia) to accomplish several dangerous labors meant to kill him—down to Hippolochus, his own father. He finishes by mentioning the directive his father gave him upon going to Troy.*

207-233 "He sent me to Troy and insistently ordered me to always be the best and to stand out among other men and not to dishonor or shame the family of my fathers, who were the best [210] in Ephyre and in wide Lycia. I boast, then, of this family and bloodline that is mine."

That's what Glaucus said. And Diomedes, good at the battle cry, rejoiced. He planted his spear in the ground and spoke to the shep-herd of men with gentle and friendly words. "If this is so," he said, "then you are an old guest-friend in my father's house. Great Oeneus once entertained Bellerophon for twenty days. At the end, the two exchanged fair gifts of friendship. Oeneus gave a belt rich with purple, [220] and Bellerophon a double cup, which I left at home when I set out for Troy. I don't remember Tydeus since he was taken from us while I was yet a child, when the army of the Achaeans was utterly destroyed before Thebes. From this moment on, however, I must be your dear host when you are in middle Argos, and you must be mine if I should ever go to Lycia. Let us consequently avoid each other's spears when the men come together. There are many Trojans and glorious allies I can kill if I overtake them and if the gods deliver them into my hands. Same with you—there are many Achaeans whose lives you may take if you can. [230] Let us exchange armor so that the men may know that we boast of guest-friendship handed down from our fathers."

With these words, they sprang from their chariots, grasped each other's hands, and bound each other together by oath.

234-403 *Diomedes and Glaucus exchange armor—but Diomedes gets the better part of the trade, obtaining gold for bronze armor.*

While they talk, Hector ventures into Troy through the Scaean gates and calls on the women to pray to the gods. He goes to Priam's house where he finds his mother, Hecuba. She offers him wine and other refreshment, but he declines, citing the ongoing battle. He commands her to go to Athena's temple to propitiate the goddess. She does. Accompanied by many older women, Hecuba lays a fine Sidonian robe on Athena's lap and prays that Diomedes' spear would be broken. Athena doesn't listen.

As they are attempting to appease the goddess, Hector runs off to discover the whereabouts of Paris. When he finds him with Helen, Hector rebukes him. Get up and fight for the people who are fighting and dying for you! he orders. Paris consents. As for Helen, she tells Hector that she wishes she had never been born—or if born, she wishes she had been the wife of a better man who knew how to feel shame in his heart. She invites Hector to sit with her while Paris dresses for battle. He turns her down, saying he must go and see his wife, son, and servants. He doesn't know if he'll return from battle or if the gods will subdue him by means of the Achaeans.

*Hector rushes off to look for his wife in his own house. But Andromache
is not there. Rather, a female slave reports that she is up on the wall because
she had heard that the Trojans were being pushed back by the Achaeans.
Learning this, Hector rushes off, making his way through the city to the
Scaean gates, where he meets his wife, one of her handmaidens, and his
"well-loved" son Astyanax (whom Hector calls Scamandrius).*

404-493 Hector smiled as he looked upon the boy, but he did not
speak. Andromache stood by him weeping.

And taking Hector's hand in her own, she said, "God-driven
man, your battle might will destroy you. You have no pity for your
infant son or for me, the unfortunate one who has no portion of
anything at all. I will be your widow when [410] all the Achaeans
rise up and kill you. And if I lose you, I'd much rather be dead and
buried—I will have nothing to comfort me when you have met your
destined end, except for pain and distress alone.

"You know how it is with me. I have neither a father nor a
mother now. Achilles slaughtered my father when he sacked great
Thebes. He killed him, but he did not strip him, for his spirit was
afraid and ashamed to do so. Instead, he burned him in his won-
drous armor and raised a mound over his ashes. And the [420]
mountain nymphs, daughters of aegis-bearing Zeus, planted a
grove of elms around his tomb. I had seven brothers in my father's
house, but on the same day, they all went down to the house of
Hades. Achilles killed them while they were tending their sheep
and cattle. And my mother, the one who ruled beneath the wooded
mountain Placus, she was carried along with all the other Achaean
plunder. But when Achilles set her free after receiving a great
amount of ransom, she died by Artemis' darts in her father's own
house. So it is that I have nothing and no one. No, Hector! *You* are
my father and queen mother [430] and brother—and you are my
vigorous husband! Come now and pity me! Stay here upon the wall
and do not make your child fatherless and your wife a widow! As
for the rest of the army, station them near the fig tree where the city
walls can best be scaled and overrun. Three times have the best of
the Achaeans attacked the wall there under the command of the

two Ajaxes, famous Idomeneus, the sons of Atreus, and the brave son of Tydeus. They did it following their own counsel or because some oracle suggested the attack."

[440] In return great Hector of the shining helmet answered, "I too have thought about all of this, woman. But I would feel ashamed before the Trojan men and women if I shirked battle like a coward. And besides, my spirit doesn't order it since I have learned always to be brave and to fight in the front ranks among the Trojans, winning great glory for my father and myself.

"Still. I know well that the day will surely come when sacred Ilium will be destroyed along with Priam and all the people. [450] But hereafter none of these will cause me as much anguish as you— not even Hecuba, nor the ruler Priam, nor my brothers, many and brave, who may fall in the dust before their foes. For none of these do I grieve as I do for you when the day will come that one of the bronze-clad Achaeans will rob you forever of your freedom and haul you away against your will, weeping. Then you'll have to work the loom of some mistress in Argos, or you'll be commanded by some woman to fetch water from the springs of Messeis or Hypereia—all against your will, by the strong force of necessity. At that time, a man who sees you weeping will say, [460] 'This was Hector's woman, Hector who was the best at fighting among the horse taming Trojans when men fought around Ilium.' This is how that man will speak. And all over again you'll feel pain and distress when you discover that you have no man to defend you against slavery. May I lie dead under a mound before I hear your frantic crying as they carry you off to bondage!"

This is what shining Hector said. And saying this, he stretched his arms and hands out to his child, but the boy cried and nestled back into his nurse's bosom. He was terrified by his father's armor—the horsehair crest nodding [470] frightfully upon his helmet. His mother and father laughed to see him so alarmed. Even so, Hector took the helmet from his head and set it gleaming upon the ground. Then he held his dear son, kissed him, and swung him around by his arms and hands. After playing with him like this, Hector spoke in prayer to Zeus and all the gods. "Zeus and the other gods, grant that this child, my boy, may be as I am. Make him outstanding among all the Trojan men, preeminent in forceful strength and noble bravery, and may he powerfully rule Ilium. And when someday he returns home [480] from battle carrying the gory spoils of the enemy man he has slaughtered—the dead man's shield and armor—may some man say, 'He's even better than his father was!' And let his mother rejoice and delight in her heart!"

With this, he put the child into the arms of his dear wife, and she took him to her own soft bosom, smiling through her tears. As her husband watched her, he felt pity for Andromache and caressed her. Then, calling her by name, he said, "God-driven woman, do not grieve too much for me in your spirit. For no man has gone down to Hades beyond what Fate had decreed. But I declare that from the moment of his birth, no man has ever been able to run away from his own fate, neither the coward nor the brave man. [490] Go, then, into the house and occupy yourself with your own work, with the loom and the distaff, and order your serving women to do the same. As for war, it is a man's work—and mine above all others born in Ilium."

494-525 *Hector picks up his helmet and rushes off, leaving Andromache to weep behind him. Returning home, she laments his fate, knowing he will die. She believes he'll never again return home to Troy.*

Meanwhile, Paris readies himself for battle and meets Hector by the gate. When Paris apologizes for being so slow, Hector explains what grieves him most about his brother—that even though Paris is strong, he is a slacker in battle, and so the Trojans speak shameful words about him. Saying that, the two brothers step off to fight.

526-529 "Let's go! We'll make amends for your behavior later if Zeus, in assembly with the everlasting heavenly gods, decides to give us the mixing-bowl of freedom to stand in our halls when we drive the well-grieved Achaeans from Troy."

BOOK 7

HECTOR FIGHTS TELAMONIAN AJAX
THE TRUCE TO BURY THE DEAD

IN BRIEF: *After Hector and Paris go out to fight, the battling finishes for the day with single combat matching Hector and Telamonian Ajax. Night falls and both sides join in assembly. The Trojans ask for a truce to gather and burn the dead. The Achaeans agree, using the opportunity to build a wall and trench around their ships.*

W ITH THESE WORDS, shining Hector rushed through the gates with his brother Alexander. And in their spirits both eagerly longed to wage war and fight.

4-66 *The Trojans are pleased to see the two leading brothers on the battlefield once again. Paris slays a man first, then Hector and Glaucus.*

From Olympus, Athena notices that the Trojans are beating the Achaeans. She flies down to Ilium where she's met by the pro-Trojan Apollo, who has spotted her from his perch on Mount Pergamus. They agree to bring the fighting to an end for the day by having Hector challenge the best of the Achaeans to single combat. At the prodding of Helenus, therefore, he does.

Hector and Agamemnon call upon the fighting men to sit down. When everyone is situated, Hector steps into the middle to make his proposition. As he does, Athena and Apollo take the form of vultures and fly to perch high in an oak tree sacred to Zeus. From there they take pleasure in all the warrior men. Down below Hector challenges the Achaeans to a fight.

67-106 "Hear me, Trojans and well-greaved Achaeans, so that I may say what I wish to say even as my spirit bids me. Sitting high in Olympus upon his throne, Zeus has refused to bring our oaths to fulfillment. [70] Rather, he intends harm for one of us—either you will take the well-fortified city of Troy, or we will overpower and conquer you by your seafaring ships. Regardless, the best men of all the Achaeans are with you now. Let the man, then, whose spirit commands him to fight me, rise as your foremost fighter against me—against godlike Hector. But here will be our agreement. Before Zeus and by my own word, if your champion slays me, then let him strip me of my armor and haul it off to your hollow ships. He may not, however, take my body. That must return to my house in Troy so that [80] the Trojans and their wives may give me my share of the fire when I am dead. In like manner, if Apollo grants me the glory-boast and I slay your foremost fighter, then I will strip him of his armor and take it to the city of Ilium where I will hang it in the temple of Apollo. As for his body, I will leave it so that the long-haired Achaeans may bury him by their well-benched ships and build him a mound by the wide waters of the Hellespont. Then men to come, as they sail in their many-benched ships over the wine-faced sea, will say, 'This mound is the marker of one who died long ago. [90] Shining Hector killed him when he was in his prime.' That's what some man will say, and, therefore, my own glory will not end."

That's what Hector said. And everyone fell silent. On the one hand, they felt ashamed to refuse his challenge; on the other, they feared to accept it.

Finally, Menelaus stood up and schooled the Achaeans with words meant to sting. "I can't believe it! Threats alone—that's what you are! Achaean women, not men! This is horrible! It'll be a dishonor for all of us if no one stands to face Hector! If not, then may you turn into earth and water [100] as you sit there like that without any courage or glory! So be it. I myself will arm and go out against him. But know that no matter the attempt, it is the gods who dwell on high that determine the winner."

With these words he put on his beautiful armor.

And the end of life would have come for Menelaus right then if the other leading men of the Achaeans hadn't darted up and seized him before Hector lay his hands on him—for Hector was by far the better man.

107-232 *Among them all, Agamemnon stops his brother, saying that Hector is better than Menelaus. It would be crazy to fight him! he declares.*

When Menelaus returns to his comrades, Nestor stands and laments the lack of Achaean will to battle with Hector. He recalls the time when his own Pylians were fighting the Arcadians by the swift-flowing Celadon, and Ereuthalion challenged all the best men of Pylos to a fight, and everyone similarly trembled. But not Nestor! No, even though he was the youngest man on his side, his much-enduring spirit and courage commanded him to fight. So Nestor battled their huge and powerful champion, and Athena granted him the glory-boast. Now he wishes he were younger. If so, then he himself would stand to fight Hector. He finishes by rebuking the Achaean leaders. You are the best men, he says, but you refuse to face him!

Feeling the sting of Nestor's words, nine men stand: Agamemnon, Diomedes, the two Ajaxes, Idomeneus and Meriones, Eurypylus, Thoas, and, lastly, Odysseus. They cast lots, and Telamonian Ajax's lot jumps out of the helmet. Everyone is pleased with this. Ajax himself rejoices since he believes he can defeat Hector.

Ajax arms as the Achaeans pray for victory and the shining glory-boast for him—or if Zeus cares for Hector too, then equal strength and glory for both. With a smile, Ajax steps out toward Hector, whose heart beats faster now—though he knows he cannot back down since he issued the challenge to fight. Ajax taunts him, telling Hector that he will learn what the best of the Achaeans is like now that lion-hearted Achilles is back by the ships.

233-306 And to him great Hector of the gleaming helmet answered, "God-born Ajax, son of Telamon, ruler of men, don't treat me as though I were some wimpy boy or woman who doesn't know warlike deeds. No, I'm quite familiar with fighting and killing men. I know how to quickly turn my shield either to the right or to the left—for I think this is important in battle. [240] I know how to charge in among the chariots and horsemen. And in hand-to-hand fighting, which I know quite well, I can delight the heart of Ares. I won't take a man like you off guard, but openly I hope to hit you."

He poised his long spear as he spoke and hurled it. And flying, it punched through the bronze layer of Ajax's thick shield and passed through the other layers until it was stopped by the last.

Godlike Ajax threw second [250] and struck the round shield of the son of Priam. Through the gleaming shield the terrible spear cut, and through his stunningly worked breastplate, before it tore the tunic against his side. But Hector dodged aside and avoided black death.

Following this, Hector and Ajax drew out the spears from behind their shields and fell on each other like savage lions or wild boars of great strength and endurance. The son of Priam struck the middle of Ajax's shield, but the bronze did not break, and the spear's tip was turned. [260] Ajax then sprang forward and pierced Hector's shield. The spear went through it, surprising Hector as he was springing forward to attack. It gashed his neck and blood poured out from the wound.

Even so Hector of the gleaming helmet didn't stop fighting. Rather, stepping back, he seized a black stone, rugged and huge, with his massive hand—a stone that was lying upon the plain. Pitching it, he struck Ajax's many layered shield right in the middle upon the boss, so that the bronze rang out. But Ajax in turn caught up a far larger stone and hurled it with incredible strength. [270] This millstone-sized rock smashed Hector's shield inwards and threw him onto his back with the shield landing near him. But Apollo raised him at once.

Hector and Ajax would have kept going, hacking at each other with their swords, had not the heralds, messengers of the gods and men, come forward, one from the Trojans and the other from the bronze-clad Achaeans. Talthybius and Idaeus, both men of understanding, parted them with their staffs. And when they were apart, the herald Idaeus, of wise counsel, said, "Dear children, stop your warring and fighting. [280] You are both dear to cloud-gathering Zeus, both warriors. That's clear—and we all know it. But look, it is nearly night, so let's give way to her, for it is always noble to obey night."

In answer, Telamonian Ajax said to him, "Idaeus, call on Hector to proclaim these quitting words—for it was his desire to battle that drove him to challenge all our best. Let him speak first and I will happily follow his lead."

Then great Hector of the gleaming helmet said, "Ajax, a god has given you great stature and strength, and wisdom, too. And in wielding the spear you excel the rest of the Achaeans. [290] Let us then stop the fighting and battle-strife for today. In the days to come we'll fight again and let some god decide who is better, giving victory to one or the other. For now, night is falling, and it's always noble to obey night. Let's stop, then, so that you can gladden the hearts of the Achaeans at your ships and even more so your clansmen and comrades. As for me, I will bring joy to the Trojans and their women, who wear long robes in the great city of Priam. They will give thanks to the gods on my behalf.

"Before we go, however, let us exchange glorious gifts [300] so that the Achaeans and Trojans may say, 'They both battled with the kind of strife that devours the heart, but when they parted, they were united in friendship.'"

On saying this Hector gave Ajax a silver-studded sword with its scabbard and well-cut belt. In return Ajax gave him a warrior's belt dyed with radiant purple. Then they parted from each other.

307-420 *Both sides rejoice in receiving their hero back alive.*

The Achaeans sacrifice and have a meal. Once they are fully satisfied, Nestor advises them to declare a truce the following day in order to gather the corpses of the fallen, burn them, and pile a mound over the remains. They should also quickly build a wall with gates and a deep trench before it to protect the ships. All the chief leaders agree to his plan.

Meanwhile, the Trojans are holding their own assembly. Wise Antenor speaks to advise returning Helen and her possessions to Menelaus and Agamemnon. He reminds them that they broke the oaths they swore before the single combat between Paris and Menelaus, and so they will not likely accomplish anything but harm. Paris accuses Antenor of senseless speech. He agrees to hand over her possessions, and he will even add to them, he promises; but he won't give up the woman. Priam stands to suggest a truce in order to gather and burn the dead. Then, he says, they'll fight until the gods grant victory to one side or the other.

The Trojan herald Idaeus ventures to the Achaean camp to report Paris' proposal and Priam's wish. Following Diomedes, who believes that Troy will soon fall and be destroyed, the Achaeans reject Paris' offer to return Helen's wealth without Helen herself. Even so, Agamemnon agrees to the truce to give the dead their share of fire.

421-432 Helios the sun was beginning to beat upon the fields, newly risen into the vault of heaven from the currents of deep Oceanus, when the two armies met on the plain. There, they could hardly recognize each dead man. But after they scraped and washed the clotted blood and gore from their bodies, shedding hot tears as they did so, they lifted them onto carts.

As for the Trojans, great Priam did not permit them to wail aloud. So in silence they heaped the corpses upon the pyre, each man lamenting his fallen comrades within his own heart. And having burned them, they went back to the city of Ilium. [430] The well-grieved Achaeans likewise quietly mourned their dead and heaped them upon the pyre. And having burned them, they went back to their ships.

433-435 *The Achaeans pile high a burial mound for all the fallen men and turn to build up their defenses.*

436-441 The Achaeans built a high wall to shelter themselves and their ships. They gave it strong gates so that the chariots could rush in and out. [440] Outside the wall, but nearby, they dug a deep and wide trench in which they planted stakes.

442-478 *As the Achaeans construct the fortifications, the gods recline by Zeus admiring their work—all but for Poseidon. He's afraid the Achaean wall will be more famous than the one he and Apollo built for Laomedon. And he's upset they didn't first consult the gods and offer sacrifice before going ahead with the construction. Zeus reassures Poseidon about his glory and fame and tells him not to worry. They can destroy the wall when the Achaeans leave so that no one will ever know about it.*

The day ends and the Achaeans feast on roasted meat and drink wine brought in Euneos' ship from Lemnos. In the distance, the Trojans likewise feast in the city. But Zeus thunders, intending bad fortune for them.

479-482 And pale fear seized them, [480] and they all spilled the wine from their cups onto the ground, nor did any man dare to drink until he had made a libation to the ultra-mighty son of Cronus. Then they fell asleep, receiving the gift of slumber.

BOOK 8

ZEUS' GREAT MIGHT
THE BACK AND FORTH OF BATTLE

IN BRIEF: *Zeus forbids divine participation in the struggle for Troy. The gods are astonished but obey. There are various battles back and forth. The scales of fate favor the Trojans. Many Achaean leaders flee. Hector pursues Nestor and Diomedes. Hera arouses Agamemnon. The Achaean Teucer shoots many Trojan men, and nearly Hector, but Hector first hits him with a stone. The Achaeans fall back once again. Hera and Athena want to help but are not allowed to—Zeus sends Iris to prevent their riding out to battle. When Zeus returns to Olympus, they sulk as he exults in his own strength. He explains what must happen before Achilles returns to battle. As night falls, Hector calls together a Trojan assembly. Their fires burn as stars in the dark sky.*

NOW WHEN YELLOW-VEILED Dawn was spreading out over all the earth, Zeus called the gods to an assembly on the topmost peak of many-ridged Olympus. Then he spoke, and all the other gods listened.

"Hear me, all you gods and goddesses, so that I may say what I wish to say even as my spirit bids me. None of you should try to act contrary to my word, but you should all consent to what I say so that I may quickly bring these works of war to an end. [10] If I see anyone helping either the Trojans or the Danaans apart from me, then I will blast him with lightning, and he will return to Olympus in a manner not befitting him. Or I will hurl him down into dark Tartarus, far into the deepest pit under the earth, where the gates are iron and the floor bronze—as far beneath Hades as the great sky of heaven is above the earth. I'll do this so that you may learn that among all the gods, I am the strongest."

18-27 Zeus goes on to dare them to test his strength and declares that if they try, they will discover how far above all the gods and men he is.

28-37 So he spoke, and all the gods were silently astonished by his speech—for he had spoken in the assembly with such power and strength.

[30] Finally, the goddess bright-eyed Athena spoke to them, saying, "Our father, the son of Cronus, highest of all rulers, we know well that your might is unyielding and harsh, yet we also feel sorry for the Danaan warriors who are perishing and coming to a bad end. Since you command us, we'll refrain from actual fighting. Still, we will offer advice to the Argives so that they won't all perish thanks to your wrath and hatred."

38-67 Upon hearing Athena's words, Zeus smiles and flies off to Mount Ida, in the Troad, and to Gargarus, its highest peak, where he has an altar. There he "exults in his glory" as he sits and looks down upon the Trojans and the Achaeans.

After eating their morning meal, the Achaeans arm, as do the Trojans. The latter men rush out from the gates of Troy eager to join in battle with the foe—out of the "dire necessity" to defend their children and women. Spears and shields clash! The groaning expressions of the slain and the triumphant voices of those who have slain them sound in abundance. The earth flows with blood. As long as it is morning, men fall to the dust.

68-77 When the sun had reached mid-heaven, father Zeus balanced his golden scales [70] and put two fates of death within them, one for the horse-taming Trojans and the other for the bronze-clad Achaeans. Then he seized it by the middle, and the scale sank down revealing the fated day of doom for the Achaeans.

So it was that the Achaean fates sank down to the all-nourishing earth while those of the Trojans rose to the broad sky above. Then Zeus thundered from Mount Ida and sent the flash of his lighting among the Achaean men. Seeing it, they were astounded, and pale fear seized them all.

78-92 Idomeneus, Agamemnon, and the two Ajaxes flee upon hearing Zeus. Only Nestor remains — not by his own free will, but because Paris killed one of the horses pulling his chariot. Noticing him all alone, Hector rushes to kill him. Diomedes observes his coming, however, and moves to save the old man. As he goes, he cries out to Odysseus for help.

93-96 "God-born son of Laertes, much-able Odysseus, why are you running off with your back turned like a coward? May some man not plant a spear in your back while you flee! Rather, stay here and help me defend old Nestor from this wild man's furious charge."

97-138 Odysseus doesn't hear him as he speeds off toward the ships. All alone, therefore, Diomedes turns to Nestor and bids him to climb aboard his own chariot so that they may together ride against the Trojans and Hector.

When they near Hector, Diomedes casts his spear at him but misses. Instead, the spear punches into Hector's driver and drops him to the ground. Now Hector fears for his own life. In fact, there would have been trouble for the Trojans if Zeus hadn't noticed and thundered and lightninged right by Diomedes and Nestor. Hearing this, Nestor fearfully pulls back on the reins and urgently speaks to the young warrior.

139-176 "Son of Tydeus, turn your horses in flight! [140] Don't you see that Zeus isn't giving you strength? No, he's giving glory to Hector today. Tomorrow, if he wills it, he'll grant us glory. Whatever the case, no man, however brave he is, may thwart the will and purpose of Zeus, for he is stronger than all men."

Diomedes, good at the battle cry, answered, "All that you have said is true. But I feel a grief that pierces me deeply in my heart. For Hector will talk among the Trojans and say, 'The son of Tydeus fled before me to the ships.' [150] This is the boast he'll make — and on that day may the earth swallow me whole!"

"Son of Tydeus," replied Nestor, "what do you mean? Even if Hector says you are a coward, the Trojans and the Dardanians will not believe him, nor will the wives of the mighty warriors whom you have slaughtered."

Saying this, he turned the horses back through the thick of the battle, and with a cry that tore through the air, the Trojans and Hector rained down their missiles upon them. From behind, [160] great Hector of the gleaming helmet shouted to him and said, "Son of Tydeus, the Danaans have honored you with a preeminent seat, roasted meat, and full cups. But now they will disdain you as a man of no account because you have acted no better than a woman. Be off you coward and thing for show alone! You will not scale our walls thanks to any flinching on my part—neither will you carry off our wives into your ships. The reason? I will kill you with my own hands!"

So he spoke, and the son of Tydeus debated in his mind whether he should turn his horses around again and fight him. Three times he anxiously thought about this in his mind and spirit, [170] but three times did the counselor Zeus thunder from the heights of Ida, providing a sign to the Trojans that he would give them strength and victory.

Hector then shouted out to them and said, "Trojans, Lycians, and Dardanians, lovers of close fighting, be men my friends, and remember the strength and valor by which you rush into the fight. I know that the son of Cronus has nodded his assent and given me victory and great glory, but for the Danaans, he's given suffering and woe."

177-272 Hector goes on to predict that the Achaean's newly constructed walls won't withstand a Trojan onslaught, and that they'll be set on fire. Declaring this, he boasts that he might slay Nestor and Diomedes and cause the invading enemy to flee in their ships. With this, Hector and the Trojans rush into the trench before the wall protecting the ships.

Hearing Hector's boast, Hera suggests that she, Poseidon, and the other divine Achaean allies go down and help their side. Poseidon balks at this, not wanting to fight with Zeus since his brother is better and stronger than all the other gods.

Regardless, Hera rouses Agamemnon to do something. Making his way around the ships and shelters, the Achaean leader calls them to arms by shaming them. What has happened to all your boasting now? he asks—

your boast to individually take on two hundred men, when now they can't even drive Hector back. Finally, Agamemnon begs Zeus to at least allow them to escape. Pitying them, Zeus nods his assent and sends an omen to confirm his will—one that consists of an eagle clutching a fawn that drops nearby his altar.

Observing the divine sign, the Achaeans rush into the trench—with Diomedes out front, followed by Agamemnon, Menelaus, the two Ajaxes, Idomeneus and Meriones, and Eurypylus. Teucer comes out ninth, firing arrow after arrow from behind Telamonian Ajax's towering shield. Homer gives him a glory report.

273-279 What Trojan man did blameless Teucer slay first? Orsilochus was first, then Ormenus, Ophelestes, Daetor, and Chromius. Next, he killed godlike Lycophontes and Amopaon, Polyaemon's son, and Melanippus. All these in turn, one after another, Teucer dropped to the ground, the much-nourishing earth. And the lord of men Agamemnon rejoiced when he saw him breaking up the Trojan battle lines with his mighty bow.

280-529 *Agamemnon praises Teucer, speaking of the glory that will come to his father Telamon, and promises him a gift of honor when they take Troy. Teucer responds by telling him that he requires no urging on, that he has already dropped eight Trojans. He fires yet another at Hector but misses him, killing instead Gorgythion, another of Priam's sons. He does this again and again. In response, Hector eagerly leaps down from his chariot, grabs a stone, and just as Teucer is pulling back the string to release another arrow at him, he throws the rugged stone and hits Teucer on the collar bone, causing him to fall to the ground. Hector rushes to kill him, but Teucer's brother, Telamonian Ajax, protects him from further harm, and the Achaeans carry him off to the ships.*

Zeus urges on the Trojans. They beat the Achaeans back into the trench, with Hector in the lead "exulting in his might." Hera takes notice and speaks with Athena. Shall we not help the Achaeans who are perishing thanks to Hector? she asks. Athena wants to help but says her father is frustrating her desires—this even though she helped Heracles in his many labors at the command of Zeus. Nevertheless, she arms to go help as Hera readies her horses and chariot. They drive through the gates of Olympus.

As they speed away, Zeus sees their flight from his perch atop Mount Ida. He's angry. He tells Iris to turn them back so that he doesn't have to thrash them, particularly his daughter, Athena. He will cripple the horses, toss them to the ground, and destroy the chariot! he threatens. Their wounds won't heal for ten years! This for Athena. For Hera, Zeus declares that he's not so upset with her since she is always thwarting his will.

Iris flies to Olympus, stops the two goddesses, and delivers Zeus' message. Hearing this, Hera says they should end their mission and let Zeus do as he pleases.

Zeus travels to Olympus and joins the other gods in assembly. Hera and Athena sit off by themselves sulking. He taunts them. They can't do a thing, he says, against his great strength. "Such is the might of my hands that all the gods in Olympus cannot turn me." If they tried, he would strike them with his thunderbolt.

Athena says nothing in return, but Hera can no longer restrain herself. She agrees to stay out of the battle but says they will nevertheless advise the Achaeans.

Zeus replies by telling her how many Achaeans will die until Hector kills Patroclus, "as is ordained," and so brings Achilles back into the battle. As for Hera's anger, Zeus declares he's not troubled by it, no matter how angry she becomes.

Hera makes no reply.

The sun sets and Hector calls the Trojans to an assembly away from the trench and the dead. He advises them to light fires and feast, and calls upon the heralds to prepare the city in case there is an ambush. Tomorrow they will battle the Achaeans again.

530-542 "But tomorrow morning toward dawn . . . I'll know whether mighty Diomedes, the son of Tydeus, will push me back from the ships to the wall or whether I'll cut him down with the bronze and carry off his armor all blood-covered and gory. We'll all know what he's made of tomorrow, whether he can withstand the approach of my spear. I think he'll be one of the first men of many of his comrades to fall at the rising of the sun. As for me, I wish that

I could be immortal and ageless all my days—just like today—[540] and honored as Athena and Apollo are honored, even as this day will certainly bring harm to the Argives."

That's how Hector spoke to the assembly, and the Trojans clapped and applauded his words.

543-561 *The Trojans shout their acclaim, gather wood, and offer heca-* *tombs to the immortal gods. But the blessed gods reject their sacrifice be-* *cause they hate Troy. Still, the Trojan fires shine in numbers comparable* *to the stars of the sky.*

562-565 A thousand fires burned and gleamed upon the plain, and in the glow of each fire there sat fifty men. Nearby, their horses champed upon white barley and rye, waiting by the chariots for Dawn to rise upon her many-colored throne.

BOOK 9

THE EMBASSY TO ACHILLES
ODYSSEUS, PHOENIX & TELAMONIAN AJAX

IN BRIEF: *Nestor reprimands Agamemnon for taking Briseis. Agamemnon admits his foolish behavior and agrees to make things right with Achilles by sending an embassy made up of Odysseus, Phoenix, and Telamonian Ajax, with the offer of many gifts, Briseis, and the hand of one of his own daughters in marriage. Despite the offer of generous compensation, and the speeches of the three ambassadors, Achilles rejects the proposal. He's still angry! Agamemnon treated him like a dishonored homeless man, he explains. The ambassadors return without success.*

S O THAT'S HOW the Trojans handled their own night watch. As for the Achaeans, all the best men were stricken with a sorrow past endurance when an unutterable panic, the comrade of ice-cold fear, took hold of them.

4-95 Agamemnon, stricken by a great worming pain and distress, calls each man to an assembly. Weeping, he explains how Zeus has tricked him, how they will not sack Troy, and so, he finishes, they might as well sail home. They can do nothing about it because Zeus is all powerful and can destroy cities or not as he desires.

Everyone is silent. Finally, Diomedes speaks up, rebukes Agamemnon for his lack of boldness, and tells him that even if he and his ships depart, he will not. He will stay with his comrade Sthenelus until Ilium falls!

Hearing his speech, the Achaeans shout their acclaim. Nestor then advises them to prepare their evening meal and take counsel after the feast. While all the men prepare their own meals, the leaders meet in Agamemnon's shelter. Once they're finished eating and satisfied, Nestor stands to speak.

96-121 "Glorious son of Atreus, ruler of men, Agamemnon, with you I will begin my speech and end it, for you are the ruler of many people, and Zeus has given you the scepter and the ability to deliberate for others and to determine what is right. [100] Therefore, it is fitting for you above all others to speak and to listen and to carry out the counsel of another who intends to speak wisely. So, I will speak in a way that appears best to me because no other man will come up with anything better. I will say what I think now and what I long ago had in mind when you angered Achilles by taking the girl Briseis from his shelter in a way contrary to what I believed best. I attempted to dissuade you, but you surrendered to your own heroic, supersized heart, [110] instead of giving way to the best of men. You took vengeance on a man honored by the immortals—for you seized and carried off his honor-prize. Now, however, let us consider how we may appease him, both with presents and gentle and soothing words."

So Agamemnon, the lord of men, answered him, "Old man, you have not falsely recounted my reckless blindness. I behaved foolishly and will do nothing to deny it. Now I see that Achilles, whom Zeus loves in his heart, is equal to many men—I see this because Zeus now pays honor to him while destroying the Achaean army. But since I behaved foolishly and blindly by obeying my wretched heart, [120] I am now willing to make amends by giving back the girl and offering a vast amount of compensation. But let me first name all the glorious gifts."

122-161 *In a glory report-like revelation that demonstrates his own wealth, Agamemnon goes on to name and number everything that he will give Achilles: tripods, gold, cauldrons, horses, women—and Briseis, about whom he will swear he never slept with her. Furthermore, Achilles will obtain prized plunder when they sack Troy—women, gold, and bronze. And when they return home, he'll be Agamemnon's son by marriage, honored like Orestes. He will receive one of his three daughters—either Chrysothemis, Laodice, or Iphianassa—without the bride price. Moreover, he'll get seven cities with farmland, vineyards, and flocks. Achilles only has to yield, he says. He shouldn't be unyielding, like Hades, who is hated by* mortals. *Rather, declares Agamemnon, he must give up his anger and submit since Agamemnon is the greater ruler and his elder.*

162-172 The horseman Nestor of Gerenia answered him, saying, "Most glorious son of Atreus, the lord of men Agamemnon. The gifts you offer are no small ones. But come, let us quickly send chosen messengers to Achilles' shelter. I'll name the men and they'll go. Let Phoenix, dear to Zeus, lead the way, and let Ajax and godlike Odysseus follow. [170] And for heralds, let Odius and Eurybates follow them. Now bring water for our hands and call on the men to avoid all irreverent speech so that we might pray to Zeus, the son of Cronus, for his pity and mercy."

173-306 *The Achaeans pray they might be successful in persuading Achilles, pour out a libation, and leave. When the three men come to the ships of the Myrmidons and Achilles' shelter, they find him playing the lyre and singing about "the glories of men," with Patroclus sitting nearby.*

After Achilles offers them food and wine, and Patroclus makes sacrifice, Odysseus speaks to Achilles. He explains the plight of the Achaeans—Hector's battle rage among the Achaean army, how the Trojans are pressing against their ships, the thousand campfires, and Hector's prayer to burn the ships when Dawn appears. Odysseus' greatest fear is that he will succeed. He explains how Achilles' father, Peleus, had charged his son with the task of restraining his own great heart by means of friendliness and kindness, and refraining from strife, the contriver of evil, so the Argives would honor him all the more. So, says Odysseus, you must give up your anger. If you do, Agamemnon will give you many gifts. Odysseus lists them just as Agamemnon did. He promises much now and much later after they sack Troy and return home. You will be honored as though a god, he assures him. Odysseus further tells Achilles that if he must hate Agamemnon, then he should at least have pity on all the other Achaeans. If you do, he promises, they will pledge themselves to you as if you were a god and raise you up in great glory. Odysseus finishes by suggesting that Achilles might be the man to slay Hector.

307-345 In answer to him, swift-footed Achilles said, "God-born son of Laertes, much-able Odysseus, I must speak bluntly, [310] exactly as I am minded to and as it will happen, so that you will not remain here and go on and on about this, that, and the other. For the man who says one thing while he hides another in his heart is hated by me like I hate the gates of Hades. Therefore, I for my part will speak in a way that appears best to me.

"Agamemnon will not persuade me, nor will the other Danaans, since he will never give the kind of gratitude or homage equal to always warring and battling against the other men without pause. The plunder portion is the same for the man who hangs back or the one who fights the most. Agamemnon honors both the coward and the brave man. [320] And the lazy man and the man who works, they must both die. Plus, there's no advantage for me—since I suffer pains in my spirit—to always throw myself into the fighting. As a bird takes a morsel of food to her nestlings when she has found one, giving the whole bit to them while she herself fares badly, even so many a long night have I remained awake, and many a bloody battle have I waged by day against those who were fighting for their women. With my ships I have taken twelve cities, and with my men by land I have stormed eleven nearby Troy. [330] From these I seized much treasure and many noble things, and I would carry them off and give them to Agamemnon, the son of Atreus. As for him, he would stay back by his swift ships. But when he divided everything, I would receive very little, while he carried off a lot. Otherwise, he gave some of the gifts to the noblest men and the chief leaders—and they still have theirs. But from me alone among the Achaeans, he has seized and holds the delightful partner of my bed. So, let him sleep with her and be pleased by her.

"But why must the Argives fight the Trojans? And why has the son of Atreus gathered and led the men here? Was it not for the sake of lovely-haired Helen? [340] Are the sons of Atreus the only ones of men endowed with speech who love their wives, their bed partners? No! The noble and sensible man loves and cares for his own wife in the same way that I loved Briseis from my spirit, even though she was won by my spear. Now, since he has seized my honor-prize from my hands and has deceived and cheated me, let him not test me—for I know him well. He will not persuade me."

346-400 *Achilles goes on to explain that when he used to fight, Hector rarely left the safety of Troy's wall. Only once did the Trojan hero fight Achilles—and he barely made it away with his life. Achilles informs Odysseus that he plans to sail away in the morning, taking everything he has won by lot with him—except for Briseis, of course, his honor-prize. No matter what he does, though, the Achaeans should be angry with shameless Agamemnon. Achilles declares he will never take any gifts from the son of Atreus—not even if the gifts outnumber all the wealth in the fabulously wealthy cities of Orchomenus in Boeotia or Thebes in Egypt. Not even if they are as many as there are grains of sand. Moreover, he explains, his own father Peleus will give him a fair wife. Then, there is the value of his own life.*

401-415 "My life is worth more to me than all the wealth of Ilium, the riches it had before the Achaeans attacked it, when there was yet peace. It is worth more than all the treasure that lies on the stone floor of Apollo's temple beneath the cliffs of Pytho. Cattle and fat sheep may be carried off as booty, and tripods and yellow-headed horses may be acquired, but when a man's life has once left him, it cannot be brought back again or won by force.

[410] "My goddess mother, the silver-footed Thetis, tells me that there are two possible fates carrying me toward the fulfillment of death. If I stay here and fight nearby the city of the Trojans, then I give up my return home, but my glory will never die. But if I return home to the land I love, then I give up my noble glory, yet my life will be very long."

416-437 *Achilles advises the rest of the Achaeans to likewise sail home since Zeus is clearly protecting Troy. Or they should consider another way to defend the ships and the army since he will not help them. He lastly requests that Phoenix stay behind with him in his shelter, so he may sail back home with him in the morning. Distressed, and fearful for the ships, Phoenix tearfully speaks.*

438-443 "The old horseman Peleus sent me with you on the day he sent you out from Phthia to Agamemnon. [440] You were then a silly child and knew nothing yet of distressing war nor of assemblies in which men stand out from others. For this reason, he sent me with you to instruct you in all these matters, to be a speaker of words and a doer of deeds."

444-599 Phoenix tells the story of how he came to Phthia from Hellas thanks to the fact that he had angered his own father by sleeping with his father's concubine at the bidding of his mother. Rather than slaying his father, who had cursed him, he fled Hellas and made his way to Phthia and to king Peleus, who received and loved him as a son, granting him land, people, and riches. Peleus charged Phoenix with rearing Achilles, and so he did. He gave him his meat in small bites and his wine, and he endured the young lad's spit up all over his tunic. His hope was that Achilles would care for him in old age.

So, he says, Achilles must give up his wrath—for even the gods, who are far greater in might and honor, change their minds when men pray and offer libations. Beware, he warns him, of blindness. Agamemnon has offered many fine gifts in recompense for his error. And now he has sent the best of the Achaeans to rectify matters. And men of old, when terribly angry, would give up their wrath if necessary and appropriate. He recounts the tale of Meleager and how he would not exchange his own anger for gifts—or give it up at all—until his fearful and weeping wife, Cleopatra, explained what happens to a city when it is sacked and taken: all the men are put to the sword, she said, the city is burned, and the children and women are taken into captivity. Fearing this (his city was being attacked), Meleager armed and fought off the enemy. Nevertheless, since he had previously scorned the gifts, he didn't receive them, even though he finally gave up his anger.

600-619 "As for you, Achilles, I hope you will think differently and that some god doesn't similarly direct you, dear man. It will be much harder to ward off fire from the ships once it is already kindled. But go and receive the gifts, for the Achaeans will honor you equally with the gods, whereas if you fight without taking the gifts, you may do well in battle, but you will not have a similar honor."

And in answer, swift-footed Achilles spoke to him, "Phoenix, old father, nurtured by Zeus, I do not need this man Agamemnon's honor. For I think that I have been honored by the decree of Zeus, which will remain with me at my ships as long as I have breath [610] in my chest and spring in my knees.

"And another thing I will tell you—and let it sink into your mind. Don't try to confound me by grieving and going on, doing a favor to the hero, the son of Atreus. You must not love that man, or you will incur my hatred—I who love you. It is a fine thing if you help me trouble those that trouble me. In doing so you may rule equally with me and share half my honor.

"So let the other messengers take my answer to Agamemnon. As for you, stay here in my shelter and sleep comfortably in your bed. Then in the morning we can consider whether we should remain here or go home."

620-642 *Achilles silently nods to Patroclus, who agrees to prepare a bed for Phoenix. Next, Telamonian Ajax speaks briefly. His advice is to return quickly to Agamemnon. He can tell Achilles will not change his mind. No, even though other great men relent and take compensation when a man seriously offends him, Achilles will not. He finishes by rebuking Achilles for his hardened heart, and he asks him once more to soften his heart and take the gifts.*

643-648 In answer to him, swift-footed Achilles said, "Ajax, god-born son of Telamon, ruler of men, you have spoken everything according to my own desire, but anger causes my heart to swell when I remember how that man, the son of Atreus, has outraged me in front of the Argives as if I were some wanderer—some dishonored homeless man."

649-709 *Achilles finishes by telling them to deliver the message—that he will not enter battle until Hector has killed many Argives, burned their ships, and come close to the Myrmidon camp.*

They have one last cup of wine before the men return without Phoenix. When they reach Agamemnon's shelter, Odysseus reports Achilles' answer.

In response, everyone is silent and full of sorrow. After some time, Diomedes speaks up and counsels them to let Achilles do as he pleases—whether he stays or goes. As for them, they should retire for the evening and sleep after eating and drinking. In the morning they should fight.

710-713 That's what he said, and the other chief leaders readily approved, pleased with the words of horse-taming Diomedes. They poured out libations, and each man walked to his own shelter where he lay down and received the gift of sleep.

BOOK 10

AGAMEMNON'S WORRY
DIOMEDES' MISSION WITH ODYSSEUS

IN BRIEF: *Held in a vice-grip of anxiety, Agamemnon cannot sleep. He therefore assembles the chief men. Nestor suggests a reconnaissance mission. Diomedes volunteers, and Odysseus goes along with him. The two capture and slay Dolon who has likewise responded to Hector's request for a spy. They later kill king Rhesus and many other Thracians before racing back to camp.*

WHILE ALL THE other chief men of the Achaeans were sleeping through the night by the ships, overcome by gentle sleep, Agamemnon, the son of Atreus and the shepherd of men, was not held by sweet sleep. Instead, he anxiously turned over many things in his mind. As when fair Hera's lord flashes his lighting to signal a flood of rain or crop-destroying hail or a bitter winter snowstorm . . . or perhaps the beginning of destructive war, even so did Agamemnon groan loudly [10] from deep in his heart, and he trembled in his core. When he looked out upon the plain of Troy, he marveled at the many fires burning before Ilium, and at the sound of pipes and flutes, and the bustling sound of men. But when he turned toward the ships and the men of the Achaeans, he tore out his hair by the handfuls before Zeus on high and groaned aloud in his great and glorious heart.

In the end, it seemed best to him to go at once to Nestor, the son of Neleus, to see if they could together find any way of [20] saving the Danaans from destruction. He stood up, put on his tunic, fastened his beautiful sandals upon his feet, flung the skin of a huge, fiery lion over his shoulders—one that reached down to his feet— and snatched up his spear.

Meanwhile, like Agamemnon, Menelaus could not check his own trembling anxiety, nor could he sate his own eyelids with sleep. Rather, he ruminated about what the Argives might suffer—and all because they had sailed over the seas to fight the Trojans for him.

29-66 Menelaus dresses in the skin of a leopard, grabs his spear, and goes to meet Agamemnon. They discuss Hector's sorrow-causing deeds from the day before and how Zeus must now favor him rather than the Achaeans. Agamemnon suggests they call the leading men together—Telamonian Ajax, Idomeneus, and the others. Agamemnon tells Menelaus how to go and do so.

67-71 "Speak loudly and clearly as you go throughout the camp, and command each man to wake up, naming each by his family lineage and his father's name so that all may be honored. Anyway, do not exalt yourself—[70] rather, it is time for us to work hard in response to the oppressive misery Zeus has hurled upon us."

72-86 Menelaus runs off while Agamemnon goes to Nestor's shelter. When Nestor asks Agamemnon to identify himself in the dark of night, he does and tells him how he cannot sleep.

87-95 "Nestor, son of Neleus, great glory of the Achaeans, know it is the son of Atreus Agamemnon—the one man among all men burdened by Zeus with the toil of war. [90] It will be this way until I die. I come here because sweet sleep will not rest upon my eyes. Instead, I worry about the war and the suffering of the Achaeans. Dreadfully do I fear for the Danaans. And so my heart is not settled, but I am sorely distressed—anxious—and my heart leaps out from my chest, and my limbs tremble."

96-337 Finally, Agamemnon suggests checking on the night watchmen and the all-too-close Trojan camp. Nestor agrees, but advises they first gather the chief men—Diomedes, Odysseus, Telamonian Ajax, Meges, and Idomeneus. Nestor says he will go and school Menelaus for sleeping while he should be working. Agamemnon assures him there is no need—

that his brother is already summoning the men to assemble by the night watchmen in the trench.

They go. Nestor first awakens Odysseus, then Diomedes. When he speaks with the latter man, he explains the Achaean either-or situation: they will either live or experience destruction. He then orders him to wake up Telamonian Ajax.

The leading men eventually make their way to the guard post where the sentinels are posted as if around a sheepfold. Nestor is happy to find them carefully guarding the Achaean camp and bids them to continue on so that the Achaeans will not become a source of delight for the enemy.

Then they go and assemble in the trench to hold council. Nestor asks for a volunteer to go spy on the Trojan camp. He dangles great fame and noble gifts before the man who will go. After a moment of silence, Diomedes offers to go and requests another man to venture out with him—as two are stronger than one, he says. Several volunteer. After Agamemnon advises Diomedes to select the best man regardless of birth or rule, he chooses Odysseus.

Diomedes and Odysseus arm, the latter putting on his battle gear, including a boar's tusk helmet, about which Homer gives its provenance. When they're finished, Athena sends them a good omen in the form of a heron flying on their right. Odysseus rejoices and prays for glory, for a good and widespread report of the great deed they will perform. Diomedes likewise offers a prayer to Athena and promises a sacrifice for success. Athena hears them. And finally they stroll off as two lions into the dark of night, walking amid all the corpses and the blood and gore from the battle the day before.

Meanwhile, Hector also asks for a volunteer to go and reconnoiter the Achaean camp. He wishes to discover their plans, he explains. To the man who goes he promises glory and gifts—Achilles' horses and chariot once he takes them. Dolon, the son of Eumedes, an ugly man but fast and rich in gold and bronze, stands forward, motivated by Hector's promise. He dresses in a wolf skin, arms, and goes.

338-381 When Dolon had left the horses and the men behind him, he eagerly sped along. [340] But god-born Odysseus saw him and said to his comrade, "Diomedes, here is some man from the Trojan camp. I don't know if he's a spy or if he's out to plunder the dead. Let him pass us so that we can spring on him and take him from behind. If, however, he's too quick for us, go after him with your spear and hem him in toward the ships, away from the Trojan camp, to prevent him from making his escape toward the city."

With this they stepped off the path and lay down among the dead. [350] Dolon mindlessly suspected nothing, and soon he rushed pass them. But when he had gone about as far as the distance by which a mule-plowed furrow exceeds one that has been plowed by oxen—for mules can plow fallow land quicker than oxen—Odysseus and Diomedes ran after him.

When Dolon heard their footsteps, he stood still. His hope was that they were friends sent to turn him back to the Trojan camp. When the Achaean heroes were only a spear's cast or less away from him, though, he saw at once that they were enemy men, and so he ran as fast as his legs could take him. The others chased him.

[360] And as a couple of well-trained hounds press forward after a doe or hare that runs screaming in front of them, even so did the son of Tydeus and Odysseus pursue Dolon and cut him off from his own people. But when Dolon had run nearby the Achaean ships and the night watchmen, Athena gave the son of Tydeus a burst of strength and filled him with fear that some other bronze-clad Achaean man would have the glory of being the first to strike him, and he would only be the second man. Mighty Diomedes therefore rushed forward with his spear and said, [370] "Stay there!—or I'll throw my spear, and you won't avoid utter destruction at my hand for long."

Diomedes threw as he spoke but missed the man on purpose— the spear flew over his right shoulder, sticking in the ground.

As for Dolon, he stood still, trembling with alarm. His teeth chattered, and he turned pale with fear.

Finally, Odysseus and Diomedes came up to him all out of breath, and they seized his hands. With this, Dolon began to weep and said, "Take me alive! I will ransom myself—for in my house I have a great store of gold, bronze, and wrought iron, [380] and from this my father will satisfy you with a very large payment once he hears that I am alive at the Achaean ships."

382-441 *Odysseus lies to the Trojan spy, advising him not to worry. But what are you doing? he queries. Dolon tells him about the promised gift to whomever would complete the mission. He also explains how Hector is holding an assembly by the tomb of Ilus, and how the camp is organized, and where the allies are sleeping—including the Thracians, with their king, Rhesus. Finishing, Dolon assumes the Achaean men will let him live for the promised ransom.*

442-464 "Now, therefore, take me to the ships or bind me securely and leave me here until you come back with the knowledge of whether I have spoken well to you or not."

Diomedes looked sternly at him and answered, "Even though you have given us good information, don't imagine that you'll now escape—not when we have you by the power of our hands. For if we ransom you or let you go, [450] you will come again to the swift ships of the Achaeans either as a spy or as an open enemy. But if I kill you and make an end of you, you'll no longer trouble us."

Hearing this, Dolon nevertheless reached up to Diomedes' bearded chin with his muscular hand in order to beg. But Diomedes struck him with his sword right in the middle of his neck. The bronze blade cut through both sinews so that Dolon's head fell rolling in the dust while he was still speaking.

They took the ferret-skin cap from his head, and also the wolf-skin, the bow, and his long spear. [460] Then godlike Odysseus raised these up in honor of Athena, the one who dispenses plunder, and prayed, saying, "Rejoice, goddess, for we give them to you before all the other immortals of Olympus. Speed us, therefore, on toward the horses and sleeping-ground of the Thracians."

465-576 *Odysseus and Diomedes make their way to the Thracian camp. They are after Rhesus' horses and other spoil. Diomedes slays twelve of the Thracians and their king, Rhesus, last. Then, just as Diomedes is considering whether he should kill more, Athena appears to tell them to return to the Achaean camp. They do, speeding off on Rhesus' horses.*

Upon returning, Nestor asks them to recount what happened. After making their report, they wash off all the battle muck in the sea.

577-579 But when they had bathed and richly anointed themselves with olive oil, they sat down to a meal, and from the mixing bowl, they drew off full cups of the honey-sweet wine and poured out a libation to Athena.

BOOK 11

AGAMEMNON'S GLORY
THE ACHAEANS FALL BACK

IN BRIEF: *The goddess Strife (Eris) stirs up the Achaeans to fight. Aga-memnon fights out front, and Homer gives him a glory report. Zeus orders Iris to tell Hector to wait until Agamemnon is wounded. Then it will be his turn to triumph. Finally, Coōn hits Agamemnon, and the Achaean leader retreats, but not before slaying and decapitating Coōn. Now Hector fires up his own men. Homer gives him a glory report as he slaughters many Achaeans. The Trojans wound many others—Diomedes, Eurypy-lus, Machaon, and Odysseus, who, at one point, is left all alone, though he stands his ground and kills Socus. Menelaus and Telamonian Ajax fly to help Odysseus. Ajax fights and kills many Trojans. Seeing his work of slaughter, Cebriones and Hector speed over to help them. Achilles sends Patroclus to find out what is happening. Nestor gives him a report. Given the fact that many of the Achaean leaders have been wounded, things are not looking well. He counsels Patroclus to ask Achilles for his consent to fight at the head of the Myrmidons in Achilles' battle gear. Patroclus agrees to this—but first he works to heal Eurypylus.*

D AWN STIRRED FROM her bed beside noble Tithonus in order to carry light to the immortal gods and mortal men. And Zeus sent Strife (Eris) to the swift ships of the Achaeans.

Now troublesome Strife held in her hand a portent of the battle to come and stood by Odysseus' large black ship, which was at the center of the long line of Achaean ships. She stood there so that her voice might carry far to both sides of the camp, to Telamonian Ajax's ship and shelter on the one side and to Achilles' on the other—for these two heroes, confident in their own strength, had bravely drawn up their ships at the two ends of the Achaean camp. [10] There the goddess took her stand and raised a cry both loud and terrible that filled the Achaeans with strength, giving them heart to fight resolutely and with all their might, to war and battle without ceasing. And straightaway, war became sweeter to them than returning home in their hollow ships to their dear fatherland.

The son of Atreus shouted out and commanded the Argives to dress themselves for battle. And he himself put on the shining bronze.

17-72 Homer details Agamemnon's preparation for the fight, describing his battle gear as he puts it on — the beautiful greaves, the breastplate, the sword and scabbard, the Gorgon-decorated shield, and, finally, the helmet and two bronze-tipped spears. Once finished, Hera and Athena thunder from Olympus to honor the Achaean leader. Then the Achaeans march out to meet the Trojans. As they do, Zeus rains down dewdrops of blood to signify how many would die and go down to Hades that day. Opposite them, the Trojans line up around Hector — Polydamas, Aeneas, and the three sons of Antenor, Polybus, Agenor, and Acamas. Both sides come upon each other as reapers clearing a field.

73-83 And Strife, who causes much sorrow, rejoiced as she beheld the two armies. She was the only god present to see the fight — the only god that went down to the battlefield when they faced each other. As for the others, they were relaxing and enjoying themselves in their own large halls on the sides of Olympus, where each had built a beautiful house.

The other gods blamed the cloud-wrapped son of Cronus for giving glory to the Trojans. He actively willed this! [80] But the father was not at all troubled by their ire. Rather, he held aloof from them all and sat apart exulting in his glory — looking down upon the city of the Trojans, and the ships of the Achaeans, and on the gleaming bronze, and on the killers and the killed.

84-89 Men fall when from both sides missiles — spears, arrows, and stones — find flesh. Nevertheless, the Achaeans eventually begin to make headway against the Trojans.

90-98 Then the Danaans, with a cry that rang through all their ranks, broke the enemy battle lines.

Agamemnon led them on. He killed the shepherd of men Bienor first, and afterward his comrade and charioteer Oileus, who sprang down from the chariot and rushed straight at him. But Agamemnon struck him on the forehead with his spear. Oileus' bronze helmet was useless as the spear punched through the bronze and the skull bone so that his brains were bashed in. The result? The Trojan hero was conquered even while he felt the desire to attack.

99-199 *Homer relates more of Agamemnon's success, revealing his many kills. After Bienor and Oileus, he slays Isus and Antiphus like a ravenous lion, and Peisander and Hippolochus. Around Agamemnon, foot and horsemen slaughter one another. Many Trojans lie dead on the plain, much dearer now to vultures than to their own wives. Agamemnon pursues Hector and the Trojan army toward the city and the Trojan wall. It's a rout as the Achaean leader devours them in battle rage. It is now that Zeus sends Iris to tell Hector that his turn will come to defeat the Achaeans and drive them to the ships when Agamemnon is wounded.*

200-209 "Hector, son of Priam, peer of Zeus in counsel. Father Zeus has sent me to you to speak the following. So long as you see the shepherd of men Agamemnon rushing along, fighting out front, and destroying the Trojan lines—up to that point, withdraw from the fight and order the other men to do battle, slaying the enemy in accord with the dictates of mighty combat. But when Agamemnon is wounded by a spear throw or an arrow and jumps into his chariot, then Zeus will grant your mighty hand the strength to slay one man after another until you reach the well-benched ships. Then the sun will make its plunge, and holy darkness will come on."

210-217 *Saying this, Iris flies off to Olympus. Hector turns to fire up his own men, urging them to fight. With renewed vigor, they go to meet the Achaeans, one army facing the other. Homer gives Agamemnon another brief glory report as he steps out front to fight.*

218-220 Tell me now, you Muses who have your houses on Olympus, what man was the first to come face to face with Agamemnon—[220] either of the Trojans themselves or of the glorious allies.

221-247 The first was Iphidamas, the son of Antenor. Homer gives his background before announcing the fight's action. And finally, after Iphidamas nearly stabs Agamemnon through the belly, the Achaean leader hacks his neck, and the Trojan hero perishes. Iphidamas' brother Coōn sees Agamemnon stripping the fallen man.

248-268 When Coōn, glorious among men and Antenor's oldest son, saw this, [250] his eyes ached at the sight of his fallen brother. Unseen by godlike Agamemnon, he moved beside him, spear in hand, and wounded him in the middle of his arm below the elbow. The shining bronze point of the spear punctured his arm, passing through and out the other side.

Pain washed over the lord of men Agamemnon, and he shuddered. Still, he did not leave the fight. Rather, gaining a second wind, he seized his spear and sprang upon Coōn, who was eagerly trying to drag off the body of his brother Iphidamas—his father's son—by the foot. As he did so, Coōn cried out to all the best men for help. But Agamemnon struck him beneath his shield [260] with a bronze-tipped spear and killed him as he was dragging the dead body through the throng of men under cover of his shield. He then cut off Coōn's head as he stood over the body of Iphidamas. And that is how the sons of Antenor fulfilled their allotted destiny and went down to Hades' house at the hands of the chief leader and son of Atreus.

As long as the blood welled warm from his wound, Agamemnon ranged through the lines of men with a spear in hand, and a sword, and big stones. But when the blood stopped and the wound grew dry, then the mighty son of Atreus was plunged into the sharp pangs of pain.

269-283 Experiencing pains as severe as those of childbirth, Agamemnon jumps once again into his chariot and races off toward the ships, commanding his men to fight off the Trojans. Hector sees this and recognizes that it is now his time to turn the battle toward the ships and defeat the invading army.

284-290 But when Hector noticed Agamemnon retreating, he called out to the Trojan and Lycian men, urging them on by shouting aloud, "Trojans, Lycians, and Dardanians who fight hand to hand with the enemy, be men, friends, and remember the strength and valor by which you rush into the fight. Their best man has gone. And now Zeus, the son of Cronus, has granted me the glory-boast. Even so, drive your chariots straight at [290] the strong Danaans, so that you may raise up an even greater glory-boast."

291-298 *Hector's speech stokes his men. And now Homer gives Hector a glory report as the Trojan hero steps out front to fight.*

299-304 What man then was the first and what man was the last to be cut down by [300] Priam's son Hector now that Zeus granted him glory? Asaeus was the first, and then Autonous, Opites, and Dolops, the son of Clytius. Then there were Opheltius, Agelaus, Aesymnus, Orus, and Hipponous, who was unwavering in battle. Hector first killed the Danaan leaders before moving on to the crowd of men.

305-312 *Seeing this slaughter and recognizing the danger, Odysseus calls out to Diomedes.*

313-319 "Son of Tydeus, what has happened to us so that we have abandoned the strength and valor by which we usually rush into the fight? Come, friend, and stand by my side—for we'll be disgraced if Hector of the gleaming helmet takes the ships."

In answer to him, mighty Diomedes said, "I will stay and endure with you. But our delight in fighting will be short since cloud-gathering Zeus wills to give strength and victory to the Trojans and not to us."

320-400 *Like wild boars, Diomedes and Odysseus injure and kill many of the enemy, and in this way, Zeus evens out the battle. Hector sees the two*

warriors and rushes at them. Observing Hector's approach, Diomedes en-
courages Odysseus to remain strong and firm, and hurls a spear at Hector.
But Apollo protects him. Then Paris shoots an arrow through Diomedes'
foot and glory-boasts over him. Nevertheless, Diomedes, though afraid, tells
Paris the arrow is nothing—no more than what a woman or child can do.
Odysseus falls back to cover his partner while Diomedes pulls the shaft from
his foot. Once finished with this gruesome task, Diomedes climbs aboard his
chariot and drives off to the ships in pain.

401-410 Now Odysseus, spear-famed, was left all alone. Not one of
the Argives stood by him since fear had seized them all. Odysseus
himself was sorely vexed—disturbed. And so he spoke to his great-
hearted spirit. "Ah me! What will happen to me? If I fear the throng
of men and flee in terror, there will be much evil. But if I am sur-
rounded and taken by the enemy all alone, it will be even worse—
for the son of Cronus has struck the other Danaans with fear and
has caused them to flee. But why does my dear spirit debate these
things? For I know that only cowards run off from a fight, and that
those who are the best in battle feel a great need [410] to make a
mighty stand, whether he hits and drops his man or the other hits
and drops him."

411-813 *Odysseus stands his ground while the Trojans charge forward*
and surround him like hunters and hounds around a wild boar. Even so,
Odysseus slays many until the Trojan Socus comes up and stabs his spear
through the Achaean hero's shield and breastplate. It passes through and
cuts his side. The thrust might have killed Odysseus, but Athena protected
him from death. Realizing this, Odysseus warns his enemy that his time
has come to die, that he will soon give him the glory-boast. Hearing this,
Socus turns to run, but Odysseus plants a spear in his back. Standing
above him and witnessing his final gasps for air, Odysseus glory-boasts
over Socus by telling him that his mother and father will not bury him;
rather, carrion birds will eat his flesh, flapping their wings while they do
so. As for Odysseus, the Achaeans will give him burial if he perishes in
battle. Finally, he pulls the spear out of the body and blood gushes from the
wound.

For the Trojans, this Achaean glory-boasting is too much! So they rush at Odysseus, who backs off and calls for help. Menelaus hears him and goes with Telamonian Ajax to aid him. They find him surrounded like a stag by wild jackals, and Menelaus speeds Odysseus off while Ajax fights and kills many Trojans.

Meanwhile, Hector is battling with Idomeneus and Nestor in the distance. Nearby, Paris shoots the healer Machaon, the son of Asclepius. When Idomeneus sees this, he tells Nestor to save him since healers are so valuable. Nestor obeys and rushes off with Machaon to the ships.

Observing that the Trojans are being routed by Telamonian Ajax, Cebriones tells Hector they should go help the Trojan foot and horsemen where they are. Hector eagerly agrees, and they speed over in their chariots—treading upon all the corpses, shields, battle gear, and gore as they go. When they arrive, Hector observes Ajax rather than engaging him in battle. The rest of the Trojans make the attempt to push him back. But Ajax holds his ground, refusing to allow them to reach the ships. When Eurypylus sees Ajax in trouble, he rushes to his side. He kills one man, Apisaon, before Paris shoots him through the thigh with an arrow. While all this action is transpiring, Nestor departs the battle with Machaon.

Achilles sees Nestor racing off in his chariot and orders Patroclus to go and ask him who he has taken out of the battle. Patroclus obeys. When Nestor reaches his shelter, Hecamede mixes him a drink of Pramnian wine, barley, goat cheese, and honey. Nestor drinks from his very heavy four-handled cup.

Patroclus shows up and sees Machaon. Nestor asks him why Achilles cares now that so many of the best of the Achaeans are struck. He lists the wounded—Diomedes, Odysseus, Agamemnon, Eurypylus. Nestor wishes that he were as strong as he used to be. He recounts the time the Pylians fought with the Eleans and how much booty they took from them in terms of animals. He offers another tale as well, about the violent contest between the Pylians and Epeians. He recalls the many men he slaughtered. Then he remembers when he and Odysseus came to recruit Achilles and Patroclus for the expedition to Troy. He recounts how hospitable Achilles was and how his father told him "to always be the best and to stand out among other men." Nestor reminds Patroclus that his job was to speak to Achilles shrewdly, wisely—and that Achilles would listen. Now, he says, Patroclus *has forgotten his charge. But still, he has time to try, and with the help of a god, he may succeed. Lastly, Nestor suggests that Patroclus should ask for Achilles' consent to fight alongside the rest of the Myrmidons—and for his permission to wear Achilles' armor into the fight.*

Excited by this suggestion, Patroclus runs off to speak with Achilles. First, though, he runs to Odysseus' ship where he encounters Odysseus and Eurypylus, who are both wounded.

814-821 Seeing them, the brave son of Menoetius felt pity for them, and wailing aloud, he spoke to them with winged words. "Wretched men! Danaan leaders and counselors! You were destined like this to satiate fast dogs with your flesh far away from your dear ones and homeland in Troy. But come and tell me this, god-born hero Eurypylus—[820] will the Achaeans be able to check great Hector, or will they now fall to him, conquered by his spear?"

822-841 *Eurypylus declares that, no, there isn't any hope now that all the best men have been wounded and await healing by the ships. He then asks Patroclus to save him since Patroclus has learned the healing arts from Achilles, who learned how to cure others from the centaur Cheiron—and because the healers Podalirius and Machaon are themselves wounded. Patroclus agrees to do so, even though he must rush off to report Nestor's battle suggestion to Achilles.*

842-848 Saying this, Patroclus grabbed the shepherd of men around the middle and led him into his shelter. When Eurypylus' attendant saw him, he spread cattle-skins upon the ground for him to lay down on. Patroclus stretched him out and cut out the sharp arrow from his thigh. He washed the black blood from the wound with warm water, and then, taking a bitter root—one that slays all bodily pain—and rubbing it between his hands, he spread it upon the wound to kill the pain. With this, the wound dried, and the blood stopped its flow.

BOOK 12

THE TROJANS ATTACK THE WALL
ASIUS & HECTOR, SARPEDON & GLAUCUS

IN BRIEF: *Like a whirlwind, Hector and the Trojans work to cross the trench and break through the enemy's wall into the Achaean camp—and this after Polydamas advises Hector to retreat. As for the Achaeans, the two Ajaxes cheer on their fellow warriors. Be men! On the other side, Sarpedon tells Glaucus they must fight. Hector throws a massive stone that bursts the Achaean wall. They're in!*

S O IT WAS that the brave son of Menoetius was in the shelter attending to and healing Eurypylus. But the Argives and Trojans fought on in groups. As for the long trench and the wide wall—the wall built to shield their ships with a trench on either side—these were not destined to defend the Danaans for very long. The reason? The Achaeans had not offered glorious hecatombs to the gods so that they might hold on to their swift ships and the bountiful spoil they had dragged inside. Instead, they had built the wall against the will of the immortal gods.

9-85 Homer explains how the trench and wall will ultimately collapse after the fall of Troy when the gods level them. During the fight, Hector blasts toward the Achaeans like a whirlwind. And like a wild boar or lion he urges his men forward across the trench. But his own horses are afraid to cross thanks to the deadly stakes the Achaeans have planted within. Unlike the horses, though, the footmen are eager to advance. Polydamas rides up next to Hector and explains the folly of attempting to ride across the trench. He advises they dismount their chariots and cross on foot while the charioteers hold back the horses and chariots. Hector jumps to the ground in agreement.

86-107 But the men divided, arranging themselves into five groups that followed after their leaders. Those that went with Hector and Polydamas were the best and most in number, and the most determined to break through the wall and fight at the ships. Cebriones joined them as third in command. The next group was led by Paris, Alcathous, and Agenor. Helenus and godlike Deiphobus, two sons of Priam, headed the third, and with them was the hero Asius— Asius, the son of Hyrtacus, whose fiery horses, great in size, had carried him from Arisbe, nearby the river Selleis. Aeneas, the noble son of Anchises, led the fourth—he and the two sons of Antenor, [100] Archelochus and Acamas, well-skilled in all the arts of fighting. Sarpedon led the glorious allies and took with him Glaucus and warlike Asteropaeus, whom he judged the best men of the others after himself—for he himself was conspicuous by far among all the rest.

But when they had joined together their well-made ox-hide shields, the Trojan groups stepped ahead, marching eagerly toward the Danaans. They felt sure that the enemy men would collapse, allowing them to fall upon the black ships.

108-309 *While the rest of the Trojans are marching across the trench, Asius decides to stay on his chariot, contrary to Polydamas' counsel, and wheels rightward to attack the Achaean left flank. It is an unfortunate move for him as Fate will catch up to him in the form of Idomeneus' spear. For now, however, he and his men speed onward, hoping to breach the Achaean wall. The fools! They encounter the sons of Lapith, the spearmen Polypoetes and Leonteus, two of the best men who stand before the wall like two trees firmly planted in the ground. Prior to the Trojan onslaught, the two had been urging on the Achaeans to the fight. Now they rush out and battle before the wall like two wild boars against huntsmen and their dogs. Above them, Achaean men sling stones from the wall down onto the Trojan crowd. The stones fall like snowflakes, ringing on the Trojan helmets and shields. Below, Asius complains to Zeus that he has lied by giving the impression that they would easily take the Achaeans. He compares the enemy to narrow waisted wasps that eagerly defend their homes. The reality is that Zeus has decided to give glory to Hector. Everywhere there is fighting. And great fires blaze, and smoke fills the air. Homer announces that he would have to be a god to tell it all.*

He tells part, though—who kills whom. Polypoetes strikes down the Trojan Damasus, stabbing him through his bronze helmet so that his brain is tossed about inside his head. By his side, Leonteus kills many with his spear and sword.

While Polypoetes and Leonteus are battle raging like this, Hector, Polydamas, and the first group of men consider what to do. Just now they have received a negative omen on their left—an eagle carrying a snake that lunged up and bit the eagle. When the eagle dropped the snake in their midst, the Trojans shuddered. What should they do? Polydamas counsels they retreat, comparing the Trojans to the eagle and the Achaeans to the snake who, in the end, bit the eagle. Hector doesn't like it—he's not at all pleased with the word of advice Polydamas has spoken. No, he claims that Zeus has promised success to him. And so he will not pay attention to omens, whether they come from the right or the left. He would rather obey Zeus, the ruler of men who die and the gods who will never die. "One bird omen is best," he declares, "to defend one's homeland." He finishes by telling Polydamas that if he holds back from the fight, he will himself strike him down.

Hector and the Trojans advance. And Zeus stirs up wind and dust against the Achaean ships and gives glory to the Trojans, who begin to dismantle the wall. But as quickly as they do, the Achaeans patch it with cattle skins.

Along the wall, the two Ajaxes rouse the men to the fight. They explain that even though all men are not equal in battle, each man has his work to do, whether he is superior and preeminent in the fight, or somewhere in the middle, or he is an inferior man and among the worst. Stay with the battle, they urge them on, in the hope that Zeus will drive the enemy back to the city.

Just then, as stones and other missiles are whizzing back and forth over both sides, Zeus stirs up his own son Sarpedon against the Argives, so that he comes out like a lion attacking cattle. Sarpedon holds his shield out before him—the shield made of bronze, cowhide, and gold stitching. Motivated in this way, he turns to his comrade Glaucus, the son of Hippolochus, and questions him.

310-330 "Glaucus, why are we greatly honored in Lycia with the best seats in the feasting hall, and the best cuts of meat, and full cups of the choicest wine? And why do all the Lycian men look at us like we're gods? And why do we have a great estate by the banks of the Xanthus? And why all the beautiful orchards and vineyards and wheat-bearing land?

"Therefore, we must now take a stand among the foremost Lycians and join in blazing battle so that many of the heavily armed Lycians may say, 'Truly our kings, who rule in Lycia, are no inglorious men! Sure, they eat fat sheep and drink [320] the best wines, honey-sweet, but their strength is good and noble since they fight amid the front ranks of the Lycians.'

"Ah friend! If we could flee from this battle and always be ageless and immortal, then I myself would not fight amid the front ranks, nor would I dispatch you into battle that confers glory on men. But now that the countless fates of death are at hand—the fates that no one can flee or escape—come, let us grab the glory-boast from some man, or some man will take it from us."

So he spoke, and Glaucus did not turn away or disobey, [330] but they led the great body of Lycians straight ahead at a marching walk.

331-437 *Seeing them marching forward and bringing evil misery with them, Menestheus, the son of Peteos, shudders. He attempts to call for help, but the clashing of arms is far too loud. Consequently, he sends a quick herald to call upon the two Ajaxes or Teucer—at least bring Telamonian Ajax, he commands. Ajax agrees and runs over with his brother, Teucer, and Pandion. When they arrive, they find the Lycians have gathered like a storm.*

Ajax crushes Epicles with a stone so huge that men now—Homer declares—could not even hold it. Then Teucer shoots Glaucus through the arm with an arrow. Glaucus leaps down from the wall and rushes off before any Achaean man notices or glory-boasts over him. Sad at seeing his comrade leave the fight, Sarpedon slays Alcmaon, the son of Thestor, who plunges to the ground. Then he pulls down a section of the wall, creating a gap for his men to pass through.

Upon witnessing Sarpedon's great deed, Ajax and Teucer fall on him. But Zeus protects his son—for now. Sarpedon falls back, yet only so much, since he desperately wishes to seize glory. He turns to the Lycians, rebukes them for forgetting their battle strength, and calls on them to help him pull down the wall. They respond, fearing their ruler.

Now the Trojans face the well-made Achaean lines of battle, and the Achaeans look out at them ready to defend their ships—like two men contending over the boundary lines of a common field, one shared by many men. Many are wounded, and blood and gore bespatter the walls. Even so, for as long as Zeus grants glory to Hector, the Lycians cannot make any progress.

438-471 The son of Priam Hector was the first to rush at the wall of the Achaeans. When he had done so, he cried out to the Trojans, [440] "Up, horse-taming Trojans! Break the Argive wall and fling fire upon their ships!"

This is what Hector said to urge them on, and they all listened and rushed straight at the wall as a mass of men. And with sharp spears in their hands, they scaled the wall.

Hector grabbed a stone that lay just outside the gates—thick at one end but pointed at the other. As men are now, two of the best could hardly lift such a stone from the ground and set it in a cart. But all by himself, Hector lifted it quite easily—[450] for the son of scheming Cronus made it light for him. As a shepherd picks up a ram's fleece with one hand and finds it no burden, so did Hector easily raise the great stone and drive it at the doors that closed the gates. These doors were double and high and were kept closed by two cross-bars. . . . He broke both hinges, and the stone fell inside the walls because of its great [460] weight . . . Then shining Hector leaped inside with a face as dark as that of flying night. The gleaming bronze flashed fiercely about his body and from the two spears he had in hand. None but a god could have withstood him as he flung himself into the gateway. His eyes glared like fire.

Then he turned around to the Trojans and called on them to scale the wall. They obeyed his urgent directive—some of them at once climbing over the wall, while others [470] poured through the gates.

The Danaans were then put to flight toward their ships, and all was an unending uproar and confusion.

BOOK 13

THE ACHAEANS FIGHT BACK
IDOMENEUS' GLORY

IN BRIEF: *When Zeus glances away from the battle for a moment, Poseidon fires up the Achaeans under various guises. There's fighting back and forth, and Homer sings the Cretan leader, Idomeneus, a glory report. Menelaus prays that the Trojans will be punished. Polydamas advises momentary retreat to plan with the other Trojan leaders. But most of them are dead. Telamonian Ajax taunts Hector. Nevertheless, Hector and his men rush the ships as the Achaeans stand firmly against the onslaught.*

N OW WHEN ZEUS had brought Hector and the Trojans to the ships, he left them to the misery of the never-ending battle toil, and he turned his radiant eyes away, gazing elsewhere. He looked down to the land of the Thracian horse-herders, and to the Mysians, who fight hand to hand, and to the noble Hippemolgi, who live on milk, and to the Abii, the most observant of custom of all mankind. As for the battle by Troy, Zeus no longer turned his radiant eyes toward it, for he did not think in his spirit that any of the immortals would go down to help either the Trojans or the Danaans.

[10] But lord Poseidon the Earth-shaker was watching—and not blindly. No, he had been looking admiringly on the battle from his seat on the topmost crests of wooded Samothrace. From there he could see the whole of Ida's range, with its plain below and the city of Priam and the ships of the Achaeans. He had come from under the sea and had taken his place there, for he pitied the Achaeans who were being conquered by the Trojans. Moreover, he strongly resented Zeus. At once Poseidon came down from his post on the rugged mountaintop. Striding swiftly, the high mountains and the

forest quaked beneath the tread of his immortal feet. [20] He took three strides, and with the fourth he reached Aegae, his goal. That's where his golden palace is—sparkling, imperishable forever in the depths of the sea.

When he got there, he prepared his swift, bronze-shod horses for the coming journey. Their manes of gold were flying in the wind. He clothed himself in a garment of gold, grasped his well-made golden horsewhip, and stepped into his chariot in order to speed off over the waves.

28-38 *Poseidon drives his chariot toward the plains of Troy and goes to join the Achaeans, who are still battling the Trojans.*

39-45 Now, close together like a storm-cloud or flame of fire, the Trojans eagerly followed the son of Priam, Hector, shouting and raising the battle cry. They hoped to take the Achaean ships and kill all their best men.

Meanwhile, Poseidon the Earth-shaker urged on the Argives. He had come up out of the deep sea and had assumed the form and voice of the seer Calchas.

46-273 *Poseidon-Calchas speaks to the two Ajaxes and inspires them and the others to be brave and fight. He strikes the two with his scepter and grants them mighty strength before taking off in the form of a falcon. The lesser Ajax, the son of Oileus, recognizes that this Calchas is actually a god and realizes he is suddenly more eager to fight. Telamonian Ajax agrees. They both rejoice in their newly experienced battle lust. Poseidon stirs up other Achaeans. What a shame! he cries. You must fight and not give up! You are the best—if you were weak and cowardly, I would say nothing. But you are not! Each one of you should have a proper sense of shame and consider the indignation others will feel toward you! This is serious—for mighty Hector is here!*

The Achaeans stand together closely, awaiting the Trojan assault. Hector rolls forward like a great stone and urges his own men and allies onward. Deiphobus, the son of Priam, steps forward. Meriones throws at him, but the spear breaks off. Angry, he runs off to get another spear.

The battle rages back and forth. Teucer slays Imbrius, the son of Mentor. Then, hoping to kill Teucer, Hector instead strikes Amphimachus, the grandson of Poseidon. The god is angry! After the Achaeans rescue the body, and after the lesser Ajax decapitates Imbrius and rolls his head to Hector's feet, Poseidon goes and speaks to Cretan Idomeneus in the form of Thoas and asks him what is going wrong. Idomeneus answers that the problem is neither the skill of the men nor their fear. No, it must be Zeus' pleasure and will that the Achaeans are perishing namelessly. Poseidon-Thoas suggests they stand and fight together—for, he declares, "Excellence comes even for very weak and cowardly men when they band together." Idomeneus arms, takes up a spear, and encounters Meriones, who is also on his way to get one. They both brag about the spears they have taken from the Trojan dead and how they have not forgotten their battle courage. Meriones finishes by telling Idomeneus that among all men, he surely must know that "he fights out front in battle that confers glory on men."

274-293 Idomeneus, the leader of the Cretans, answered Meriones, "I know that you are a brave man. You don't have to tell me. For if by the ships we were now choosing the best of all men for an ambush, you'd want to go first. Let me tell you, Meriones, that it is under circumstances like an ambush that the warlike excellence of a man is discerned, and there that the cowardly man or the brave man reveals himself. For while the coward's skin changes from this color to another—[280] and he can't sit without trembling or restrain the spirit in his chest, but he keeps shifting his weight from one knee to the other as his great heart rapidly beats, and he frightfully pictures the fates of death taking him, and his teeth begin to chatter—the good, noble, and brave man's skin doesn't change, nor is he excessively alarmed when he's chosen first to participate in an ambush of men. Rather he prays to quickly mix in the deadly battle. No, Meriones—in such a situation no man would find fault with your courage and the strength of your hands. If you were struck by an arrow or a spear, you would not be hit from behind in your neck or your back. [290] But the weapon would hit you in the chest or your belly as you were pressing forward to take your place in the front ranks.

"But come, let us no longer stay here talking as though we were little children, in case some man reproaches us excessively."

294-360 *They march out and Meriones asks Idomeneus where they should enter the fight — whether in the center of the army's ranks, or the right or left flank. Idomeneus explains that the two Ajaxes and Teucer are defending the middle. And Telamonian Ajax will stand against any mortal man who eats the grain of Demeter — he would even stand against Achilles! He recommends going to the left where they will soon find out if they win the glory-boast or give it over to another.*

When the Trojans see Idomeneus entering the fray, they surge after him. The men on each side eagerly desire to slay the men opposite them amid the confusion and hard work of war.

As for the gods, the two sons of Cronus, Zeus and Poseidon, are at odds. Zeus wants to give glory to Achilles and Thetis by helping the Trojans; Poseidon, however, fears for the Achaeans and encourages them under the guise of different men. He resents his brother — even though Zeus is older and knows more. Whatever the case, the two gods tie the knot of mighty strife and distressful war, and many men die.

361-362 And now Idomeneus, though his hair was already sprinkled with gray, called aloud to the Danaans. He rushed at the Trojans and spread panic and flight among them.

363-423 *Raging among the Trojans, Idomeneus drops the Trojan ally Othryoneus, who had promised to fight off the Achaeans, and so Priam had pledged his daughter Cassandra to him in marriage. It never happened. Rather, Idomeneus mocks him by promising him an Achaean bride as he drags him off by the foot to the ships. Seeing this, Asius comes to fight for Othryoneus' corpse, desiring most of all to strike Idomeneus. Instead of getting his wish, however, the Cretan warrior kills him with a throw of his spear that flies through his throat. And the son of Nestor, Antilochus, drives a spear through Asius' fear-stricken charioteer's belly. As Antilochus speeds off, Deiphobus throws at Idomeneus. But the latter ducks, and the spear hits another Achaean, Hypsenor, the son of Hippasus. Deiphobus brags that he will make a good traveling companion for Asius on his way to Hades. All*

the boasting bothers the Achaeans! Still, Antilochus remembers his duty to
rescue Hypsenor's body. He covers him with his shield, and two other men,
Mecisteus and Alastor, carry him off to the ships.

424-454 Idomeneus kept on, never relaxing his great battle might. His constant desire was to cover some Trojan warrior with the darkness of night—or he himself would fall with a heavy thud while warding off destruction from the Achaeans.

It was then that the hero Alcathous, the dear son of god-nourished Aesyetes, fell. He was Anchises' son by marriage, having married his eldest daughter Hippodameia. [430] Now this girl was dearly loved by her father and queenly mother since she excelled all her generation in beauty, weaving, and understanding. Because of this, the best man in all of Troy had taken her as his wife. It was this man that Poseidon dropped by the hand of Idomeneus . . . who struck him with a spear right in the middle of his chest. The spear shattered his tunic made of [440] bronze that had always protected his skin from injury and destruction. The ringing sound was harsh as the spear punched through the bronze. And Alcathous fell heavily to the ground just as the spear struck his still-beating heart—and above him, the spear's end quivered until strong Ares put an end to his life.

Then Idomeneus vehemently glory-boasted, loudly shouting out, "Deiphobus, since you yourself are inclined to boast, what about this—have we achieved a balance now that we have killed three men to your one? You are blind! You are god-possessed! But you should also stand and face me yourself. Then you would know what kind of Zeus-begotten man I am—I who have come to this land. For Zeus [450] first brought Minos into the world to watch over Crete. And Minos in his turn engendered a son, the blameless man Deucalion. And Deucalion begot me to be the ruler over the many men in Crete. So now have my ships brought me here to bring harm to you, your father, and the other Trojans."

455-619 Deiphobus debates whether he should remain to fight Idomeneus,
or not. Yet rather than staying to face him alone, Deiphobus runs off to
Aeneas—who, Homer explains, always hangs back, upset at Priam for not

*honoring him. He asks Aeneas for help in rescuing Alcathous' corpse be-
cause the fallen man is Aeneas' brother-in-law.*

*When Idomeneus sees the two coming, he doesn't back off in fear, even
though he is afraid. Instead, like a wild boar, he holds his ground and calls
on his friends for help. Hearing this, Aeneas likewise calls out to his own
men. There follows a huge brawl over Alcathous' body. Idomeneus and
Aeneas swing at each other's flesh. They cast their spears, and missing,
strike other men.*

*Deiphobus hits and kills Ascalaphus, the son of the war god Ares. Mer-
iones strikes Deiphobus through the arm. As a result, he races off from the
battle with his brother Polites. They head to the city. Meanwhile, Aeneas
slays Aphareus.*

*On the opposite side, Antilochus, protected by Poseidon, drops the Tro-
jan Thoön. Witnessing him do this, Adamas, the son of Asius, vainly casts
at Antilochus before withdrawing to the Trojan lines. Meriones doesn't let
him escape, though. Instead, he pursues Adamas and plants a spear be-
tween his genitals and bellybutton. Squirming in pain, the young Trojan
hero dies.*

*Homer pans over to the Trojan Helenus, the son of Priam, who just
killed Deipyrus. Observing this, and taken by distress, Menelaus steps out
against Helenus with his spear as the latter man simultaneously comes
against him with his bow. Helenus fires an arrow, but it ricochets off Men-
elaus' breastplate. Then Menelaus throws his spear. It hits Helenus, pass-
ing through his hand. Defeated, he retreats, and Antenor bandages his
hand. Now Peisander comes at Menelaus. Peisander strikes his shield, joy-
fully driving through his spear. But it doesn't hit the Achaean leader. In
turn, Menelaus stabs him through the face above the nose, causing his eye-
balls to pop out and fall to the ground. In rage, Menelaus calls out, glory-
boasting.*

620-639 "Even so, will you arrogant Trojans leave the ships of the
Danaans, though you are proud and can't get enough of battle. Nor
will you go without first tasting the same dishonor and shame that
you mistreated me with—you cowardly dogs!

"You had no fear in your spirits of the hard wrath of loud-thun-
dering Zeus Xenios, the god of hospitality and guest-friendship, the

god who will one day utterly destroy your lofty city! Why? You stole my wedded wife and much wealth when you were her guest. And now you wish to set our ships on fire and kill our heroes. [630] But, however eager you are for war, the day will come when we stop your fighting.

"Father Zeus—you who they say are above all the other gods and men in wisdom, and by whom all these things have come into existence—how can you favor the Trojans in this way, men who are so proud and insolent, who are always so reckless in their might that they are unable to find satisfaction in distressing battle? For I declare that all things find satisfaction—sleep, love, sweet song, and the stately dance. With these things a man hopes to find fulfilment—*not* with war. But with battle, the Trojans are insatiate!"

640-722 Menelaus strips Peisander and gives the bloody armor to his comrades. The fight volleys back and forth. Meriones drops Harpalion, the son of Pylaemenes. In anger at this, Paris kills the Corinthian man Euchenor, who knew ahead of time that he would either die of disease at home or perish at Troy.

As the battle rages on the left, the Achaeans winning much glory, Hector and his men fight inside the walls at the center. Hector has no idea about the Trojan losses on the left. The Boeotians, long-tunic wearing Ionians, Locrians, Phthians, Epeians, and others battle against him, among them the Athenians, who are led on by their leader, Menestheus. Homer gives a catalogue of many of the leaders. Pheidas, Stichius, and Bias are with the Athenian Menestheus. Meges, Amphion, and Dracius lead the Epeians, as do Medon and Podarces the Phthians. The two Ajaxes fight near each other like two oxen stoutly pulling the plow. As the Trojans come on, the Locrians fire and sling a storm of arrows and stones upon them, dashing them together in confusion.

723-747 Then, pathetically, the Trojans would have withdrawn from the ships and shelters back to windy Ilium, had not Polydamas stood beside bold Hector and said, "Hector, what means are there to persuade you? None. Because some god has granted you skill in war, you wish therefore to know more than every other man in counsel.

But let me tell you something—you can't win in everything. [730] The gods have given to one man skill in war and to another skill in the dance. To others they've given the ability to play the lyre or sing. To still others far-seeing Zeus gives a noble mind. And many are able to share in its profit, as when many are saved . . . Therefore, I'll declare what I think will be the best for us.

"The fight is all around us like a circle of fire. And look, even now that we've made it past the wall, some of our men stand back from the fight in full armor while others are fighting scattered and outnumbered near the ships. [740] Draw back, therefore, and call upon all the best men to gather in an assembly. Then we will consider all our options, whether to fall upon the many-benched ships—if the gods will give us victory—or to retreat from the ships while we are still unharmed. My greatest fear is that the Achaeans will pay us back in full for yesterday—for there is still one man at their ships who is never weary of battle, and who will not hold back from the fight for much longer."

748-812 Hector gladly listens. He goes off to look for the best men to call them to an assembly. When he finds Paris, his brother reports that most of them are dead. They rush off to Polydamas and the others who are battling the Achaeans. Telamonian Ajax taunts Hector.

813-837 "Your spirit now surely hopes to storm our ships—but here are our hands to repel you! No, it is far more likely that we will first take your populous city and sack it, razing it to the ground. The time is near when in flight you will pray to father Zeus and all the other immortals that your beautifully maned horses may fly faster than a falcon [820] as they raise dust on the plain while carrying you toward the city."

While Ajax was shouting these words, a bird flew by on his right-hand side, a high-flying eagle, and the Achaean army shouted with joy, encouraged by the omen.

But shining Hector answered, "You're a confused man, Ajax, a braggart of jumbled words . . . *For I'm sure* this day will deliver much harm to the Argives. And among them all, you will fall by my own spear—if you endure and [830] await my long spear. It will cut your skin and puncture your body. And when you die by the Achaean ships, you will glut the dogs and birds of prey with your fat and flesh."

With these words Hector led the way, and the others noisily followed him while the army shouted behind them.

For their part, the Argives roared from the other side, nor did they forget their battle strength, but they stood firm against the best of the Trojans as they came on. And the cry from both sides rose into the sky and to the light of the sun surrounding Zeus.

BOOK 14

HERA TRICKS ZEUS
HECTOR FALLS AND THE ACHAEANS ATTACK

IN BRIEF: *Nestor ventures out to see what is going on. On the Achaean side, there is word of slipping away at night. Odysseus can't believe Agamemnon's word! Wounded as we are, we must return to the battle! he says. Diomedes advises the wounded leaders to go out and urge everyone on. Poseidon reassures Agamemnon. His superhuman shout rouses the Achaeans. Hera considers how to turn Zeus' attention away from the war. With the help of Aphrodite, she seduces him atop Mount Ida, with the goal of tricking him into falling asleep. He does. Now her side, the Achaeans, can fight. Hector is taken out when Telamonian Ajax hurls a huge anchor stone at him. Now the Trojans are winning! Now the Achaeans! The battle and revenge rages back and forth. Given his speed, Ajax, the son of Oileus, kills the most.*

NESTOR HEARD ALL the shouting rising up from both armies even though he was off at some distance drinking his wine at his ship. And so with winged words, he addressed the son of Asclepius:

"Consider what will happen now, godlike Machaon. The cries of all the young men full of strength are now growing louder and louder by the ships. Anyway, sit here and drink your sparkling wine while fair-headed Hecamede heats you a bath and washes the clotted blood from your wound. As for me, I'll go look around to find out what is going on."

That's what Nestor said . . . [10] . . . He took up a strong spear, tipped with sharp bronze, and stood outside his shelter. Right away he saw something shameful. The high-spirited Trojans were troubling the Achaeans from behind, driving them on in confusion. And the Achaean wall was tumbling down!

16-156 *After considering whether he should join the battle or consult with Agamemnon, Nestor runs off to find the Achaean leader. He eventually joins up with Agamemnon, Diomedes, and Odysseus, and he suggests they plan what to do rather than enter into battle wounded.*

Agamemnon advises retreat by cover of night; they should drag their ships into the sea from the beach. His reason is straightforward: Zeus is presently glorifying the Trojans as he glorifies the blessed gods, whereas he is hindering the Achaean effort.

Odysseus isn't pleased with his advice; rather, he angrily replies, "Son of Atreus, what kind of word has escaped the barrier of your teeth?" He goes on to claim that the Achaean army is no inglorious one to be led by a man who would say such things. Odysseus scorns Agamemnon's thoughts and mind. If they leave, he argues, then the Trojans will get what they want—they will be the victors, and we will face destruction.

Accepting Odysseus' censure, Agamemnon wishes that someone would offer better counsel than he has given, whether young or old. Diomedes stands to speak. After giving his lineage to demonstrate that he is neither "a coward nor a weakling," the young man advises they go down to the battle to urge everyone on. They all agree.

On their way, Poseidon appears as an old man and takes hold of Agamemnon's hand. He reassures him of the blessed gods' support, curses Achilles for his heart bent on destruction, and foretells the fall of the Trojans. Then, taking off, he shouts as loud as thousands of men, and so he rouses the Achaeans to battle. Hera observes Poseidon from Olympus and rejoices.

157-165 Then Hera turned her eyes to Zeus as he sat on the topmost crests of Ida with its many springs, and she hated him. The cow-eyed queenly goddess anxiously thought about [160] how she might beguile and deceive the mind of aegis-bearing Zeus in order to turn his attention away from the war. Finally, she came up with what she thought was a good plan. She would travel to Ida looking beautiful so that Zeus might long for her and desire to make love to her. She subsequently hoped to pour a warm and harmless sleep over his eyes and his much-knowing mind.

166-291 With this plan in mind, Hera beautifies herself and goes off to ask Aphrodite for help even though the two are fighting the war on opposite sides. Her request is for sexual love and desire. She falsely claims that she is going to use the gifts to bring Oceanus, "the origin of the gods," and his spouse, Tethys, together again to end their ongoing squabbling—for, thanks to anger, Hera reveals, they haven't visited their love bed for a long time. Aphrodite agrees to provide the gifts since Hera is Zeus' lover. She gives her an adornment filled with sexual love, desire, and fond discourse, and tells Hera that she will return with her desires fulfilled.

Hera smiles before speeding off. From Olympus she goes south, and from Athos she steps across the sea to Lemnos where she meets up with Sleep, the brother of Death. There, she asks him to lull Zeus to sleep after they've made love. If he does, Hera will give him many fine gifts. The god hesitates, recalling the last time Hera asked him to lull Zeus to sleep—when Heracles sacked Troy many years before. Zeus would have hammered him if Night had not saved him. Recognizing the danger, Hera promises Sleep one of the younger Graces for his wife—Pasithea, the one he has desired for a long time. Sleep rejoices at this and asks Hera to swear to what she has said. She swears. And they fly off to Mount Ida where Sleep hides from Zeus in a silver fir tree while Hera approaches the father of gods and men.

292-296 Hera went up to Gargarus, the topmost peak of Ida, and the cloud-gatherer Zeus spotted her. When he saw her, desire flooded his perceptive mind. It was just like the first time, when Zeus initially fell for Hera, and they mingled together in love and slept with each other without their dear parents knowing anything about it.

297-312 Standing, Zeus asks Hera where she's going. She lies and tells Zeus the same story she told Aphrodite, the one about Oceanus and Tethys. Zeus tells her the mission can wait.

313-316 "Hera, go some other time on your visit to Oceanus. For now, let us take delight in love. For never yet have I been so overpowered by desire—neither for a goddess nor for a mortal woman—as I am overpowered at this moment by desire for you."

*317-401 Zeus goes on to give an Olympic account of the many times he
was seized with desire for various women and goddesses, including Alc-
mene, the mother of Heracles, and Semele, the mother of Dionysus, "the
delight of mortal men."*

*Regarding Zeus' proposition, Hera demurely chastises him. How can
they make love on the top of the mountain in plain view? She suggests they
go to Zeus' house. He tells her not to worry, though, that he will create a
shining cloud of gold to hide them. Not even the sun god Helios will be
able to see them. Without waiting for Hera's reply, Zeus grabs his wife,
tosses her down to the earth, and makes love to her. Beneath them and their
lovemaking, grass, lotus, and much else springs up in new life to cushion
their encounter.*

*Afterward, while Zeus is conquered by sleep, Sleep journeys to tell
earth-shaking Poseidon to help the Achaeans and grant them glory. Posei-
don fires up the Achaean men. He explains that if they give their all, they
won't need Achilles, that they can defeat Hector on their own. He advises
the foremost of men to take the best of the shields, the largest ones, and the
longest spears, and give to the lesser, inferior men the smaller shields. The
rule: good armor for good and brave men, and inferior armor for inferior,
worse men. Diomedes, Odysseus, and Agamemnon help Poseidon make
this exchange among all the men. Meanwhile, Hector is gathering his
army. Finally, the two sides clash.*

402-20 Shining Hector first aimed his spear at Ajax, who was facing
him full-on. He didn't miss. Nevertheless, the spear struck him
where his body was most protected . . . As a result, Hector was an-
gry that he'd thrown his spear in vain, so he withdrew to the cover
of his men to avoid death.

As he was retreating like this, great Telamonian Ajax struck him
[410] with a large stone, one of the many that propped up all the
swift ships along the shore. Ajax lifted one of these and struck Hec-
tor above the rim of his shield close to his neck, and the blow made
him spin around in every direction. As an oak falls over when up-
rooted by father Zeus' exploding lightning and there rises the terri-
ble smell of sulfur . . . even so did mighty Hector quickly fall to the
ground amid an exploding cloud of dust. His spear fell from his

hand, but everything else—his shield [420] and helmet and all his bronze battle gear—rang about him.

421-439 *Shouting, the Achaeans run at Hector, hoping to strike him dead and drag him off. Seeing this, the Trojan leaders defend their fallen comrade and carry him off from the battle. When they reach the immortal Xanthus, they pour water over him and he revives—only to vomit blood and pass out again in darkness.*

440-441 When the Argives saw Hector going off from the fight, they upped the attack on the Trojans and remembered how much they delighted in fighting.

442-507 *Little Ajax, the son of Oileus, leaps out first and wounds Satnius, the son of Enops. Both sides battle over him. During this fight, Polydamas wounds and drops Prothoënor to the ground and glory-boasts over him. The Argives grieve at this bragging. Hoping for revenge, then, Telamonian Ajax casts at Polydamas and misses as the Trojan hero leaps to the side to escape "black death." Even so, Archelochus, the son of Antenor, is hit by the spear because the gods planned his destruction. Ajax boasts that his death is a payment for Prothoënor. In turn, grief seizes the Trojans. So, the Trojan Acamas slays Boeotian Promachus in recompense for Archelochus' death and glory-boasts over him loudly. He explains that this is what kinsmen are supposed to do.*

As before, the Argives feel distress at his boasting—especially Peneleos, who goes after Acamas with his spear, misses him, and kills instead Ilioneus, the only child of Phorbas. When Peneleos decapitates Ilioneus with his sword, he holds up his spear with Ilioneus' eyeball stuck on it like a "poppy flower's round head," and he glory-boasts over him. It's his death for Promachus' own death! Neither of their wives will ever welcome them home! Everyone trembles at this remark, considering how to flee destruction. Homer finishes with a brief glory report in honor of the Achaeans.

508-510 Speak now to me, you Muses who have your houses on Olympus, what mortal man was the first of the Achaeans [510] to take up the spoils of the fallen enemy men when the glorious Earth-shaker Poseidon altered the course of the battle?

511-519 *Telamonian Ajax is first, then Antilochus, Meriones, and Menelaus.*

520-522 But it was Ajax, the swift son of Oileus, who killed the most men since, given his speed, he could best catch up to all the fleeing men when Zeus awakened fear in them.

BOOK 15

THE BATTLE AT THE SHIPS
ZEUS & POSEIDON

IN BRIEF: *The Trojans retreat. Zeus wakes up angry, and Hera swears she didn't mean to trick him. He relents and smiles before foretelling what will happen—including Patroclus' and Hector's deaths and the sack of Troy. Hera is afraid. Through the messenger Iris, Zeus orders Poseidon to stop fighting for the Achaeans. Poseidon balks, citing the three equal portions of each brother—the sky, the sea, and the underworld. Apollo heals Hector. The fight goes on, the Trojans advancing. Hector battle rages. He commands his men to set the Achaean ships afire. Ajax urges on the Achaeans.*

WHEN THE TROJAN flight had taken them past the trench and its sharpened stakes, and after many had fallen by the hands of the Danaans, the Trojans finally stood still upon reaching their chariots, routed and pale with fear.

It was then that Zeus awoke on the heights of Mount Ida where he was sleeping with golden-throned Hera by his side. He sprang to his feet, and, looking down, he saw the Trojans and the Achaeans — the one group stirred up and the others driving them on in confusion, with lord Poseidon himself among them. Then he saw Hector lying on the ground with his comrades gathered around him. [10] He was painfully gasping for breath, senseless, and vomiting blood—since it was not a weak Achaean man who had struck him. Seeing him, the father of men and gods had pity on Hector. And turning to Hera and flashing her a terrible look from beneath his brows, he said to her, "You're irresistible! It is your skill at causing harm that has stopped the fighting of godlike Hector and the fearful route of the whole Trojan army. Who knows—maybe you'll be the first to know the results of your own grievous mischief when I strike and whip you."

18-58 *Zeus reminds Hera of the time he hung her from the clouds when Hera had contrived painful labors for Heracles. There she was, suspended by her wrists that were tied with gold, with two heavy sky-fallen stones dangling from her feet. None of the gods could do anything to help her. Zeus fended them off, tossing them down to earth by his mighty power. He finishes the point by assuring Hera that their lovemaking will not protect her.*

Hearing this, Hera shudders. She swears by Earth, the broad Sky, the river Styx—"the most frightful oath made by the blessed gods"—Zeus' head, and their love bed that she didn't command Poseidon to help the Achaeans and harm the Trojans. Hera supposes Poseidon must be helping because he wants to help. "It is doubtlessly his own spirit that commands and urges him on," she suggests.

Zeus smiles. He then commands Hera to go and fetch Iris and Apollo. Iris is to go tell Poseidon to stop fighting for the Achaeans. Zeus goes on to explain what will happen during the battle to come.

59-77 "Phoebus Apollo will urge Hector into the fight, [60] breathing battle strength into him again. He will forget the bodily pain that now distresses his mind and senses, and he will turn the Achaeans back in pathetic rout until, fleeing, they fall back to the well-benched ships of Achilles, the son of Peleus. Achilles will then send his comrade Patroclus into battle as the Achaean champion. But shining Hector will slay him in front of Ilium after Patroclus has destroyed many young warriors, among them my own godlike son Sarpedon. But in anger, godlike Achilles will kill Hector to avenge Patroclus.

"From that moment on I will make it so that the Achaeans [70] will incessantly drive the Trojans back from the ships until they fulfill the counsels of Athena and sack lofty Ilium. But for now, I will not stop the march of my wrath, nor will I allow any of the other immortals to help the Danaans until I have satisfied the son of Peleus' longing desire—just as I promised Thetis by nodding my head that day when she grabbed my knees in supplication and begged me to give honor to Achilles, the sacker of cities."

78-103 *Obeying without question, Hera flies off to Olympus as fast as the speed of a man's thoughts that travel to one place or another. There she sits down with Themis, who immediately notices her distress and guesses its source. Hera bids her not to question her, though. She says that many of the gods will be unhappy with Zeus' intentions. Hearing this, the gods are troubled. In response, Hera simultaneously laughs and frowns, before haranguing the gods by telling them they are no match for Zeus and can do nothing about his plans.*

104-109 "We are fools to be madly angry with Zeus like this. We want to approach him and stop what he is doing by force or by persuasion, but he sits apart from us not worried about anyone. The reason is simple. He knows he is much stronger than any of us immortals. Here's what I advise, then. Make the best of whatever harm he may choose to send your way."

110-183 *Hera goes on to tell Ares about the death of his own son Ascalaphus. Ares says he will go down to the ships to avenge his death, even if Zeus strikes him with his thunderbolt. Athena prevents him, however, telling him that his son was not the first or best of mortals to die. Furthermore, if Ares acts in this way, Zeus will thrash them all!*

While Athena is speaking with the god of war, Hera orders Apollo and Iris to go meet with Zeus on Mount Ida. They do, and Zeus is pleased with their quick obedience. He first tells Iris to go and command Poseidon to stop his warring on the side of the Achaeans. Remind my brother of my own might and that I am older by birth, he says, even though Poseidon insists we are equal.

Iris ventures off and delivers the command. She finishes by relaying Zeus' threat that he will come down to fight his brother if Poseidon doesn't obey.

184-217 And greatly troubled, the glorious Earth-shaker spoke to her, "Shameful words! Zeus has spoken presumptuously if by force he wants to control me against my will—I who am honored like him. Rhea bore three brothers to Cronus—Zeus, myself, and the third, Hades, who rules the dead beneath the earth. All things have therefore been divided into three parts. Each brother has received his own portion of honor. [190] When the lots were shaken, I got the gray sea to live in forever, Hades won the dark and murky underworld, and Zeus was allotted the broad and bright sky up in the air and clouds. But the earth and tall Olympus belong to all in common. Therefore, even if Zeus wants me to walk off the battlefield, I won't. Sure he's strong—but let him be satisfied with his own share of things without threatening to lay hands on me as though I were some coward. Let him hold his bragging talk for his own sons and daughters who have to listen to him."

[200] Iris, who is speedy as the wind, answered, "Come now, Poseidon. Should I really take this daring and unyielding message to Zeus, or will you reconsider your answer? Sensible people are open to argument. Plus, you know that the Erinyes always side with whomever is older."

Poseidon the Earth-shaker again answered, "Goddess Iris, you have spoken appropriately. It is good when a messenger shows so much discretion. Nevertheless, it cuts me deeply that anyone [210] should angrily school another whom Fate has given an equal portion. Even so, I will withdraw now from the fight despite the shame I feel. But let me tell you this—and I promise what I say. If without my agreement, or the agreement of Athena, the driver of spoil, Hera, Hermes, and Hephaestus, Zeus decides to spare lofty Ilium and will not let the Achaeans sack the city, then let him understand that he will incur my implacable wrath."

218-317 *After offering his speech, Poseidon leaves the fight and plunges into the sea. Zeus sends Phoebus Apollo, along with the terrible aegis Hephaestus made for him, to frighten the Achaeans and rouse Hector to battle. Apollo ventures down to the battlefield, revealing himself to Hector and suffusing him with great might. Healed like this, Hector struts out among the Trojan army and inspires them to fight. Observing his surprising return—they hoped he was dead—Thoas, the son of Andraemon, calls out to the best Achaeans to stand against Hector and fight. The other Achaean leaders—Ajax, Idomeneus, Teucer, Meriones, and Meges—echo Thoas in his call to battle. As for the crowd of Achaean men, they are ordered back to make a stand by the ships.*

Hector and his men advance, allied with Apollo. Opposite them, the leading Argives close together and await Hector's coming.

318-329 So long as Phoebus Apollo held his aegis quietly and without shaking it, the weapons on either side hit their targets, and the people fell. [320] But when he shook it straight in the face of the Danaans and raised his mighty battle cry, he bewitched them, and they forgot the strength and valor by which they usually rushed into the fight. As when two wild beasts spring in the dead of night on a herd of cattle or a large flock of sheep when the cowherd or shepherd is not there, even so were the Achaeans running in pathetic rout. Apollo cast fear on them and gave glory to Hector and the Trojans.

328-483 *Homer sings that man conquers man as the Achaean battle line breaks up. Hector and the other Trojans slaughter many Achaean men as they flee through the trench inside the wall. Hector commands his men to leave the spoils and pursue the enemy. They do. Apollo easily knocks down a portion of the wall — like a child breaking up a sandcastle upon the shore of the sea. He drives the Achaeans on in rout.*

At the ships Nestor, among other men, raises his hands and prays, reminding Zeus and the other gods about the sacrifices he has made so that he and the other Achaeans would safely return home. Zeus hears and thunders.

The Trojans, taking the thundering sign favorably for themselves, rush forward so that the Achaeans must fight them from the ships.

Hearing the Trojan advance, Patroclus leaves Eurypylus' shelter where he had been soothing his pain with healing herbs, and he runs off to confer with Achilles.

Along the ships, the Achaeans and Trojans maintain the battle — Telamonian Ajax and Hector prominent among them. Ajax calls on his brother, Teucer, to loosen arrows on the enemy. Teucer drops one man and then moves to hit Hector, but Zeus defends him and robs Teucer of the glory-boast by turning the arrow aside. Then, at the prodding of his brother, Teucer leaves his bow and arrows behind, arms himself, and runs to the side of Ajax to assist him and the other Achaeans.

484-499 When Hector saw that Teucer's arrows had been hindered, he shouted out to the Trojans and Lycians, "Trojans, Lycians, and Dardanians, lovers of close fighting, be men, my friends, and

remember the strength and valor by which you rush into the fight—
for I see with my own eyes that Zeus has hindered the flight of the
arrows of one of their best men. [490] It is easy to know when Zeus
is increasing an army's strength or decreasing it—both the one he is
granting glory and the one he is taking it from. Even now he is re-
ducing the Argives' battle strength, and he is helping us. So let's fight
around the ships in groups, men. If anyone of you is struck by a spear
or a sword and loses your life, well then, may you die and follow
your destined end. It is no shameful thing to die while fighting for
your homeland. Rather, you save your wife and children, and no one
plunders your house and land. Ah, but this will only happen if we
can drive the Achaeans off, making them sail home in their ships."

500-560 *Across the battle lines, Telamonian Ajax similarly urges his com-
rades on by commanding them to have a sense of shame and either be de-
stroyed or save the ships from evil. Don't you hear Hector? he asks. He's
not inviting you to a dance but to fight! We must either be killed or kill the
other man and live!*

*Homer glances back and forth, glory reporting. Hector kills the Phocian
leader, Schedius, first. Then Ajax slaughters Laodamas, the son of Antenor
and leader of the footmen, followed by the Trojan Polydamas, the son of
Panthous, who drops Otus of Cyllene. When the Achaean Meges casts at
Polydamas, he misses and hits Croesmus instead. While Meges is strip-
ping him, Dolops leaps at him and has a drawn-out fight with Meges, until
Menelaus sneaks up and spears Dolops from behind. The Achaeans begin
to strip Dolops of his armor. When Hector sees this, he calls on Melanip-
pus, the son of Hicetaon, to go rescue his kinsman. They advance together.
Seeing this, Telamonian Ajax calls out to the men.*

561-564 "Dear friends, be men! Feel shame in your hearts and be-
fore one another in the mighty fight. More men are saved than
struck from behind when shame is found among us. But when we
flee, there is neither glory nor strength."

565-740 *The Achaeans make a defensive bronze wall with their shields and
spears. Still, the Trojans advance, spurred on by Zeus.*

Menelaus turns to young Antilochus and challenges him to leap out from the line and strike down a Trojan man. He does. Antilochus throws and hits Melanippus on his chest and kills him. Just as he's stripping him, however, Hector hurries toward him, and Antilochus flees.

The Trojans attack, and Zeus robs the Achaeans of their glory, giving it instead to Hector so that he might cast fire onto the ships and so that Thetis' prayer might be fulfilled. From that moment on, Zeus will reverse the course of battle and give glory to the Argives. But for now, Zeus honors and glorifies Hector as he blazes toward the ships like a fire. Homer sings that, in truth, Hector's time to live is growing short. Like a great wave, or like a lion, Hector falls upon the Achaeans, driving them in rout to the ships. As they run, Periphetes of Mycenae, the son of Copreus, trips over his shield and falls, giving Hector the chance to plant his spear in his chest and so take glory from him.

At the ships, Nestor calls on the Achaeans to be men and have shame in their hearts. He tells them to remember their children and wives, along with their wealth and parents back home. As Nestor speaks, Ajax thunders up and down the ships while Hector flies like an eagle toward Protesilaus' ship on the right.

Now the battle rages with weapons appropriate for close, hand-to-hand combat—battle-axes and hatchets. And the earth flows with blood. When Hector reaches the ship, he calls for fire—for revenge against all the harm and sorrow the Achaeans brought with them when they came to Troy.

Ajax shouts out to the Achaeans, bidding them to be men and remember their strength. They're pressed up against the sea, he explains, with no other help and no route of escape!

741-746 "But in our own hands is the light of life—not in softer fighting!"

As Telamonian Ajax spoke, he urged the Achaeans on with his sharp-pointed spear. And when any Trojan man came with burning fire to the hollow ships in order to delight Hector and obey his earlier command, Ajax would greet him by stabbing him with his long spear. He stabbed twelve men in this way in hand-to-hand combat before the ships.

BOOK 16

PATROCLUS FIGHTS
TWO HEROES DIE

IN BRIEF: *Patroclus chastises Achilles for his anger and asks permission to go out and fight in Achilles' armor. Achilles agrees, but only after he recounts Agamemnon's offensive behavior once more. As they speak, the Trojans finally cast fire upon the Achaean ships. Observing this, Achilles knows it is time to act. He sends Patroclus with the Myrmidons out to fight. Achilles prays to Zeus, but Zeus fulfills only half the prayer—that Patroclus and the rest will push back the Trojans. During the fight, Sarpedon perishes. There's an epic fight for his body before Apollo zips him off to Lycia. As for the other half of the prayer, that Patroclus would return safely, Patroclus dies after scrumming before the city walls. He foretells Hector's death prior to perishing.*

THE ACHAEANS WERE fighting like this around the well-benched ships. Then, shedding hot tears, Patroclus drew near to the shepherd of men Achilles. . . . When swift-footed godlike Achilles saw him weeping in this way, he felt pity for him and said to him with winged words, "Patroclus—why do you stand there weeping like some foolish little girl that runs up to her mother and begs to be taken up and carried? Even though her mother is in a hurry, she takes hold of her dress to prevent her from going [10] and looks tearfully up until her mother carries her. This is what you look like, Patroclus. You look like this little girl shedding tears.

"Well, tell me, do you have anything to say to the Myrmidons or to me? Or do you have news from Phthia that you alone know? I hear that the son of Actor, Menoetius, is still alive, as is the son of Aeacus, Peleus, among the Myrmidons. If we lost these men, we two would bitterly mourn. Or are you lamenting the Argives and the way they are being killed at the hollow ships on account of their own transgressions? Do not hide anything from me, but tell me so that both of us may know about it."

[20] Then with a heavy sigh the horseman Patroclus answered, "Achilles, son of Peleus, the best and bravest of the Achaeans, do not be annoyed with me, for the Achaeans are really hurting."

23-28 Patroclus briefly outlines how the Achaean army is being destroyed and how many of the leaders are wounded. Then he rebukes Achilles.

29-90 "You've become useless, Achilles! [30] May I never be possessed by such an anger—the kind that possesses you, that you stand guard over, you brave man! Who in the future will speak well of you unless you now save the Argives from ruin? You know no pity! I doubt the horseman Peleus was your father or Thetis your mother. Rather, as though you are some monster, the gray sea gave birth to you and some sheer cliff begot you since your mind is so unbending and hard.

"If, however, some oracle keeps you from fighting, or if your queen mother, Thetis, has told you some word from the mouth of Zeus—if this is how it is, then at least send me with the Myrmidons so that I may become the light of life to the Danaans. One more thing. [40] Let me wear your armor. If you do, the Trojans may mistake me for you and keep away from the battle. And then the warlike sons of the Achaeans may have a chance to rest and revive since they are presently hard-pressed. You know how rare it is in battle to get a chance to catch your breath. Anyway, since we Myrmidons are fresh, we should be able to drive these battle-weary men back from our ships and shelters to their own city."

That's what the big fool Patroclus said when he begged Achilles to go out—fool because he was begging for his own apportioned death and evil doom.

Greatly disturbed, swift-footed Achilles answered him, "Ah me! God-born Patroclus, what a word you have spoken! [50] I know of no oracle, nor has my mother told me anything from the mouth of

Zeus, but I am cut to the core that my equal should dare to take back again and deprive me of my honor-prize simply because he is more powerful than I am. The whole matter has been a terrible distress to me; I've suffered painful grief in my spirit. Think about it: the girl I won with my spear when I sacked the well-fortified city, the one the sons of the Achaeans chose for me as my honor-prize— this is the one that the son of Atreus, lord Agamemnon, snatched out of my hands as if I were some dishonored homeless man.

[60] "Still, let it pass. I can't be angry forever. Even though I said that I would not surrender my anger until the fight had reached my own ships, you should now fasten my armor upon your shoulders and lead the Myrmidons into battle. For now, the dark Trojan cloud has burst over our fleet with overwhelming might, and the Argives are driven back upon the beach, trapped in a narrow space. Why? The whole city of Troy [70] dared to march out when they looked and didn't see my shining helmet. But know this. If they had seen me enter the fray, then soon the waterways would have been filled with their dead as they fled backwards. That's how it would have been if only king Agamemnon had been gentle and kind with me. As it is, the Trojans have come out to fight the whole army. The son of Tydeus, Diomedes, no longer wields his spear to defend the Danaans. Neither have I heard the voice of the son of Atreus coming out of that mouth I hate. On the other hand, man-slaying Hector's shouting is everywhere as he gives orders to the Trojans. And they hold the plain before Troy with their shouts of victory as they prevail over the Achaeans in the battle.

[80] "Even so, Patroclus, fall on the Trojan army and save the ships. Otherwise, they will cast burning fire upon them and snatch from us our cherished return home. Do as I now bid you so that you may win for me great honor and glory from all the Danaans. Then they will return to me the most beautiful girl and deliver to me glorious gifts. When you have driven the Trojans off from the ships, come back again. Even if Hera's thundering husband chooses to give you glory, do not in my absence stay to fight [90] the battle-loving Trojans, or you will add to my lack of honor."

91-111 *Achilles explains that not only will Patroclus' increased honor de-tract from his own, but Achilles is also afraid that some god will contrive to slay Patroclus.*

While Achilles advises Patroclus in this way, Telamonian Ajax is being hammered by a variety of missiles—arrows, stones, and anything else the Trojans can hurl at him. His helmet and shield ring with the sound of these projectiles. He's sweating, struggling to breathe, with harmful evil sur-rounding him. It's now that Homer offers a glory report for the Trojans.

112-129 Tell me now, you Muses who have your houses on Olym-pus, in what way did fire first fall upon the Achaean ships?

Hector approached Ajax. And coming near to him he swung his great sword at Ajax's ashen spear. The sharp blade flew humming through the air and cut the spear's pointed head from its shaft so that the bronze head flew off and fell to the ground with a ringing noise some distance away.

Now Ajax had nothing but a headless spear. Immediately he rec-ognized [120] the action of the gods in his blameless spirit, and he shuddered at them. High-thundering Zeus was spoiling his battle plans since he willed victory for the Trojans. And so, Ajax fell back to avoid all the missiles.

Then it was that the Trojans threw fire that never rests upon the swift ship. And suddenly and quickly the unquenchable flame poured out over the vessel so that the whole rear end of the ship was engulfed. Achilles struck his thighs with alarm. And turning to Patroclus, he said, "Up godlike Patroclus, driver of horses! I can see burning fire by the ships and hear it roaring. May they not seize our ships—for if they do, there will be no way to escape. So rise up and quickly get into my armor. As for me, I'll go gather the men."

130-274 *Patroclus arms with Achilles armor—with greaves, a breastplate, a sword and shield, a helmet upon his head, and two spears. While he's arming, he orders Automedon to ready the immortal horses that the Harpy Podarge bore to Zephyrus, the West Wind, as well as the mortal horse Pedasus. Achilles simultaneously gathers the Myrmidons together. They arm and quickly emerge from their shelters as ravenous wolves.*

Now Homer catalogues the ships that came with Achilles, fifty in all,
with fifty men rowing each one, commanded by five hegemons—Menes-
theus led the first; the second was commanded by Eudorus, the son of the
maiden Polymele and the god Hermes, whom Eileithyia, goddess of birth
pangs "led out into the light so that he saw the light of the sun"; the third
was directed by Peisander, a man distinguished among the Myrmidons;
the fourth was commanded by the old horseman Phoenix; and the fifth by
Alcimedon, the son of Laerces.

Having gathered his men, Achilles reminds them of how they have re-
sented him for commanding them to stay out of the battle against the will
of each man. So now, he says, they should remember and fight with heart.
It works. His speech stirs up the might and spirit of each man. Upon hear-
ing him, the Myrmidons march out in close formation with Patroclus and
Automedon leading the way, eager to do battle with the Trojans.

As they march, Achilles returns to his shelter in order to pour out a
libation and pray to father Zeus of Dodona, in Epirus, who is served by
the Selli, the priests that guard Zeus' oracle there and live an austere life,
sleeping on the ground with unwashed feet. He asks Zeus to answer an-
other prayer, even as he did before, that the Myrmidons led by Patroclus
would be given glory and courage to beat back Hector and the Trojans, and
that Patroclus would come back safely with all his armor. Zeus grants the
first half of his prayer but not the second—as Patroclus will not return
from the fight. Achilles then goes out to watch the battle.

Like angry wasps pouring out of their nest to defend it against foolish
boys who always disturb their home, the Myrmidons stream out from the
ships, shouting enthusiastically for battle. Patroclus bids them to be men
in order to honor Achilles, "the best of the Argives by the ships." Then, he
declares, Agamemnon will know how utterly blind he was to dishonor "the
best of the Achaeans."

275-306 With these words, Patroclus stirred up battle strength in
the spirit of each man, and together they fell upon the Trojans. At
long last the ships echoed again with the battle cry of the Achaeans.

When the Trojans saw the brave son of Menoetius and his battle
partner shining in their fighting gear, [280] they felt unsettled, agi-
tated. And their battle lines were thrown into confusion—for they

thought the swift-footed son of Peleus must now have put down his anger in order to take up friendship once again with Agamemnon. Each man, therefore, desperately glanced around to see how he might flee from unavoidable destruction.

But Patroclus was the first to cast his spear. He hurled it right into the middle of the crowd of men, right where they were most driven in confusion by the rear end of Protesilaus' ship. He hit Pyraechmes, who had led his Paeonian horsemen and charioteers from Amydon and the wide-flowing Axius. The spear punched through his right shoulder, and with a loud groan, he fell backward, [290] dropping on his back into the dust. Seeing this, the Paeonian men trembled all around—for by killing their leader, who was the best fighter among them, Patroclus struck panic and flight into them all. He therefore drove them from the ship and quenched the blazing fire, leaving the half-burnt ship where it was.

The Trojans were now driven back amid a storm of noise, while the Danaans rushed after them from their hollow ships, shouting. . . . [297-300] . . . When the Danaans had pushed back the burning fire from their ships, they took a break for a moment to revive. But the storm and rush of the fight was not yet over since the Trojans were not yet completely driven back in rout by the Achaeans, dear to Ares, from the black ships. Rather, the Trojans turned to make a stand even though they had earlier withdrawn from the ships by force of necessity. Then, as one leading man killed another, the battle became a disordered mess.

307-357 *Patroclus drops Areilycus with a spear through his thigh. Menelaus stabs Thoas through the chest. And many other Achaean heroes make their own kills. Homer explains that they take and slaughter the Trojans just as wolves take the young sheep out of their flock despite the careful watch of a shepherd.*

358-363 Meanwhile, great Ajax kept on trying to drive a spear into bronze-armed Hector, but Hector was so skillful in battle that [360] he covered himself with his ox-hide shield while always looking out for and avoiding the whizzing of the arrows and the heavy thud of the spears. Even though he knew that victory was changing sides, he nevertheless stood his ground and tried to save his faithful comrades.

364-393 *In the end, the Trojans flee in disordered rout, Hector included. Patroclus rides after them pell-mell, past the wall and across the ditch, crushing fallen men beneath his chariot wheels as he goes. He's after Hector! As they ride and run, the Trojans roar—just like the sound Zeus' angry rain makes, Homer says, when it pours down from the sky against those who make crooked judgments in the assembly, and the rivers flood bringing to nothing the work of men.*

394-410 Patroclus now cut off the men and battle lines that were nearest to him and turned them back in the direction of the ships. These were doing their best to reach the city, but the Achaean warrior would not let them. Instead, in the space between the high walls of the city and the river and the ships, he rushed upon the Trojan masses and slaughtered them so that they ended up paying the penalty for the many Achaean dead.

Patroclus first cast his radiant spear at Pronous. He hit him [400] on the chest where he was naked near the rim of his shield, and Pronous fell heavily to the ground. Next, he dashed over to Thestor, the son of Enops, who was hiding in his chariot. The man had become stricken with terror when the reins of his chariot were yanked from his hands. Patroclus went straight up to him and plunged his spear into his right jaw. Doing so, he hooked Thestor by the teeth and pulled him with the spear over the side of his chariot. Even as a man who sits at the end of some jutting rock draws a strong fish out of the sea with a gleaming bronze hook on a flaxen line, so did Patroclus draw Thestor all gaping from his chariot with the radiant spear. [410] Then he threw him down on his face—though he died while falling.

411-478 *Patroclus gloriously continues to slaughter the Trojans one man at a time—Erylaus, Erymas, Amphoterus, Epaltes, Tlepolemus, Echius, Pyris, Ipheus, Euippus, and Polymelus.*

Seeing this, Sarpedon, the son of Zeus, calls down shame upon the Ly-cians for fleeing. He jumps down from his chariot to face Patroclus. They fly at each other like screeching vultures!

Observing his son meet up with Patroclus, Zeus pities him and his fate to be conquered by the Achaean hero, and so he tells Hera so that he may save him from death. Hera balks at this. What a word you have spoken! she says. You think you may save a mortal man from the fate that was declared long before. "Do it. But know that we other gods will not approve of you or your deed." If you save your son today, she goes on, another god will likewise contravene fate tomorrow and save his own son. No, let Patroclus vanquish him and then send Death and sweet Sleep to bear him away. Zeus obeys her advice.

Patroclus and Sarpedon approach each other. Spears fly, and Sarpedon strikes the mortal horse Pedasus, and the horse shrieks and breathes his last. Automedon cuts the chariot loose from the now motionless animal. Again, Sarpedon throws, but his spear flies over Patroclus' left shoulder, missing its mark.

479-503 Finally, Patroclus rushed furiously on him with the bronze. [480] And when he threw his spear, the missile didn't fly uselessly from his hand, but it slammed into Sarpedon's chest, right into his pounding heart. Sarpedon fell like some oak or silver poplar or tall pine that woodsmen cut down upon the mountains to make wooden planks for shipbuilding. And falling, he lay stretched out at full length in front of his chariot and horses, moaning and clutch-ing at the blood-soaked dust. . . . [487-490] . . . Lying there, he called on his dear comrade in arms and said, "Glaucus, friend, you war-rior among men. Now you must be the foremost spearman and a daring warrior. First go out among the Lycian leading men and stir them up to fight for me. Then you come and do battle for me as well—your friend Sarpedon. Let me tell you, you'll know nothing but shame and blame if the Achaeans [500] strip off and take my battle gear now that I've fallen near their ships. Whatever you do, mightily stand your ground and urge on the whole army."

Saying this, death closed Sarpedon's eyes and he took his last breath.

504-782 *Standing above Sarpedon, Patroclus steps on his chest and pulls the spear from his body. Heartbroken, Glaucus begs Apollo to heal the wound he had earlier received from Teucer's arrow. He prays for strength so that he may fight for his comrade's fallen body. Apollo hears him and does his bidding. Knowing he's been healed, Glaucus spurs on his men and the other Trojans, calling Polydamas, Agenor, Aeneas, and Hector to fight by his side to defend the best man Sarpedon from shameful treatment at the hands of the Achaeans. Hearing about Sarpedon's death, the Trojans weep, feeling a profound grief. And they rush to Sarpedon.*

Patroclus calls on the two Ajaxes to help strip Sarpedon's body, treat it shamefully, and fight off the oncoming Trojans. As they do, Hector and the Trojans rush forward until the two sides clash. Hector first strikes the Myrmidon Agacles, the son of Epeigeus, with a stone. In turn, Patroclus likewise strikes the son of Ithaemenes, Sthenelaus, crushing his neck. With this, the Trojans step back as far as a man can cast a spear. Finally, though, they turn and fight.

Glaucus strikes and kills Bathycles, the son of Chalcon, whose happy bliss and riches distinguished him above the other Myrmidons. The Achaeans are upset that such a brave, noble, and good man has fallen. On the other side, the Trojans rejoice and dart forward to surround him. But the Achaeans are not yet finished making war. Meriones drops the Trojan priest of Zeus and son of Onetor Laogonus, a man who's honored like a god among the people. Then Aeneas casts at Meriones, but the latter dodges to the side. Aeneas shouts out that he can't always dance his way out of danger like that. Meriones responds by taunting Aeneas, declaring that he may yet get glory from him. Patroclus tells Meriones to fight rather than tossing words as in the assembly.

The battle continues around Sarpedon's corpse, which is by now unrecognizable, pierced as it is with many missiles and covered with blood. Homer sings that the men from both sides buzz around his body just as flies buzz around wooden bowls full of milk.

Looking on, Zeus debates whether Hector should slay Patroclus. He decides to let Patroclus live a while longer so that he may kill many more Trojans. Accordingly, he causes Hector to turn in weakness — for Hector realizes Zeus' scales have fallen against the Trojans. The Lycians also flee, leaving behind Sarpedon, whose corpse is covered with the many fallen comrades who perished to defend him from mistreatment. As the Trojans flee, the Achaeans strip Sarpedon and send his bronze armor back to the ships. Zeus commands Apollo to take Sarpedon's body, clean and anoint it with ambrosia, and give it to Sleep and Death, who will convey it to Lycia for burning and burial, "the honor-prize of the dead."

While Apollo carries out Zeus' order, Patroclus foolishly presses on contrary to Achilles' command—the very one that would have defended him from the fates of black death if he had only obeyed it. But Patroclus didn't have a chance. No, Zeus drove him on in his fury. Homer sings one last glory report for Patroclus. "At that time, which man did you kill and strip first, and which man last, Patroclus, now that the gods were calling you to your death?" In order, he slays Adrastus, Autonous, Echeclus, and Perimus, as well as Epistor, Melanippus, Elasus, Mulius, and Pylartes. The others run from him.

If not for Apollo, the Achaeans may have taken Troy that day. Patroclus rushes the wall three times. Upon the fourth, Apollo shouts at Patroclus to stop, explaining that Fate has not given the sacking of Troy to him. That has not even been fated for Achilles, who is better, he explains. Patroclus backs off, not wishing to anger Apollo.

Meanwhile, Hector is pondering what to do. As he considers the matter, Apollo appears to him in the guise of Asius, his uncle, and advises him to ride out against Patroclus in the hope that Apollo may give him the glory-boast when he slays him.

After speaking to Hector in this way, Apollo rejoins the work of war, the toil of men, and causes a panic among the Achaeans in order to give glory to Hector and the other Trojans. Hector drives at Patroclus, hoping to slay him. Seeing him come on, Patroclus jumps from his chariot with his spear in one hand and a stone in the other. He throws the stone at Hector, but rather than killing him, the stone drops his chariot driver Cebriones. The stone slams into his head, knocks out his eyes, and Cebriones falls like a deep-sea diver to the ground. Seeing this, Patroclus vaunts over the fallen driver, comparing him to a diver going down for pearls. Patroclus and Hector both leap down to fight for Cebriones—like lions they both want to cut the other man's skin with the pitiless bonze. Hector grabs Cebriones' head and Patroclus his feet. Neither let go as the mass of men battle around them. Finally, the Achaeans outdo the Trojans and take his armor.

783-800 Then Patroclus leaped out like Ares with thoughts of evil harm, and with a terrible shout equal to Ares, he sprang upon the Trojans. Three times he rushed at them and killed nine men each time. But as he was coming on like some god for the fourth time—then, for you Patroclus, the end of life appeared when terrible Apollo met you in the mighty battle.

Patroclus didn't see Apollo as he moved about in the swirl of men [790] since the god was covered with a thick fog. But then the god struck him from behind with the flat of his hand so that Patroclus' eyes rolled with dizziness. Next Phoebus Apollo beat the helmet off his head. It rolled on the ground and rattled under the horses' hooves, and it was all begrimed with dust and blood. Never had that helmet taken such a beating—for ordinarily it protected godlike Achilles' beautiful head. Now, however, Zeus delivered it to Hector [800] so that he could wear it on his head. Even so, Hector's destruction was near at hand.

801-811 *Apollo continues to disarm Patroclus by breaking his spear, dropping his shield, and loosening his breastplate. Most importantly, blindness seizes Patroclus, and he stands there astonished by what's happening. Finally, the son of Panthous, Euphorbus, who has already killed many Achaean men, sneaks up and spears Patroclus from behind.*

812-584 This was the sort of man who speared you Patroclus, the first man to drive his weapon into you. But he didn't overpower you. Rather, after drawing his ashen spear out of the wound, Euphorbus ran back into the crowd of men and would not fight the Achaean hero even though he was now unarmed. As for Patroclus, who was unnerved by the blow the god had given him and by the spear wound, he drew back under the cover of his men, fearing for his life.

But Hector forced his way through the battle lines when he saw great-hearted Patroclus retreating because he had been cut by the sharp bronze. [820] And when he had come near to him, he struck him with a spear in the lower part of his abdomen, just below the ribs. And he drove the bronze through his belly so that Patroclus tumbled heavily to the ground.

Seeing this, the Achaeans mourned greatly. . . . [823-828] . . . But the son of Priam, Hector, glory-boasted over him, and with winged words he said, [830] "Patroclus, you thought that you would sack our city, rob the Trojan women of their freedom, and carry them off in your ships to your own homeland. You fool! Hector and his swift horses did everything they could to defend them. I stand out among the other war-loving Trojan warriors to ward off the day of bondage from them. As for you, vultures will devour you here. Ah, unhappy wretch! Even that brave man Achilles cannot ward off your death! No, even though he ordered you, I imagine, to fly back [840] to the hollow ships when you had slain and stripped Hector, you did not!"

Then, as your life was leaking from you, horseman Patroclus, you answered, "Glory-boast all you want, Hector, for Zeus, the son of Cronus, and Apollo have readily given you victory over me. It is *they* who have vanquished me so easily, and *they* who have stripped the armor from my shoulders. If twenty men like you had attacked me, all of them would have fallen before my spear. But it was Fate and the son of Leto, Apollo, who have overpowered me, [850] and among mortal men Euphorbus. You yourself are third in line! Moreover—and hold my saying in your heart—you too will live but for a little while. Death and mighty Fate are close upon you, and they will lay you low by the hand of Achilles."

855-865 *Saying this, Patroclus closes his eyes in death, and his life-breath flees down to Hades' house. Though dead, Hector explains to Patroclus that he may yet slay Achilles. Who knows? Regardless, Hector draws out his spear and runs after Automedon, the driver of Achilles' chariot, wishing to strike him down.*

866-867 But the swift immortal horses carried Automedon off—the horses that the gods had given to Peleus as glorious gifts.

BOOK 17

THE BATTLE FOR PATROCLUS' BODY
MENELAUS' DILEMMA AND COURAGE

IN BRIEF: *Now the struggle is over Patroclus' body. Menelaus stands over it in defense. When he moves off to get help, Hector strips it of Achilles' armor. Telamonian Ajax arrives to defend it. Apollo spurs on the Trojans and many die. There's a great battle around Patroclus' corpse. The Trojans nearly retreat but for the encouragement of Aeneas. The fight rages on. The attempt is made to capture Achilles' immortal horses. Antilochus is sent to report Patroclus' death to Achilles. The action ends with some of the Achaeans retreating with Patroclus' body in tow, the others battling the Trojans.*

IT DID NOT escape the notice of Atreus' son Menelaus, dear to Ares, that Patroclus had been overpowered by the Trojans in the battle strife. And so, wearing a bronze helmet that flashed with the sun, he stepped out among the foremost fighters and stood over him. . . . [4-6] . . . And before him he held out his spear and his round shield.

8-89 *Euphorbus warns Menelaus to draw back so that he can strip Patroclus of the blood-stained armor and have great glory. In response, Menelaus rebukes Euphorbus in the guise of a prayer to Zeus, declaring that it is not noble to glory-boast excessively. "Father Zeus, it is not noble to glory-boast with all your strength." Leopards, lions, or wild boars do not even have such exaggerated feelings, he explains. He finishes by warning the Trojan warrior to back off.*

But he doesn't. Instead, Euphorbus details how Menelaus will pay for killing his brother Hyperenor. His parents and widowed wife will be pleased to receive Menelaus' head and armor. Euphorbus then throws his spear, striking Menelaus' bronze shield without success.

In response, and praying to Zeus, Menelaus attacks the young Trojan hero and stabs him through the throat. The wound gushes with blood as Euphorbus falls to the ground. When Menelaus begins to strip him, Apollo calls out to Hector in the form of Mentes, the leader of the Cicones. He asks him to stop chasing Achilles' immortal horses and help defend Euphorbus' body. He does. And so Menelaus looks up to see Hector coming straight at him!

90-101 Feeling disturbed and frustrated at this sight, Menelaus spoke to his great-hearted spirit. "Ah me! If I forsake Patroclus, the man who has fallen fighting for my honor, and leave his fine battle gear behind, then will not one of the Danaans rightly feel resentment toward me, some man who sees my flight? Still, if I fight Hector and the Trojans all alone, motivated by a sense of shame, then they may be too much for me, for Hector of the gleaming helmet is leading all the Trojans here. But why does my dear spirit debate these things? When a man chooses to fight against a god-inspired man, one honored by a god, then soon there is much misery as he squirms in the dirt. [100] Therefore, no Danaan man will be angry with me when he sees me give way to Hector, since that man fights with the help of a god."

102-318 *Saying this to himself, Menelaus moves off like a defeated lion to get help from Telamonian Ajax.*

Meanwhile, Hector and his men advance. Hector strips Patroclus and readies to drag him away in order to sever his head from his body. But as he does, Menelaus and Telamonian Ajax approach—the latter warrior with his massive shield. Seeing him, Hector backs off, handing the spoils to his men to take to the city.

Now Ajax stands over Patroclus' body with the shield. Glaucus upbraids Hector for earlier leaving Sarpedon to the Achaeans and now for retreating from the fight over Patroclus' body. He finishes his rebuke by declaring Ajax's superiority over Hector.

Hector scoffs! He's not afraid of battle with anyone—even though, he affirms, Zeus is the one who decides who wins or not. He invites Glaucus to fight by his side to see whether he is a coward. Hector shouts out to all the warriors to be men and remember their strength. Then he puts on Achilles' armor that he stripped from Patroclus.

When Zeus sees this, he pities Hector for his ignorance—that he doesn't realize he will soon die, and Andromache will never receive him home again. Still, Zeus grants him strength, and War itself—Ares—enters Hector.

Hector fires up his men and allies by telling them that whoever succeeds in dragging Patroclus into the Trojan camp will get half the spoils, and his glory will be the same as Hector's. Hearing this, they charge on the Achaeans, hoping to drag the body from beneath Telamonian Ajax's shield. The fools! Many eventually lose their lives at his hands.

As the Trojans rush toward them, Ajax fears imminent death. So he has Menelaus call to the other Achaean leaders to defend Patroclus—the men who share a common table with the sons of Atreus, give commands, and those to whom Zeus gives honor and glory. The son of Oileus, the lesser Ajax, comes, as do Idomeneus and Meriones, along with many others—so many, Homer sings, that one man could not possibly name them.

The Trojans close together in battle with the Achaeans, who have encircled Patroclus' fallen body. They push the Achaeans back and begin to drag Patroclus' corpse away.

But soon, Telamonian Ajax rallies them. And like a wild boar he scatters the Trojans from the body, those who hoped to seize glory. He first slaughters the young man Hippothous, who was busy dragging Patroclus off by the foot; he will never be able to repay his parents for his upbringing. No, his life was very short. Seeing this, Hector casts at Ajax and misses, hitting instead Schedius, the son of Iphitus. To pay him back, Ajax strikes Phorcys, the son of Phaenops. The Achaeans drag off their bodies as Hector steps back some.

319-323 Overpowered and without strength, the Trojans [320] would have fled up to the walls of Ilium again, goaded along by the Achaeans, dear to Ares. And opposite them the Argives would have seized glory even beyond the plan of Zeus thanks to their own strength and might. All this would have happened if Apollo had not roused Aeneas in the likeness of the herald Periphas, the son of Epytus.

324-334 Apollo shames Aeneas into fighting. Knowing the presence of the god, Aeneas turns to Hector to urge him on.

335-343 "Hector—and all you other Trojan and allied leaders! What a shame this is to be overpowered and without strength, fleeing up to the walls of Ilium, goaded along by the Achaeans, dear to Ares! But some god just stood nearby me and told me that Zeus, the highest counselor, is our ally in the fight. [340] Therefore, let us go straight against the Danaans so that they cannot easily carry off the dead man Patroclus to the ships."

That's what Aeneas said. And he jumped way out front and made a stand there. And so the Trojans rallied and amassed themselves opposite the Achaeans.

344-555 The battle rages on, the Achaeans defending Patroclus and the Trojans attempting to get his body. The earth grows dark purple with the blood of the many fallen from both sides. Both Antilochus and Thrasymedes have no idea that Patroclus has fallen. Neither does Achilles know.

Meanwhile, Achilles' immortal horses weep for Patroclus, and Zeus pities them—that he gave them to a mortal man since for him mortal men are the most miserable among all living things on earth. Still, he will not let Hector capture them even though he plans to give glory to the Trojans one more time. Nevertheless, Hector, Aeneas, and Chromius try to seize the horses. They move against Automedon and Alcimedon, who is presently driving them. Automedon calls on Menelaus and the two Ajaxes to help ward off the Trojans. Either way, he judges, the result is with the gods. He casts and drops the Trojan Aretus like a great ox. When Hector in turn throws a spear at Automedon, the latter dodges and the weapon stabs into the ground. Hector, Aeneas, and Chromius back off just as the two Ajaxes approach. As they do, Automedon strips Aretus, wishing that he had been a greater man to pay for Patroclus' death. Then Automedon boards the chariot, looking like a lion bloody after eating.

The fighting continues over Patroclus. Athena, sent by Zeus, rouses the Danaans to battle. She speaks to Menelaus in the form of Phoenix.

556-574 "Menelaus," she said, "it will surely be shame and blame for you if the faithful comrade of noble Achilles is dragged about by swift dogs and torn beneath the Trojan walls. But be strong and urge on all the other men."

[560] And Menelaus, good at the battle cry, answered him, "Phoenix—you old father full of years. If only Athena would grant me strength and defend me against the many missiles, then I would stand by Patroclus and ward off the enemy—for his death has truly struck me to the core. But look! Hector's might is like a raging fire as his bronze weapons kill and kill! And all because Zeus is giving him glory."

That's what Menelaus said. And the bright-eyed goddess Athena rejoiced that of all the gods he prayed to her first. Therefore, she put strength into his shoulders and knees, [570] and into his breast she sent the courage and audacity of the fly, which, though driven off, it will come yet again and bite if it can—so much does it love human blood. Even so did Athena fill Menelaus' dark chest with much courage so that he stood over Patroclus and swung the radiant spear at whatever man drew near.

575-757 *Despite Menelaus' success, Zeus causes the Achaeans to run in rout. Polydamas wounds Boeotian Peneleos, and Hector cuts Leitus, the son of Alectryon. As Hector runs by, Idomeneus vainly strikes at him. The latter casts at Idomeneus but misses, hitting instead Coeranus, the follower and charioteer of Meriones. Idomeneus returns to the ships in fear after Meriones explains that the Achaeans have lost their strength. Telamonian Ajax and Menelaus recognize the same—that every Trojan man is finding success, whether a brave and good man or a bad and cowardly man. Zeus guides their weapons. Ajax suggests that someone go and tell Achilles about Patroclus' demise. He prays to Zeus to protect the Achaeans from the misty darkness. With pleasure, Zeus drives the mist away, and the sun shines brightly. And following Ajax's bidding, Menelaus runs off to find Antilochus, the son of Nestor. Antilochus is to report Patroclus' death to Achilles so that Achilles might save his corpse from the Trojans. When he learns the bad news, Antilochus is speechless, his eyes full of tears. Nevertheless, he trots off to deliver the message.*

Menelaus returns to the men guarding Patroclus and suggests they devise a plan. Achilles, he foretells, will not come out to fight until he gets new armor since Hector has his. Telamonian Ajax advises Menelaus and Meriones to pick him up and rush off while he and the other Ajax ward off the Trojans. They do that—and the Trojans attack! But when the two Ajaxes charge them, they back off, afraid, the color of their skin changing. Even so, Hector and Aeneas run after them again like falcons flying into a cloud of smaller, madly chirping birds.

758-761 Just like this, then, like screeching birds, did the Achaean men flee from Aeneas and Hector forgetting their every desire for battle. [760] As they fled, the Danaans dropped much of their battle gear in the trench. Still, there was no rest from the battle.

BOOK 18

ACHILLES' GREAT SORROW AND SHOUT
HEPHAESTUS—THE SHIELD AND ARMOR OF ACHILLES

IN BRIEF: *Achilles learns of Patroclus' death and mourns. Out of his mind with grief, and near to suicide, he vows revenge. But he needs new armor. Thetis speeds off to Olympus to ask Hephaestus to make it. The Trojans nearly retake Patroclus. Hector's goal: his head on a stake! Achilles comes out, and with a goddess-supplemented shout, he drives off the Trojans. Ahhh! The sun sinks and the battle ends for the day. In the Trojan assembly, Polydamas advises retreat. Hector refuses. He'll fight Achilles tomorrow! The Achaeans wash and mourn Patroclus. Achilles promises a hero-sized sendoff, including a great fire, Hector's head, and twelve young Trojan males. Meanwhile, Thetis is sipping nectar with Charis, asking Hephaestus for new armor. He makes it, including Achilles' famous shield.*

S O WHILE THE Achaeans fought on like blazing fire, swift Antilochus went as a messenger to Achilles.

3-15 *As Antilochus races toward him, Achilles ponders why the Trojans are winning again and whether it means Patroclus is dead just as his mother foretold would happen.*

16-22 When the noble son of Nestor came up to Achilles and stood nearby him, he was shedding hot tears as he delivered the painful message. "Alas, son of battle-wise Peleus, the news is horrible—the sort of message that should never be spoken. [20] Patroclus has fallen and lies low in the dust! And now they're fighting around his naked corpse. Yet another thing—Hector of the gleaming helmet has carried off his battle gear."

That's what Antilochus said. And hearing his words, a black cloud of sorrow enveloped Achilles.

23-53 Achilles immediately dusts himself with ashes, pulls at his hair, and his women beat their breasts in sorrow. Antilochus joins in the wailing, tears pouring from his eyes. He holds Achilles' hands to prevent the groaning man from cutting his own throat with an iron knife. Finally, Achilles laments loudly to his queen mother, Thetis. In response to his sorrow, the goddess gives way to grief, wailing loudly. Hearing her howl like this, all the other sea nymphs, the daughters of Nereus, join her in the depths of the salty sea. And Thetis leads the chorus of lamentation.

54-64 "Ah me! I'm wretched—the unhappy mother of the best of men! Ever since I gave birth to this man, who is blameless, strong, and outstanding among all the heroes, he shot up as a sapling does, and I tended him as a caring gardener would a plant in a wonderful garden. Then I sent him with his ships to Ilium to fight the Trojans. But I will never welcome him back again. [60] There will be no return to his house, to Peleus' home. And now while he lives and looks upon the light of the sun, he grieves, and I am unable to help him. Nevertheless, I will go so that I may see my dear son and hear about the sorrows he has known, even though he has been out of the battle."

65-72 Thetis leaves her father's cave with the other sea nymphs and goes to Troy. There they join Achilles who is weeping in his profound grief. And throwing her arms around him, Thetis questions him.

73-82 "My son, why are you weeping like this? What sorrow has now befallen you? Tell me—do not hide it from me. Surely Zeus granted you the prayer you made to him when you lifted your hands up and prayed that the Achaeans might be penned in by their ships and bitterly regret that you were no longer fighting alongside them."

Achilles groaned and answered, "My mother, Olympian Zeus has indeed fulfilled my prayer. [80] But what delight is all of that to me since my dear comrade Patroclus has perished? For he is the one companion that I honored above all the others—I honored him equally with myself."

83-106 *Achilles goes on to wish that Thetis had never slept with Peleus and says that she will experience great sorrow when he dies. Either way, he must kill Hector in repayment for killing Patroclus. Thetis replies by announcing Achilles' looming death: "For your own death awaits you after Hector dies." Achilles wishes to die since he could not aid his comrade and ward off death—even though he is the best of the bronze-clad Achaeans in battle, though not the best in the assembly, he admits. Then he prays.*

107-121 "May strife utterly perish from among both the gods and men, and anger that incites a wise man to be savagely upset—an anger that drips like very sweet honey [110] and expands like smoke in the breast of a man, growing ever larger. Even so has the lord of men Agamemnon now provoked me to anger.

"But now, though grieving, we will let these things go, allowing the dear spirit in our chest to be conquered since we must. I will go. I will pursue Hector, who has slain the man I dearly loved. As for my own fated death, I will take it when Zeus chooses to accomplish it—and the other immortal gods. For not even was the mighty Heracles able to flee from death—he who was dear to the ruler Zeus, the son of Cronus. Rather, Fate conquered him as well in the form of Hera's troublesome anger. [120] It will be like this for me too if a similar fate has been prepared for me. So will I lie asleep when I die. But now may I take hold of noble glory!"

122-214 *Achilles goes on to describe all the women that will weep when they lose the Trojan men that he will slaughter. Thetis responds by raising the fact that Achilles no longer has his armor since Hector stripped Patroclus and is wearing it. She promises him new armor from the smith god Hephaestus. Then she speeds off to Olympus, telling her sisters to inform the old man of the sea of her plans.*

As she goes, the Trojans continue their pursuit of the Achaeans and their attempt to seize Patroclus' naked body. Three times Hector grabs at his foot, and three times the two Ajaxes fight him off as shepherds fight off

a fierce and hungry lion. Hector, who wishes to cut off and fix Patroclus'
head on a stake, would have seized unspeakable glory if Hera hadn't sent
Iris to Achilles to shame him into action, threatening Achaean reproach if
Patroclus is left to the dogs of Troy. In response, Achilles asks how he
might enter the fight without his arms. There is no other battle gear that
will work for him except for Telamonian Ajax's—but he's fighting. Iris
says she knows all this and gives him her plan. All he must do is go and
show himself to the Trojans to give the Achaeans a momentary break from
the battle. Achilles goes. Glowing as a golden cloud with a pillar of flame
rising from his head, he ventures out.

215-218 Achilles went from the wall and stood by the trench. But
following his dread mother's wise command, he didn't join the
other Achaeans there. Rather, he stood there shouting as loudly as
he could. And standing apart, Pallas Athena joined him, also shout-
ing loudly. Hearing this, the Trojans were thrown into confusion.

219-231 *Trojan hearts beat furiously as their horses back up and their*
charioteers feel great fear. Three times Achilles shouts out above the trench,
and three times the Trojans and their allies are panic-stricken. As the Tro-
jans rush off in alarm, twelve of their own die at the hands of their own
men and spears and beneath the wheels of the fleeing chariots.

232-238 While the Trojans fled in disorder, the Achaeans welcomed
the chance to drag Patroclus' body from the hail of missiles and put
him on a flat board to carry him off. And standing around him, they
melted into tears. Swift-footed Achilles was also there shedding hot
tears when he saw his faithful friend stretched out on the wooden
bier all cut up by the sharp bronze. It was this man that he'd sent
out with his horses and chariot into battle. Ah, but he would never
again welcome him home upon his return!

239-304 *Hera commands the Sun to descend behind Oceanus so that dark-*
ness comes on. With this, the battle stops for the day.
    The Trojans, now desperately afraid because of Achilles' appearance,
meet in assembly. Polydamas, the second in command to Hector, speaks

first. He urges immediate retreat from the battle plain now that Achilles has once again joined the fight. The Achaean hero will go straight for the city, he predicts, and for their wives. If this happens, many of them will die and be devoured by wild dogs and vultures. May it never be that I hear of this happening! he says. He advises them to sleep in the city's assembly area and fight from the walls in the morning.

Grimly raising his brows at him, Hector is not satisfied with Polydamas' speech. Haven't you had enough of being trapped inside the walls? he asks. He tells of the great wealth that Ilium used to have and how men used to speak of it all. Not anymore! So now that Zeus is granting Hector glory by trapping the Achaeans by the ships, he will neither fall back nor have any of his men retreat. No, they will take their meals and keep watch through the night, and in the morning they will fight.

305-313 "And if godlike Achilles truly makes a stand to fight by the ships, the worse it will be for him if that's what he wants. Whatever the case, I won't flee from hateful war. No, I'll stand face to face with him, whether he pulls off a great victory, or I do. The war god Ares, furious in battle, is common to all men—he kills the killer."

[310] That's how Hector addressed the men. And they applauded his speech, the fools! They did so because Pallas Athena had sacked their minds. While they approved Hector's harmful deliberation and advice, not one man among them recognized what Polydamas pointed out or supported his beneficial plans.

314-613 *As the night goes on, the Myrmidons mourn Patroclus, with Achilles leading them. Speaking to the men, Achilles bemoans the fact that he vainly promised his friend a return home along with great wealth. On the contrary, they will both perish in Troy land, staining the earth with their dark blood. He promises a great funeral pyre and burial for Patroclus, including Hector's head and twelve young Trojan males, whom he will sacrifice by slitting their throats. And the women and men will lament his passing.*

The Myrmidons wash Patroclus' body with warm water and anoint him with fine nine-year-old olive oil. Finally, they cover him with soft linen cloth and a white mantle. In this way they weep all night long.

Seeing this, Zeus turns to Hera and congratulates her on rousing Achilles. Hera, who claims to be the best of the goddesses, balks.

Meanwhile, Thetis comes to Hephaestus' house. She finds the god drenched with sweat, constructing mechanized tripods that will serve the assembly of the gods from his house. Charis, Hephaestus' wife, sees Thetis and asks why she has come. But before she's able to answer, Charis sets the gifts of hospitality before her and calls Hephaestus to their side. When he enters and sees Thetis, he reminds her of the time she saved him from Hera. He spent nine years in hiding with her and Eurynome, making all sorts of jewelry. So now he will certainly repay the favor.

While Charis sets out the gifts of hospitality, Hephaestus limps around arranging his tools, wiping the sweat off his face and hands, and dressing, assisted by young girls made of gold, but who are nevertheless like living girls. They have minds, human voices, and they know well the work of the immortal gods. Finally, he sits next to Thetis and asks why she has come and what she needs. He promises to fulfill her wish if he can.

Crying, she bemoans her many sorrows. She explains how Zeus forced her to sleep with Peleus and how she endured his bed. And now he's old! But she has other sorrows. She then repeats her earlier speech, the one she made to her sister sea nymphs—that Achilles will never return home. She explains how Agamemnon took back her son's honor-prize, and how upset he was. And then, she goes on, Achilles refused to receive compensating gifts from Agamemnon and finally sent Patroclus out to fight. But Apollo gave Hector glory when he killed Patroclus and took his battle gear. Now she begs Hephaestus for new armor—for a shield, a helmet, and greaves.

The smith god agrees to the task and goes to make them of bronze, tin, gold, and silver. First, he makes the famous shield of Achilles with its great circle encompassing the earth and heavens, the sea, sun, moon, and all the stars.

He also puts two cities on the shield. In one city, people come together to feast and celebrate marriage. But in the assembly of that city, two men are wrangling over the blood price of a man who had perished. The one says he has paid a fair price; the other disagrees. The gathered elders consider both sides while the people cheer one side or another. In the middle are two talents of gold for the elder who will give the straightest judgment following custom.

Two armies face each other at the second city. One is defending the city while the other is laying siege to it. The besieging army offers an ultimatum: either they will overwhelm and sack the city, or the defending city must pay them off. The besieged city refuses to give payment even though their women and children are there with them. In the end, there is a ferocious battle joined by Strife and Death.

Far away, Hephaestus makes a peaceful farming scene where men work hard plowing and drinking wine. There is also a great ruler's estate with ripened fields of grain and clustered vineyards propped up on silver posts. The laborers there gather the grapes in baskets to make wine. In the distance, there are cattle and sheep, and lions prowling for prey.

Last of all, Hephaestus adds a dance floor where young men dance with young and beautiful girls, well-adorned and worth many cattle. He encloses the whole shield with Oceanus.

Once the shield is complete, he makes a breastplate, a helmet, and greaves for Achilles.

614-617 But when the glorious god, the one with two disabled feet, had finished working all the armor, he set it before Achilles' mother. And like a hawk, she flew down from snowclad Olympus carrying Hephaestus' shining battle gear.

BOOK 19

THE GREAT RECONCILIATION
ACHILLES & AGAMEMNON

IN BRIEF: *Thetis gives Achilles his new shield and the rest of the armor. Achilles "unsays" his anger against Agamemnon. The latter man accepts, declaring that it was not his—Agamemnon's—fault. He claims that divine Bewilderment and other gods made him do it. Nevertheless, he offers Achilles gifts to make up for the wrong done. After admonishing Agamemnon, Odysseus suggests they should feast. Achilles counters, saying they should fight instead. The Achaeans move ahead with Odysseus' plan. They feast and drag in Agamemnon's compensatory gifts, including Briseis, who weeps for Patroclus. When Achilles refuses food, Athena gives him ambrosia and nectar. He likes his new arms. When the immortal horse Xanthus prophesizes his death, he is disturbed. Still, they ride off to fight.*

NOW WHILE DAWN with a yellow veil stirred from behind Oceanus' streams in order to carry light to the immortal gods and to mortal men, Thetis came down to the ships carrying the gifts of the god. She found her dear son lying with his arms around Patroclus, loudly weeping for him. Surrounding him, many of his comrades were shedding tears.

Standing there with them, the noble goddess took Achilles' hand in her own, and calling him by name, she said, "My child, since Patroclus was overpowered by the will of the gods, we must leave him alone despite all our sorrow for him. [10] But here—take these glorious arms from Hephaestus. They're more beautiful than any other arms ever worn by any other man."

12-64 Looking at them, Achilles rejoices. He says he will arm, but he's afraid that flies will enter Patroclus' wounds and his corpse will rot. Thetis promises to defend his friend's body against such an infestation by means of ambrosia and nectar. She commands him to call an assembly, renounce his anger, and arm to fight.

Many men come to the assembly, including a wounded Diomedes, Odysseus, and, lastly, Agamemnon. Achilles speaks. He says it would have been better if they had not fought over the girl, if she had earlier been slain with an arrow. But now so many Achaeans have died thanks to his ongoing wrath. It was only profitable for the Trojans.

65-67 "But now, though grieving, we will let these things go, allowing the dear spirit in our chests to be conquered since we must. And now I put a stop to my anger—of necessity I will not rage forever."

68-85 *Achilles finishes by declaring that he will go out against the Trojans. Hearing his resolution, the men are happy that he has finally renounced his anger. In response, Agamemnon speaks, recounting how many of the Achaeans have blamed him for all that has happened. Then he defends himself.*

86-91 "But I was not culpable, I tell you! It was Zeus and Fate and the Furies who come under cover of darkness—they are to blame since in the assembly they bewildered and blinded me on the day that I snatched Achilles' honor-prize. [90] But what could I do? All things are accomplished by some god. It is Bewilderment who is to blame, the august daughter of Zeus—she blinds everyone and everything, that destructive one!"

92-133 *Agamemnon goes on: Bewilderment moves with hardly any sound and ensnares all manner of men and women. She even blinded Zeus once, the best of the gods, by allowing Hera to deceive him about Heracles' birth and rule. Whereas Zeus wanted Heracles, his son by the mortal woman Alcmene, to rule over all men, and he bragged about how his birth would happen that very day, Hera—with Zeus' blind agreement—guilefully arranged it so that the Argive Eurystheus, the son of Sthenelus and grandson of Perseus, was born that day and ruled in his place. In pain, therefore, Zeus threw Bewilderment down to earth so that she might bewilder all the men there. And every time he saw Heracles sweat in his labors, he would*

sigh and groan. Agamemnon claims that he was similarly blinded by Be-
wilderment.

134-144 "Even so did I grieve when mighty Hector of the gleaming
helmet was killing the Argives at their ships, and all the time I kept
thinking of Bewilderment who had blinded me. I was blind, and
Zeus robbed me of my mind. Still, I will now make up for it and
will add much treasure to pay the penalty. But stir yourself to battle
and urge all your men on to fight. [140] As for me, I will hand over
all the gifts that Odysseus offered you yesterday in your shelter . . .
gifts that will satisfy your desires."

145-269 *Achilles is indifferent to the gifts. He replies by saying that Aga-
memnon can give the gifts or not right now. Either way, they must arm
for battle and go fight—for there is much work to be done.*

*Odysseus submits, however, that the men need to eat and drink first in
order to have strength for the daylong battle. He also recommends that
Agamemnon deliver the gifts to the place of assembly, so that all the men
may look at them and rejoice in the repayment, and so that Agamemnon
will have the chance to swear he never slept with Briseis. Achilles should
in turn be gentle with him. Lastly, he tells Agamemnon to behave in a
better way in the future, according to just custom. Agamemnon agrees and
further commands his henchman Talthybius to prepare a wild boar to sac-
rifice to Zeus and the Sun—all to appease Achilles.*

*Achilles begs off, telling Agamemnon he's too anxious and angry to
eat—not when so many dead men are lying in the field, undefended and
unavenged. He vows not to eat until they have redressed the many wrongs.*

*Odysseus responds, first explaining that even though Achilles is the
best of the Achaeans in battle, he is better in counsel since he is older and
knows more. So Achilles must endure his speech. In short, those who sur-
vive in battle must eat to carry on in the fight. Meanwhile, they must
harden their hearts to the battle dead.*

*Upon saying this, Odysseus and many others go to Agamemnon's
shelter to gather the gifts—the tripods, cauldrons, horses, gold, women,
and, with them, beautiful-cheeked Briseis. They bring them back and "put
them in the middle of the assembly's meeting place." Then Agamemnon*

slits the boar's throat, and prays to Zeus, the best of the gods, and swears to him and to Earth, the Sun, and the Furies, that he never slept with Briseis or touched her in any way. He calls down pains upon his head if he is swearing falsely. Upon cutting the boar's throat, Talthybius takes it and flings it into the sea to be the food of fish.

In response, Achilles rises and speaks to Zeus and the men.

270-275 "Father Zeus, great is the bewildering blindness you give to men! Otherwise, the son of Atreus would have never stirred fierce anger within my breast, nor would have he so stubbornly taken Briseis against my will. Surely Zeus must have willed it for so many Achaean deaths to happen. Even so, we should now go and eat so that we'll be able to join Ares in the fight."

276-418 *After Achilles speaks, the assembly breaks up, and the Myrmidons take all the treasure and women back to their camp. Arriving in Achilles' shelter and seeing Patroclus mangled with his many wounds, Briseis wails, bemoaning her wretchedness now that he is dead, he who was alive not long before. She recounts all her relatives whom she likewise saw torn to pieces by the pitiless bronze—her husband and three brothers.*

The Achaean leaders leave Achilles' shelter—all but for Agamemnon and Menelaus, Odysseus, Nestor, Idomeneus, and Phoenix. They try to comfort him in his sorrow. Achilles vows, nevertheless, not to eat until he has won revenge in bloody battle. He mourns Patroclus, declaring to his fallen comrade that no greater sorrow could have come to him, not even the knowledge of his father's own death nor that of his son, Neoptolemus. He explains that he had hoped to be the only one to die before the walls of Troy, that Patroclus might have lived to take care of his son and show him all his things—his acquisitions, slaves, and his great house. By now, he finishes, Peleus must be dead.

The other men weep and remember what they left behind in their great halls. Looking down, Zeus pities them and calls on Athena to give Achilles nectar and ambrosia to sustain him. Hearing him, she zips down from Olympus like a falcon and does as he suggested.

As she does so, the Achaeans begin to leave their ships to go into battle, their armor shining in the sun. Achilles likewise arms with Hephaestus' gifts — the greaves, the breastplate, the bronze sword, and the great shining shield that reflects in the sun as the moon does. After these, he fits the helmet on his head; it shines like a star. The armor all fits very well as wings do on a bird. Lastly, he takes up his father's heavy spear while his men ready the horses and chariot.

Stepping aboard the chariot, he commands the immortal horses Xanthus (Chestnut) and Balius (Spotted) to bring them back safely. In reply, and speaking with Hera's help, Xanthus bows and promises to save him this time. But, he says, the day of your own destruction draws near. A god and mighty Fate will achieve it. Besides, says Xanthus, Apollo was responsible for stripping Patroclus; the horses were not at fault. No, he and Balius can run as fast as Zephyrus, the West Wind. He finishes by reiterating that Achilles is destined to be conquered by a god and a mortal man.

419-424 Greatly troubled, swift-footed Achilles spoke to the horse. [420] "Xanthus, why do you foretell my death? You don't need to since I know well that it is my fate to die here far away from my dear father and mother. But you should know that I won't stop until the Trojans have been glutted with war."

Once he had said these words, he turned his horses toward the front with a shout.

BOOK 20

THE GODS FIGHT
ACHILLES FIGHTS AENEAS & HECTOR

IN BRIEF: *The gods assemble, and Zeus gives them permission to fight as they wish. As for Zeus, he will stay and watch the battle from Olympus. Hera, Athena, Poseidon, Hermes, and Hephaestus aid the Achaeans. The Trojans have Ares, Apollo, Artemis, Aphrodite, Leto, and the divine river Xanthus. Achilles encounters Aeneas and fights him until Aeneas is spirited away. Achilles goes on a slaughtering rampage, killing Polydorus, among others. He fights Hector, who is saved by Apollo.*

SO IT WAS that around you Achilles, son of Peleus, the battle-insatiate Achaeans readied themselves for the fight by their curved ships. Opposite them, the Trojans armed themselves upon the rise of the battle plain.

Meanwhile, from the top of many-ridged Olympus Zeus ordered Themis to gather the gods into an assembly. She did. She went from here to there and called them to the house of Zeus. There was not a river absent, but for Oceanus, nor one of the nymphs that dwell in the fair groves or springs of rivers and meadows of green grass. [10] When they reached the house of cloud-gathering Zeus, they sat down beneath the polished portico that Hephaestus had constructed for father Zeus with his knowing mind.

In this way, therefore, all the immortals gathered inside the house of Zeus. The Earth-shaker Poseidon also obeyed the call of the goddess and came up out of the sea to join them. Sitting among them, he asked Zeus what his plan was. "Why have you, bright with lightning, called the gods together in council? Are you mulling over something having to do with the Trojans and the Achaeans? I ask because the blazing battle is on the verge of raging again."

Cloud-gathering Zeus answered him and said, [20] "Come now, Earth-shaker. Doubtlessly you perceive my plans and why I have gathered you all here. I care for them—even in their destruction. As for me, I'll stay seated on Mount Olympus and follow the battle from here, delighting my mind. But you other gods should go out among the Trojans and the Achaeans and help either side as each of you is minded to do. If Achilles fights the Trojans without hindrance, they will be unable to make a stand against him. They have always trembled at the mere sight of him. And now that Achilles's spirit is roused to such dreadful anger for his comrade, [30] I fear that he will storm the city wall in a manner that is beyond fate."

That's what the son of Cronus said. And turning aside he stirred up unending battle. As for the gods, they departed and made their way down to the fight even though their desires carried them in two directions. Hera, Pallas Athena, the earth-carrier Poseidon, and the ready-helper Hermes, who is most excellent in cunning, went down among the ships. And Hephaestus went with them, exulting in his strength, even though he was limping along, his thin legs rapidly moving beneath him. On the other side, Ares with the shining helmet joined the Trojans, and with him long-haired Phoebus Apollo, the archer goddess Artemis, [40] Leto, the river Xanthus, and laughter-loving Aphrodite.

So long as the immortal gods held themselves aloof from the men, the Achaeans won great glory because Achilles, who had long refused to fight, was now with them. There was not one Trojan in the field who did not melt with fear when he saw the swift son of Peleus shining in his armor, the equal of man-plaguing Ares. But when the Olympians came down among the mass of fighting men, mighty Strife, who rouses men to battle, urged them on. And Athena raised her loud voice, now standing by the deep trench that ran outside the wall, [50] and now from the shore of the thundering sea. And Ares bellowed out to the other side, dark as a raging thundercloud, and he called on the Trojans at the top of his voice from the city's heights or along the river Simois as he sped toward the beautiful hill.

In this manner the blessed gods urged both armies to come together, and heavy strife broke out between them. From above, the father of men and gods thundered terribly, while from below Poseidon shook the boundless earth and the tops of the lofty mountains.

59-155 While the earthquakes and the gods clash, Hades fears that if the ground above breaks apart, then the horrible mansions of the dead below will be revealed. Nevertheless, the immortals line up one god against another: Poseidon against Apollo; Ares versus Athena; Hera opposite Artemis; Hermes facing Leto; and fire in the form of Hephaestus raging against the river Xanthus, called by men Scamander.

Ranging along the battlefield, Achilles looks to fight Hector. Apollo, however, rouses Aeneas to action, taking on the form of Lycaon, Priam's son. He taunts him, asking him to match his present actions with his former boasting over cups of wine about how he would fight Achilles. Aeneas responds with a story recounting how he was previously vanquished by Achilles and would have perished if Zeus hadn't saved him. He claims that it is impossible to defeat him as long as a god fights by his side. Apollo nevertheless advises Aeneas to pray to the gods and favorably compares Aeneas' mother and grandfather—Aphrodite and Zeus—with Achilles' own—Thetis and the old man of the sea. Finally, Apollo breathes great might into Aeneas, and the warrior goes out to fight.

White-armed Hera witnesses Aeneas' move and urges her side—the best of the immortals, she says—to turn back Aeneas or fight by Achilles' side. At the very least, they must protect Achilles for today, even though he will later experience whatever Fate has spun for him on the day of his birth. Poseidon suggests they hold off before mixing in strife with the other gods. Yet, he says, if Ares or Apollo enter the fray, he will not hesitate to likewise join the struggle and cause the defeated gods to hurry back to Olympus.

They all agree and go off to a high point to watch the battle under cover of a cloud. They sit opposite the other gods, who similarly sit observing the action. Both sides are hesitant to begin the battle with each other. Not the men. Below, the earth shakes with action.

156-164 The whole battle plain shone with the bronze of warriors and their horses, and the earth shook beneath their feet as the gods urged them on together. Then it was that two of the best and most outstanding men from both sides met between the armies eager to do battle. [160] They were Aeneas, the son of Anchises, and godlike Achilles.

Aeneas stepped out first, threatening Achilles—his strong helmet nodding at the other while he held out his fighting shield before him and shook his bronze spear. And from the other side opposite Aeneas, the son of Peleus furiously rushed forward like a lion.

165-258 *When they finally meet, Achilles asks Aeneas why he's challenging him. Is it for power or an estate? He reminds him of the time Aeneas ran from him in flight and how he was saved by Zeus and the other gods. Achilles advises Aeneas to fall back into the crowd of men to avoid getting hurt.*

Aeneas scoffs at him, declaring that he knows how to trade taunts. Then he compares their family lineage and claims that one set of parents will mourn this very day. He goes on to give his full pedigree, glory-boasting in it: from Zeus to Dardanus to Erichthonius to Tros to Assaracus to Capys to Anchises to Aeneas. As for excellence—including battle strength and courage—Aeneas declares that Zeus gives or takes it away. He ends by suggesting that they can go on talking all day like women do when they angrily argue with each other in the middle of the street. Instead, they should fight with bronze-tipped spears.

259-317 As he spoke, he drove his spear at Achilles' great and terrible shield, [260] which rang out as the point struck it. At this, the son of Peleus thrust the shield out with his strong hand, afraid that Aeneas's spear would easily go through it. But what a foolish thought! He didn't know in his mind and spirit that the glorious gifts of a god were unlikely to give way before the blows of mortal men. Aeneas's spear didn't punch through the shield—for the layer of gold, the gift of the god, stopped it. The spear passed through two layers. [270] But the god had made the shield with five—two of bronze, the two innermost ones of tin, and one of gold. It was in this gold layer that the spear came to a stop.

Achilles threw his spear next and struck Aeneas' round shield at the very edge where the bronze was thinnest. The spear of Pelian ash shot through, and the shield rang out at the blow. Aeneas was afraid at this. He crouched down and held the shield out from him. But the spear had already flown over his back [280] and stuck in the ground quivering, after having gone through both circles of the sheltering shield. And now, even though Aeneas had avoided the spear, he stood still, blinded with fear and grief because the weapon had come so near him.

Nevertheless, Achilles drew his sharp sword and eagerly sprang on him with a fearful shout. Opposite him Aeneas seized a great stone—so huge that two men now would be unable to lift it, but Aeneas wielded it quite easily. Aeneas would have then struck Achilles as he was rushing toward him, either on the helmet or on the shield that defended him from sorrowful destruction, [290] and the son of Peleus would have come near and taken his life with the sword, if Poseidon the Earth-shaker had not noticed what was going on.

Turning to the immortal gods, he said, "Alas, I'm distressed for great Aeneas, who will now go down to the house of Hades, vanquished by the son of Peleus. He was a fool to listen to far-shooting Apollo's counsel. Apollo will never save him from destruction. But why should this man suffer when he is guiltless? There is no point. And it is another man's quarrel anyway. Does he not offer acceptable gifts of sacrifice to those of us who possess the broad sky?

[300] "Come on—we must go and save Aeneas from death! The son of Cronus will be angry if Achilles slays him. Rather, his fate is to roam far from here so that Dardanus' family line will not be destroyed and vanish without posterity. Don't you know? The son of Cronus loves Dardanus above all his children born to him from mortal women. As for Priam's family line, the son of Cronus has come to hate it. But now strong Aeneas will be lord over the Trojans as well as his sons' sons and those sons to come."

In return the cow-eyed queen Hera said, [310] "Earth-shaker, consider this matter yourself, whether you will rescue Aeneas or let Achilles, the son of Peleus, overpower him, even though he is a noble man. Whatever you decide, let me tell you that Pallas Athena and I have many times sworn oaths before the immortals that we would never preserve the Trojans from the day of evil harm, not even when we learn that Troy is burning in the raging fire that the warlike sons of the Achaeans will cast on the city."

318-406 *Poseidon takes Aeneas from the battle. After setting him down, he advises him not to go up against Achilles anymore since Achilles is stronger and dearer to the immortals. If he does, Aeneas may go down to Hades in a manner contrary to fate. He should only fight the Achaeans after Achilles has met his own destined death.*

Far away on the battlefield, Achilles discovers Aeneas' absence and realizes a god has taken him away. Then he calls on his men to fight. While the battle rages on, Apollo warns Hector to drop back into the crowd rather than fight out front as a champion against Achilles. As for Achilles himself, he battle-rages, first killing Iphition, the son of Otrynteus, by cleaving his head in two. Achilles glory-boasts over him after he falls and dies and as the Achaean chariots rip him to shreds. Next Achilles slaughters Demoleon, Antenor's son, dashing his brains all over the inside of his bronze helmet. Then he drops Hippodamas with a spear to his back. And next, the youngest son of Priam, Polydorus.

407-454 But stepping out with his spear, Achilles raced against Polydorus, the son of Priam. Polydorus' father had always refused him permission to fight because he was the youngest of his sons [410] and the one he loved best. He was also the fastest of his sons and could beat any other man with his feet. So it was that right then, when Polydorus was foolishly showing off his excellence by darting through the foremost fighters, godlike Achilles struck him in the middle of the back as he was racing past him. He struck him upon the golden fastenings of his belt, where the breastplate overlapped. The point of the spear punched through his stomach, exiting his body through his belly button. Immediately, Polydorus fell to his knees, groaning, and a cloud of darkness passed over him as he collapsed, holding his own guts in his hands.

When Hector saw his brother [420] cradling his own guts and sinking down to the earth, a mist came over his eyes. He knew he could no longer bear to stay out of the fight. He therefore readied his sharp spear that flashed like a flame and went to face Achilles.

But when Achilles saw Hector, he jumped up and boastfully said, "Nearby is the man who has upset me the most—for he struck and killed the comrade I most honored. But we won't hang back from each other for long, hiding behind the battle lines!"

That's what he said. Then glaring at him from beneath his brows, he called out to godlike Hector, "Come nearer to me so that you may quickly experience your destruction."

[430] Without fear Hector of the gleaming helmet answered him, "Son of Peleus, you shouldn't hope to frighten me with words alone as if I were a little child. I too know how to jeer and say shameless words. I also know that you are a mighty warrior and that the strength of my hands is not like yours. Nevertheless, everything rests with the gods. Even though I am inferior, I may yet take your life when I throw my spear for the simple reason that my spear is also very sharp."

Hector hurled his spear as he spoke, but Athena breathed on it. And though her breath was light, she turned the spear back in its flight toward Achilles [440] so that it returned to Hector and lay at his feet in front of him. As for Achilles, he eagerly sprang on him with a fearful shout, ready to kill Hector, but Apollo snatched him away as easily as a god can and hid him in a thick darkness.

Even so, godlike Achilles jumped at him three times with his spear in hand. But three times the spear met with nothing but air. When he rushed forward again for the fourth time as though he were a god, he shouted aloud terribly, and with winged words he said, "Now you have again escaped death, you dog!—even though [450] evil death was near you. Phoebus Apollo has saved you again, the god you pray to before you go into battle. That's fine. If I have a friend among the gods, I will kill you when I encounter you again some other time. For now, I'll chase after other Trojans—whatever ones I meet."

455-494 *Upon saying this, Achilles moves on and slaughters many other Trojans—Dryops, Demuchus, and Laogonus and Dardanus, two sons of Bias. When Tros, the son of Alastor, begs for his life by clasping his knees in the hope that Achilles will take him for ransom, Achilles instead stabs him through the liver and kills him. Next Achilles kills Mulius, Echeclus, and Deucalion, whose head flies from his shoulders to the earth. Rhigmus falls thanks to a spear to his belly, as does his attendant Areithous due to a spear to his back. Achilles rushes along like a wildfire, slaughtering everyone. And the dark earth flows with blood.*

495-503 As one who yokes broad-browed oxen so that they may tread barley upon a well-made threshing-floor—and soon the barley is crushed to pieces under the hooves of the loud-bellowing cattle— even so did the horses of great-spirited Achilles trample on the shields and corpses of the fallen. The axle [500] beneath, and the railing that ran around the chariot's body, and the wheels—these were all bespattered with clots of blood thrown up by his horses' hooves.

But the son of Peleus hurled forward to seize even more glory, though his invincible hands were dirty with blood and gore.

BOOK 21

ACHILLES AND THE RIVER XANTHUS
AGENOR FACES ACHILLES

IN BRIEF: *Achilles kills so many that the river Xanthus (known to mortals as the Scamander) fills up with corpses, those of Lycaon and Asteropaeus included. The river commands him to stop, but Achilles refuses. Xanthus thus begins to drown Achilles. When he voices his concern, Poseidon and Athena assure him that he will not be conquered by the river. Finally, Hera sends Hephaestus to fight and defeat the river—fire against water! He does. The gods battle one another. Priam calls for the gates of Troy to be opened wide. The Trojans flee into the city as Agenor debates whether to stand his ground or flee. He faces Achilles and Apollo saves him.*

NOW WHEN THE Trojans came to the best place to cross the fair-flowing river, the whirling Xanthus begotten of immortal Zeus, Achilles divided them and chased off half of the men to the plain before the city . . . [4-7] . . . while the other half were trapped by the deep-flowing, silver-eddying river.

As Achilles ran at them, they fell into the water with a great up-roar. And around them the waters [10] thundered as the river flowed past its high banks. Screaming and shouting, the men splashed and floundered this way and that in the water amid the river's battling currents. [12-14] . . . So it was that as Achilles came on, the whooshing waters of the whirling Xanthus were chaotically filled with men and horses.

17-96 Achilles goes after the confused men in the river and hacks at them with his sword. It is a slaughter, and the water grows red with blood. Taking a rest, Achilles seizes twelve living boys to pay the blood price later for Patroclus' death. Then he spots Lycaon, Priam's son, who had previously

been his captive and sold for a ransom of one hundred cows. Clasping his
knees, Lycaon begs Achilles to spare him. He hopes to flee evil death and
black fate. But now, he remarks, Fate has put him back into Achilles' un-
kind hands.

97-128 That's how Lycaon, the glorious son of Priam, addressed
Achilles—with begging words of supplication. But in return he
heard harsh words.

"Fool!" Achilles judged him. "Don't tell me about ransoms and
make speeches like we're in the assembly. [100] Until Patroclus fell
on his fated day, I preferred to spare the Trojans, and I sold many
of the captives that I had taken alive. But now, do not even think
about it. If a god throws a man into my hands before the walls of
Ilium, that man will die. No Trojan will escape death, and surely
not the sons of Priam. No, dear man, you too will die—so why do
you moan and wail like this? Patroclus died, and he was a much
better man than you. And don't you see what kind of a man I am?
I'm tall and good looking. And my father is a good man, noble and
brave. And the mother who gave birth to me is a goddess. [110]
Even so, the mighty hands of Fate and death hold me too. The mo-
ment will come, either at dawn or dusk, or perhaps in the afternoon,
when some man will take my life in battle, either with his spear or
with an arrow flying from his bow."

That's what Achilles said, and Lycaon's knees gave way, and his
heart melted within. He let go of the Achaean hero's spear and fell
over to the earth on all fours. Above him Achilles drew his sharp
sword and stabbed him by the collarbone on his neck. The blade
plunged in all the way, and Lycaon sprawled out on the ground.
Around him, the dark blood pooled until the earth was soaked.
[120] Then Achilles caught him by the foot and flung him into the
river so that his body would float downstream. As he drifted away,
he glory-boasted over him speaking winged words, "Lie there
among the fishes! They'll lick the blood from your wound without
a thought of you. And so your mother will never lay you out to
mourn you, but the whirling waters of the Scamander will take you
to the wide gulf of the salty sea. There, the fish will feed on the fat

of Lycaon as they swim under the dark waves. In this way, may all you Trojans perish until we reach the walls of sacred Ilium!"

129-271 *Achilles explains that even though Lycaon sacrificed to the river, the river won't help him. No, they will all pay for Patroclus! Hearing this boast, the river Xanthus grows angry.*

Out of the river, the Trojan Asteropaeus faces Achilles who declares those parents "unhappy" whose children will face him in battle. At Achilles' request, Asteropaeus gives his lineage, including his grandfather, Axius, a river. Then he challenges Achilles to a fight, and they fight. Being ambidextrous, Asteropaeus throws two spears at once. One is stopped by the Achaean hero's great shield; the other cuts his right arm but passes by. Next, Achilles throws and misses. Finally, he pounces on the Trojan and kills him by plunging his sword into his belly. As Asteropaeus' guts and blood leak out, along with his life-breath, Achilles glory-boasts over him, responding to Asteropaeus' prior genealogical revelation. He declares that he's from the line of Zeus through Peleus and Aeacus. And Zeus is stronger than a divine river, he observes. And so it follows that the offspring of Zeus is stronger than that of a river. Not even Oceanus, the source of all the rivers and seas, fights with Zeus who thunders.

Achilles moves off, leaving the river fish to nibble on Asteropaeus. He slays many of Asteropaeus' comrades. The river Xanthus becomes upset and tells Achilles to go kill the Trojans somewhere else. Go slaughter them on the plain! he commands. He complains that the Achaean hero is stopping up the flow of his waters with all the dead men. Finally, at Apollo's urging, Xanthus floods, tossing the dead to dry land. Then he rushes to engulf Achilles and drown him.

At this, Achilles prays to Zeus. He's afraid he'll die like some nameless swineherd boy. But he would rather have a better death. He wishes that Hector had killed him!

272-297 And the son of Peleus looked up into the broad sky, and wailing, he prayed, "Father Zeus, will none of the gods pity me and save me from the river? I don't care what happens after—I'll suffer what I have to. But of all the heavenly ones, I blame my dear mother the most. She tricked me with false words. She told me that my fate was to fall under the walls of Troy, that Apollo's swift-flying arrows would destroy me. It would have been far better if Hector, the best of the Trojans, had cut me down. [280] Then a good, noble, and brave man would have killed one of the same kind—for that's what I am. But now I receive as my fated portion this wretched death, trapped in a big, surging river like some swineherd boy who gets carried along with the torrential waters while trying to cross the river during a storm."

That's what Achilles said. And quickly Poseidon and Athena came and stood near him in the likeness of two men. They took him by the hand and spoke to reassure him.

Poseidon spoke first. "Son of Peleus, don't be such a coward or fear too much. For we are helpers sent by the gods [290] with Zeus' approval—I, Poseidon, and Pallas Athena. But listen. It is not fated for you to be conquered by a river. He will very quickly give the flooding a rest—you'll see.

"But now we will offer you some shrewd advice, if only you'll listen and obey. Don't let your hands stop the distressful battle until you've trapped the Trojan men behind the glorious walls of Ilium— those, at least, who flee your wrath. As for you, take Hector's life and return to the ships. We grant you to raise high the glory-boast."

298-460 *Hearing the latter promise, and filled with Athena-given strength, Achilles darts into the flooded, corpse-strewn battle plain. Seeing this, Xanthus calls out to his brother river Simois for help against the battle-crazed Achilles. Surge! he commands him. Raise a wave! Let us check this wild man! They attack and nearly submerge Achilles before Hera notices and calls to Hephaestus for help. The smith god, who was earlier matched with the river Xanthus, calls upon Zephyrus and Notos, the West and South Winds, and they drive Hephaestus' great fire across the plain, burning up all the dead and trees and other vegetation, and causing Xanthus to boil as when many fires cause a cauldron to boil.*

Xanthus complains to Hera. Why is Hephaestus picking on me? Hera calls off the smith god and tells him it is not fitting for an immortal god to strike another one on behalf of a mortal. Hephaestus stops the burning, Xanthus flows, and their great battle ends.

Even so, the other gods continue in strife. On Olympus, Zeus laughs and delights in his heart. Ares fights Athena—the god of war hoping to make the goddess repay him for how she previously wounded him when Diomedes was battle raging. He strikes her goatskin shield. She steps back, grabs a huge black stone, and bowls him over. She laughs, glory-boasting over him that she is so much stronger than he is. She says it is payback for how he deserted the Achaeans to help the Trojans.

Aphrodite comes over to lead Ares off the battlefield. When Hera sees this, she orders Athena to go after her, calling Aphrodite the shameless "dog-fly." Hera doesn't have to ask again. Athena drops her to the ground and glory-boasts over both, the goddess of love and the god of war. She claims that Ilium would have fallen long before if they had not helped the Trojans.

Seeing all this happen, Poseidon suggests to Apollo that they should fight as is fitting since the other gods have joined in battle. It would be shameful if they didn't battle each other, he claims. Then he urges Apollo to begin since he, Poseidon, is older and knows more. Yet before Apollo can start, Poseidon reminds him of how foolish it is to help the Trojans. He recalls the time they labored for Laomedon, the ruler of Troy and father of Priam, for a year to build a wall around the city. At the end of the year the king defrauded them by not paying the promised wage. More, he threatened to disfigure the two and sell them into slavery.

461-467 Then lord Apollo, who works from afar, answered him, "Lord of the earthquake, you would have no respect for me if I were to battle with you over miserable mortals who flourish now like green leaves in springtime, eating whatever the earth provides, but soon waste away and decay, falling lifeless to the ground. No, let us not fight. Rather, let them settle it themselves."

468-525 *With this, Apollo turns away from Poseidon, ashamed to fight his father's brother. Artemis schools him for this, for fleeing and giving Poseidon the glory-boast. Apollo ignores her.*

As he walks away, Hera challenges Artemis to a fight so that Artemis will know how much mightier she is. She takes Artemis' weapons and beats her with them. As she does, the younger goddess weeps and flies away.

*Witnessing this, Hermes tells Leto he doesn't want to fight with her.
He says she can glory-boast that she beat him if she wants. Instead of glory-
boasting, however, Leto just takes up her daughter's fallen weapons — her
bow and arrows — and follows Artemis to Olympus. There, Artemis plops
down on Zeus' lap and complains about Hera. Zeus laughs at this.*

*Meanwhile, Apollo is upset that Troy's wall may fall before the fated
time. The other gods return to Olympus, some angry, some exulting.
Down below on the battle plain, Achilles keeps up his slaughter.*

526-572 Old Priam stood on the tower of the god-built wall looking
down on mighty Achilles as the Trojans helplessly fled panic-
stricken before him. Presently, he stepped down from the tower
moaning and groaning. [530] He passed along the wall urging on
the highly renowned gatekeepers. "Hold wide the gates with your
hands, men. Open them like a sail and keep them open until the
people come flying into the city. Achilles is nearby, driving them
on in confusion, and I foresee ruin. As soon as the men are safely
inside, close the strong gates again, for I fear that destructive man
will jump inside the wall."

That's what Priam said. And the gatekeepers drew back the
bolts and opened wide the doors letting in the light of day. As for
the people, Apollo sprang out to meet them in order to ward off
ruin from them in the form of Achilles' mighty rage. [540] They fled
straight to the city and the high wall, their throats itching with thirst
and their bodies covered with a cloud of dust from the plain. Be-
hind them, the violent man Achilles came on waving his spear as
one with fury in his heart and an eager desire to win glory.

Then the sons of the Achaeans would have taken the lofty gates
of Troy if Phoebus Apollo had not sent out Agenor, the blameless
and mighty son of Antenor. The god filled his heart with courage
and stood by his side to ward off the heavy hands of death. There
he was, leaning against the oak tree and shrouded by a cloud of
mist.

[550] But when Agenor observed the sacker of cities Achilles, he
stood still, and his heart swirled with doubts about staying or go-
ing. And troubled, he spoke these words to his own great spirit:

"Ah me! If I run before mighty Achilles and go where all the others are fearfully being driven in rout, then he will seize me and cut me down like a powerless woman. But what if I leave them alone and flee to safety elsewhere, through the plain before Troy and to the foothills of Mount Ida where there are bushes I could hide in and trees. [560] Later on, after washing the battle grime and sweat from my body, I could return to the city.

"But why does my dear spirit debate these things? He'd likely see me as I rush off from the city and run over the plain. Then he would chase me with all his speed. And there's no way I would then avoid the fates of death. What, then, if I go out and meet him in front of the city? I imagine his flesh is surely vulnerable to sharp bronze. And he's only got one life—men say he's mortal. [570] The problem is Zeus, the son of Cronus, is covering him with glory."

Saying this, Agenor stood ready to meet Achilles, and he urged his brave heart on to battle and fight.

573-605 *Agenor waits there like a leopard facing a man and his dogs, and when Achilles approaches, he threatens him with the destined loss of his life. He casts and strikes Achilles' greave-shielded leg. Achilles throws in turn. But as the spear flies forward, Apollo takes up Agenor, refusing to grant Achilles glory. In this way, Agenor returns home from the great war in peace. All the while Achilles is chasing Apollo in the form of Agenor as the rest of the Trojans flee into the city.*

606-611 Some distance away, the rest of the Trojans ran until they gladly came to the town's gates. And the city was filled as they were shut in one after another. Usually, they would have waited outside the gates to account for each man—the man who fled [610] and the man who fell. Not now. Rather now they yearned to pour into the city—those saved by their own feet and legs.

BOOK 22

HECTOR BATTLES ACHILLES
ATHENA'S DECEPTION

IN BRIEF: *Priam and Hecuba beg Hector to fight from a safe distance. The Trojan hero debates back and forth in his own mind. Achilles chases him. Disguised as Deiphobus, Athena fools Hector into fighting Achilles. They finally face each other. And after trading taunts, bargaining for and refusing deals, and throwing spears, the Achaean hero kills him by means of a spear through his throat. He strips Hector, glory-boasts over him, and drags him behind his chariot. Witnessing all this from atop Troy's walls, the Trojans mourn their hero—Priam, Hecuba, and Andromache most of all.*

S O NOW, UP and down the city, those who had fled like fawns were cooling off by fanning their sweat and drinking to quench their thirst as they rested against the well-made fortifications. Outside, the Achaeans drew nearer to the wall, their shields up against their shoulders.

But a deadly fate bound Hector so that he stayed where he was in front of Ilium and the Scaean gates.

Then Phoebus Apollo spoke to the son of Peleus, saying, "Why, son of Peleus, do you chase me with your swift feet—you who are a mortal man, while I am an immortal god? Do you still, even now, fail [10] to perceive that I am a god—you who rage without ceasing? Don't you care about all those Trojans, the ones you worked so hard to rout? Well, they've shut themselves in the city, and you, you've gone way out of the way here. Anyway, you will not kill me. I'm not one fated to die."

14-97 Achilles realizes Apollo's ploy, that he distracted him while all the Trojans were being saved. And by doing this, Apollo stole glory from him.

Ah! He would avenge himself if only he were as powerful as the god! Achilles turns and runs off toward the city wall.

Standing high on the wall, Priam sees him speeding along like the Dog of Orion that signals evil to come. He begs Hector not to face Achilles alone and reminds him of how many sons he has already lost. Come inside the walls, he bids, save your fellow Trojans, and don't give glory to the son of Peleus when he slays you. Have pity on me! Priam goes on to foretell Troy's doom, and his own, and his sons' fated deaths and their wives' enslavement. His own dogs will eat him once he's gone! Young men who have fallen in battle have a certain beauty, he observes, but what a shame battle death is for an old man. Even though Priam pulls at his hair, Hector refuses to listen. Then his mother Hecuba joins in, bearing her breast to him, begging and crying.

Neither she nor his father can persuade Hector. He just stands there holding his ground, awaiting Achilles' furious approach. Still, as he watches him come on, his mood shifts.

98-116 And troubled, Hector spoke to his own great-hearted spirit, "Ah me! If I make my way into the city, behind the gates and walls, [100] Polydamas will be the first to lay blame on me. He called on me to lead the Trojans back to the city on that destructive night when godlike Achilles stirred himself against us. I refused to listen then, but it would have been far better if I had!

"Now my recklessness has destroyed the army, and I feel shame before the Trojan men and the Trojan women with their long trailing robes. What if some cowardly man says of me, 'Persuaded by his own bodily strength, Hector has destroyed the men of the army!' Surely it would be better for me to face Achilles in a fight before I return. [110] Then I could kill him. If not, at least I'll be destroyed gloriously before the city.

"On the other hand, what if I lay down my shield and helmet, lean my spear against the wall, and go straight up to blameless Achilles? I could promise to hand over Helen with all her possessions, everything that Alexander carried with him in his hollow ships to Troy."

117-121 *Hector considers the option of splitting half of Troy's wealth with Achilles.*

122-130 "But why does my dear spirit debate these things? If I go and come up to him, he will neither show me pity nor will he respect me. No—as soon as I have taken off my armor and am naked, he'll slay me like a woman. There's no talking to him now by some large rock or tree as young men and young maidens do, chatting on and flirting with one another. No—it would be better to encounter each other in combat quickly [130] to see which one of us the Olympian will grant the glory-boast."

131-247 *Hector thinks these thoughts as Achilles comes barreling on toward him, the bronze flashing in the sun. As soon as the Achaean hero nears him, Hector begins to quake and tremble. On second thought, he takes off from the gates, fleeing before Achilles, who chases after him as a hawk chases after a dove. They run past the wall and by the wild fig tree. And by the fountains bubbling up from Xanthus, one cold, the other warm. And by the wide tanks where the women used to do the laundry when there was peace. There's a good man running ahead but a better man trailing. And what is the prize? They aren't competing for any ordinary prize but for Hector's own life! They circle the city three times while all the gods watch.*

Witnessing the hell-bent race and Hector's likely demise, Zeus considers aloud whether to save him from death—the man who has been very faithful in burning sacrifices to him high upon the ridges of Mount Ida. Athena balks. She reminds Zeus that Hector is a mortal man fated to die. Do it, she says, but we other gods will neither approve of you nor your act. Zeus backs off, and Athena darts down from Olympus to make an end of Hector.

Hector tries, but he cannot make it to the wall where his men will be able to fend off Achilles with arrows. Rather, Achilles drives him out to the battle plain. Still, as in a dream, neither can Hector make it away nor can Achilles reach him. Apollo appears to urge Hector on. Achilles forbids his men to cast their spears or fire their arrows at his opponent. He doesn't want them to steal his glory. A fourth time they come to the springs in their mad dash. Now Zeus' golden scales fall against Hector, signaling his fated day, the day he will die.

Athena appears to Achilles and tells him to rest, that she will go persuade Hector to fight. She goes in the form of Deiphobus, Hector's brother, and convinces him to make a stand together against Achilles. Hector is pleased with Deiphobus and promises to honor him for his offer. Deiphobus-Athena explains how everyone, parents and friends, tried to talk him out of it, but seeing Hector's sad misfortune, he had to help. So now, he says, let's fight and see who will win. In this way, Athena tricks Hector into fighting Achilles.

248-366 Now when the two were near each other, great Hector of the gleaming helmet was first to speak. [250] "I will no longer run from you in fear, son of Peleus, as I have up to now. I've run around godlike Priam's city three times, but I've not dared to await your attack. Now my spirit urges me to make a stand and face you. Either I will overpower and kill you, or I will fall into your hands. But come here, let us freely give these words before the gods, who are the best witnesses and guardians of all agreements. If Zeus gives me endurance and I take your life, I will not dishonor you in any exceeding manner. But when I strip your glorious arms from your dead body, I will give your corpse back to the Achaeans, and you will do the same for me."

[260] Then glaring at him from beneath his brows, swift-footed Achilles said, "Hector, don't go on and on about nice arrangements. There can be no agreements between men and lions. Wolves and lambs hate and plan harm for each other—every time and all the way. There's no friendship or oath-making, not until one of us has fallen and satisfied Ares, the warrior with the thick bull-hide shield, with blood. Rather, put in mind all your excellent strength and bravery. Now you must be a spearman and a daring warrior. [270] There's no more escaping. Pallas Athena will vanquish you by my spear. And now you will pay me in full for all the grief you have caused me when you battle raged, killing all my comrades."

Achilles readied his shadow-casting spear as he spoke and hurled it. But shining Hector saw it coming and avoided it. He crouched down so that the bronze spear flew over his head and stuck in the ground. Even so, Athena invisibly snatched it up and gave it back to Achilles so that the shepherd of men Hector didn't notice.

And Hector said to the blameless son of Peleus, "You've missed, godlike Achilles! [280] And I imagine you thought you knew my fate, straight from Zeus! You were a cunning, fast-talking liar when you tried to make me forget my battle strength and valor so that I would cower before you. But if some god grants you the victory, you'll not drive your spear into my back as I flee. Rather, you'll have to drive it into my chest as I eagerly come straight at you. And now for your own part, try to avoid my spear if you can. I wish that you would receive the whole of it through your skin and body. If you died, the Trojans would find the war much easier—because you have harmed them most."

Hector readied his shadow-casting spear as he spoke and hurled it. [290] He hit the middle of Achilles' shield, but the spear was deflected. Seeing this, Hector was angry when he saw that the missile had sped from his hand in vain. And now he stood there quietly in dismay since he had no second spear. With a loud cry, then, he called out to Deiphobus and asked him for one. But the man was not there.

Now Hector realized the truth and spoke to himself, "Alas! The gods have lured me to my death. I thought that the hero Deiphobus was by my side, but he's far away, safely within the wall. The goddess Athena has deceived me. [300] And now evil death is very near to me and there's no escape—for so have Zeus and his far-shooting son Apollo willed it, though before they were ever ready to protect me. Now my fate has come! Let me not then die ingloriously and without a struggle, but let me first do some great thing that men to come will hear about!"

As he spoke, he drew the sharp sword that dangled by his side. And gathering himself together, Hector sprang on Achilles like a soaring eagle that swoops down from the clouds [310] onto some lamb or timid hare. Like this, Hector brandished his sword and swooped down on Achilles.

Wild with rage, Achilles darted toward him . . . [313-316] . . . And as the evening star shines brighter than all other stars through the stillness of night, even so did Achilles' spear gleam [320] in his right hand as he planned harm for godlike Hector. He looked over his beautiful body to see where he could best strike and wound it, but his skin and flesh were protected by the bronze armor that Hector had stripped from strong Patroclus when he had slaughtered him. Ah!—but there was a spot upon his neck where the collarbones divide the neck from the shoulders. The throat! It is the spot where death's destruction comes most swiftly to the life-breath.

So as Hector was eagerly rushing on him, godlike Achilles drove his spear through his throat. The point of the bronze spear plunged in and went straight through the fleshy part of the neck. But it did not sever Hector's windpipe. No, the Trojan hero could still speak.

[330] Regardless, Hector fell headlong into the dust, and godlike Achilles glory-boasted over him. "Hector, you thought you would safely escape when you were stripping Patroclus. You had no regard for me while I stood apart from the battle. You fool! I was still alive at the hollow ships. He had a helper—me! And I am far better than the man you killed! But now, look. I've loosened your knees so that you have fallen. And when the Achaeans give Patroclus the funeral rites we owe him, dogs and vultures will shamefully tear at your flesh."

Then, as the life ebbed out of him, Hector of the gleaming helmet said, "I beg you by your life and knees, and by your parents, do not let the dogs devour me by the ships of the Achaeans. I beg you— [340] accept the pile of gold and bronze that my father and mother will give you. As for my body, send it home so that the Trojans and their wives may give me my proper share of fire in death."

Then glaring at him from beneath his brows, swift-footed Achilles said, "You dog! Don't mention knees or parents to me! No, I wish that I could cut your flesh into pieces and eat it raw for all the harm you've done me! Nothing will save you from the dogs! Not even if your parents bring a much larger ransom, [350] and even larger than that, and weigh it out for me on the spot with a promise of even more in time to come! Not even if the son of Dardanus, Priam, offered me your weight in gold—even then would your mother never be able to lay you out to mourn the son she bore. But dogs and vultures will eat every part of you!"

Then, with his dying breath, Hector of the gleaming helmet said, "I now know what kind of a man you are and see that I will not move you, for your heart is as hard as iron. Make sure, though, that I do not become the cause of the gods' anger against you on the day when Paris and Phoebus Apollo, [360] noble though you are, destroy you at the Scaean gates."

When he had spoken these words, death's end covered him, and his life passed out of him and flew down to the house of Hades lamenting its sad fate that it should no longer enjoy youth and strength.

But godlike Achilles answered the dead man, "Die! As for me, I will accept my death when Zeus and the other immortal gods choose to accomplish it."

367-394 *Achilles yanks the bronze-tipped spear from Hector's throat and strips him. The other Achaeans run up to him, gazing upon Hector's admirable form and body. As each looks upon him, they wound him with spears and swords, joking about how much softer he is now in comparison to when he was burning the ships.*

After briefly wondering whether the Trojans will remain in the city now that their champion Hector is dead, or whether they will flee, Achilles orders his men to return to the ships. They have won great glory by slaying Hector—the man the Trojans looked to and prayed as if a god. Furthermore, he says, they must give Patroclus his last rites—for Achilles will never forget his dear friend. Let us return to the ships singing a paean, a song of triumph.

395-404 Upon saying these words, Achilles devised shameful things for godlike Hector. He pierced the sinews at the back of both his feet from heel to ankle and passed thongs of ox-hide through the slits he had made. In this manner he fastened Hector's body to his chariot, letting the head trail behind on the ground. Then, when he had put the glorious armor on the chariot and had himself mounted, [400] he lashed the horses on, and they sped forward.

Behind him, the dust rose from Hector as he was being dragged along. His dark hair flew this way and that, and his once beautiful head dragged along the earth. But so much for that. Zeus had finally delivered him to his enemies so that they might treat him shamefully in his own land.

405-436 *Seeing this, Hector's mother, father, and all the people lament his ruin. Priam wants to go down to the ships and beg "that reckless man" Achilles for his body, hoping that Achilles will respect his age and the fact that he is like his own father, Peleus. He explains that of all his sons, he grieves the most for Hector.*

Following Priam and tearing out her hair, Hecuba wails for all her unhappiness and suffering. "I am wretched!" she cries. Hector was her boast and a great glory for all the Trojans. But now he's gone!

437-515 That's how Hecuba spoke in tears. Meanwhile, Hector's wife had learned nothing about what had happened because no truth-bearing messenger had come to tell her that her husband had remained outside the gates. [440] No, Andromache was at her loom in the innermost part of the lofty house, weaving a large dark purple mantle that folded over and embroidering it with many colorful flowers. She told her handmaidens to set a large tripod on the fire— so that a warm bath would be ready for Hector when he came in from battle. Poor foolish woman! She didn't know that he was now beyond the reach of baths, that bright-eyed Athena had laid him low by the hands of Achilles.

Just then Andromache heard all the wailing and lamentation coming from the direction of the tower upon the wall. And her limbs trembled, and the weaver's shuttle fell from her hands to the floor.

Again she spoke to her serving women. [450] "Two of you— come with me so that I may learn what has happened. I just heard the voice of my husband's honored mother. My own heart beats into my mouth, and my limbs refuse to carry me. I know it—some great misfortune has struck Priam's children. May that news never find my ear! Still, I fear that godlike Achilles has cut off brave Hector's retreat. He has chased him out to the plain where he had to stand all alone. I fear he may have put an end to the reckless daring that possessed my husband. He never stayed back among all the men, but would run out front, yielding to no other man's battle might."

[460] Andromache's heart thumped within her chest, and as she spoke, she frantically flew through the halls and from the house like a mad woman. The handmaidens followed her. When she reached the tower upon the wall and the crowd of men gathered there, she stood looking out from atop the wall, searching. And there! Down below she spotted Hector being dragged away in front of the city, the swift horses carelessly dragging him over the ground toward the hollow Achaean ships.

Seeing this sight, the darkness of night shrouded Andromache's eyes, and she fainted, falling backward, giving up her life-breath. As she fell, she tore the glittering headdress from her head and flung it from her along with [470] the veil which golden Aphrodite had given her on the day when Hector of the gleaming helmet took her with him from the house of Eetion, after having given countless gifts for her sake. Her husband's sisters and his brothers' wives crowded around her and supported her, for she was overwhelmed with fear.

When she finally breathed again and came to herself, she sobbed and lamented among the Trojans, saying, "Hector! I am wretched! Unhappy! We were born to the same fate, both of us—you at Troy, in the house of Priam, and I at Thebes, under the wooded mountain of Placus, [480] in the house of Eetion. He brought me up when I was a child—ill-fated and doomed to a horrible end. I wish that he had never begotten me. And now you are going down to the house of Hades, into the depths of the earth. You leave me a widow in your halls, full of grief.

"And our child—the one we brought into this world who was born to two ill-fated parents—he is only an infant. Now that you are dead and gone, Hector, you can do nothing for him, nor will he ever be able to do anything for you. Even if he survives the horrors of this unhappy war with the Achaeans, his future life will later be full of hard labor and troublesome care. Others will progressively take his land. [490] The day that robs a child of his father and makes of him an orphan—that day cuts him off from those who would have been his friends. His head is bowed, and his cheeks are wet with tears. While he misses his own father and stands in need of him, he goes up to his father's feasting friends and tugs at one by his mantle and another by his tunic. One of these may pity the boy and hold out his cup for a moment so that the boy may moisten his lips. But he must not drink too much, taking whole mouthfuls. Otherwise, one whose parents are still alive will drive him from the feasting table with blows and angry words of reproach. "Get out of here!" he'll say. "Your father doesn't feast with us!" And the boy will run off crying to his widowed mother. [500] Astyanax will do this, the young boy who used to sit upon his father's knees eating nothing but the best—bone marrow and the fat of sheep. And when he had played his heart out until he was tired and went to sleep, he would lie in a soft bed knowing neither want nor care while his nurse lay with him and stroked him to sleep. But now that he has lost his father, he will suffer much harm. Astyanax! The one the Trojans called by this special name because you alone, Hector, defended the gates and great walls of Troy!

"And now that you're far from your parents at the curved ships, Hector, twisting worms will eat you after the dogs have glutted themselves upon your [510] naked corpse. There you'll be, unclad, when in your house you have beautiful clothes made by the hands of all your women. I'll burn these now so that before the Trojan men and women they'll be your glory."

That's what Andromache said when they were crying. And surrounding her, the women joined in the lamentation.

BOOK 23

THE FUNERAL GAMES
THE ACHAEANS MOURN PATROCLUS

IN BRIEF: *Patroclus appears to Achilles while he is sleeping. Though his friend speaks to him, Achilles cannot touch him. The Myrmidons mourn the loss of Patroclus, honoring him, sending him off with a great funeral pyre. Achilles holds funeral games in honor of him: a chariot race, boxing, wrestling, a footrace, single armed combat, the iron-weight throw, archery, and a spear throw. Prizes are distributed after each contest. Antilochus reconciles with Menelaus after wronging him.*

SO IT WAS that the Trojans wailed and lamented Hector and the other fallen men throughout the city.

As for the Achaeans, when they reached the camp and the Hellespont, they each dispersed to their own ships. But Achilles would not let the Myrmidons go. Instead, he spoke among his war-loving comrades. "You Myrmidons with swift horses, my own trusted friends in arms. Let us not unyoke our horses yet. No, let us draw near to Patroclus with horses and chariots and mourn him—for that is the honor-prize of the dead. [10] Then, when we have satisfied ourselves with sorrowful weeping, we will release the horses and eat together."

That's what Achilles said. So they lamented together, with Achilles in the lead. Doing so, they drove their chariots around Patroclus' body three times, shedding tears as they went, . . . [14-17] . . . and Achilles put his man-slaying hands on Patroclus' chest.

"Goodbye Patroclus, you who are now in the house of Hades. But listen, [20] I am already doing what I promised. I have dragged Hector through the dust and will give his flesh to dogs to divide among themselves. And I will cut the throats of twelve glorious

Trojan boys before your funeral pyre to satisfy the anger I feel at your slaying."

24-61 *After drenching the earth with tears, Achilles and the Myrmidons sit down to a feast suitable to their desires—cattle, sheep, goats, and wild swine.*

Sometime later, Agamemnon calls Achilles to his shelter to convince him to wash himself with warm water. But Achilles refuses, saying that he will not wash until Patroclus is given the final rites of fire. He asks Agamemnon to have the men gather wood for the great fire.

After feasting, and while all the other Myrmidons are asleep, Achilles remains on the beach, weeping for his fallen comrade.

62-84 When sleep took hold of him, releasing his deepest cares and sinking him in sweetness—he was bone-tired, after all, from chasing Hector around windy Ilium—the phantom-life of Patroclus, wretched man that he was, came to him. It appeared just as he had been in life—in size, the expression of his eyes, his sound, and his clothing, too.

Patroclus stood over his head and spoke a word to him. "You sleep, Achilles, and have forgotten me. [70] You loved and cared for me while I lived, but now that I'm dead, you don't think about me anymore. One thing I ask: bury me quickly so that I may pass through the gates of Hades. The phantom-lives of men drive me away from the gates, the man-images that no longer toil. Since they won't let me join the dead beyond the river, I wander aimlessly around the wide gates of Hades' house. So I beg you now with tears, give me your hand. Let me take it—for I will never again come up from Hades when you have allotted me the fire. We won't ever sit together again apart from our dear comrades knocking around ideas and coming up with great plans. Instead, hated death gapes for me, the one allotted me when I was born. [80] But it is also your fate, godlike Achilles, to be utterly destroyed beneath the walls of the wealthy Trojans.

"One more thing I will tell you if you will listen. Let not my bones be laid to rest apart from yours, Achilles, but let them rest together—even as we were brought up together in your own home."

85-90 *Patroclus explains how his father Menoetius brought him to Achilles' house when Patroclus quarreled with and accidentally killed the son of Amphidas.*

91-107 "Let our bones rest in a single urn, the golden amphora given you by your queenly mother."

In reply, swift-footed Achilles said, "Why, honored friend, have you come here to prod me about each thing? I hear you and will accomplish all these things just as you urge me on. But stand nearer to me. Let us once again throw our arms around each other so that we may find satisfaction in sorrowful weeping."

That's what Achilles said. And when he finished, he opened his arms toward Patroclus to embrace him. He would have closed them around him, too, [100] but there was nothing! The phantom-life vanished with a shrill cry beneath the earth even as smoke vanishes around a fire.

The Achaean hero sprang to his feet, clapped his hands together, and spoke a word of lamentation, saying, "Ah friend! Even in the house of Hades there is something—phantom-lives and man-images—though there is no mind at all in these. All night long the wretched phantom-life of Patroclus has hovered over my head, weeping and flowing with tears, and prodding me about each thing I am to accomplish for him. And he looked wonderfully like himself."

108-351 *Led by Meriones, the companion in arms of Idomeneus, the Achaeans gather wood for the great funeral pyre. They stack the wood where Achilles hopes to pile a mound for both his own and Patroclus' bones. Then the Myrmidons, some on chariots and many more afoot, all armored in bronze, convey Patroclus' corpse to the pyre. The body is covered with their shorn hair. When they set him down, Achilles cuts his own hair to offer to the hero Patroclus—the hair that he had previously promised to the river Spercheios along with sacrificed animals upon his return home.*

While many of the Achaeans go off to take their evening meal, those closest to Patroclus stay and prepare the funeral pyre for his burning. They set him atop the mountainous pile along with sheep and cattle, all flayed, and amphoras of honey and sweet-smelling oil, as well as nine horses. Achilles adds two of Patroclus' dogs and the twelve noble sons of Troy; he kills both groups by slitting their throats with a bronze knife. Finally, he lights the fire. As he does so, he reminds Patroclus of all he has promised him and explains how he is fulfilling the promises. And Hector will be given to the dogs, he says. But despite the promise, Aphrodite protects Hector from the dogs, and Apollo hides him beneath a dark cloud.

When the fire doesn't light as Achilles would like it to, he prays to the North and West Winds for help. Iris delivers his message, and they, though they are feasting, answer his prayer by driving a great wind toward the funeral pyre. When it hits, the fire explodes skyward and burns all night long. Next to it Achilles pours out libation after libation, calling on the wretched phantom-life of Patroclus, and weeping. At long last, as morning comes and Dawn rises, the fire dies out. Achilles finally sleeps.

Sometime later, Agamemnon and his men come by, and Achilles commands them to put out the fire with wine. They are to gather Patroclus' bones, set them in the golden urn, the one Achilles will eventually share with him, and pile a fitting mound over him—one they will make larger once Achilles is buried there too. They do as he ordered.

Achilles has the men sit in a wide assembly and collects prizes for the funeral games. First is the chariot race. After declaring he would win if he were racing, Achilles calls on the men to step up to compete. Five do—Eumelus, Diomedes, Menelaus, Antilochus, the son of Nestor, and Meriones. Nestor advises Antilochus to be cunningly wise during the race—since cunning wisdom often beats sheer strength, he declares. He warns his son not to crash into the turning stones that mark the point where the chariots return, or his disgrace will be a source of joy for the others. Be wise and mind well what you are about.

352-441 They stepped into their chariots and cast lots. When Achilles shook the helmet, the lot of Antilochus, the son of Nestor, sprang out first. Next came that of lord Eumelus, and after his, those of the son of Atreus, Menelaus, and of Meriones. The last place fell to the lot of the son of Tydeus, Diomedes, who was the best man of them all.

Knowing who was first and who last, they took their places in line. Achilles showed them the distant post in the plain around which they were to turn and race back. There he stationed [360] godlike Phoenix, his father's comrade in arms, as the watchman so that he might remember what happened and declare the truth.

Right then they all lashed their horses, striking them with the reins and shouting at them with all their might. Away from the ships, they flew out over the plain, and the dust rose from under them as if it were a cloud or whirlwind. The horses' manes danced in the wind. At one moment the chariots seemed to touch the ground; the next they shot into the air. All along, [370] the drivers stood in the chariot's car, their hearts pounding as each man longed for victory. Each kept calling out to his horses as they darted along the dust-cloud-covered plain.

It was when they had reached the end of the racecourse and were on their way back toward the gray sea, that the skill and ability of each man and horse came to light as the horses were raced at top speed. Eumelus' horses now took the lead, and near behind them came Diomedes' Trojan stallions. . . . [380] The horses were so close that Eumelus could feel their warm breath on his back and on his broad shoulders—their heads and nostrils right there as they sped along the racecourse.

Just now, when the son of Tydeus would have overcome Eumelus to win, or they would have passed through the finish line together making the race hard to call, Phoebus Apollo made Diomedes drop his horsewhip because he bore an angry grudge against him. Tears of anger consequently fell from Diomedes eyes as he saw Eumelus' horses going on faster than ever while his own were hindered and losing ground because he had no way to drive them on. Athena wasn't blind to all this. She saw the trick that Apollo had played on the son of Tydeus, so she chased after the shepherd of men and [390] gave to him his horsewhip. Then she filled his horses with renewed vigor and racing strength. Moreover, she went after Eumelus, the son of Admetus, bearing an angry grudge against him. She broke the crossbar that yoked his horses so that one horse fell to one side of the track and the other went to the other side. When this happened, the pole that connected the chariot to the crossbar suddenly dropped to the ground and Eumelus was thrown headfirst from the chariot's platform. When he landed, his mouth, nose, and elbows were stripped of skin, and his forehead and the ridges above his eyes were crushed. Laying there speechless, his eyes filled with tears.

But the son of Tydeus turned his horses aside and shot far ahead since Athena [400] had put fresh strength into them and gave him glory.

Yellow-haired Menelaus, the son of Atreus, came next behind Diomedes. Yet from behind, Antilochus called out to his father's horses. "Go!" he shouted. "Reach for your best speed! I'm not asking you to beat the horses of the battle-minded son of Tydeus—for I know that Athena has increased their running pace and has given Diomedes glory. But you must at least reach Menelaus' horses and not be left behind, or Aethe, who is but a female horse, will cover you with shame. Why are you, the best horses, falling behind? [410] Let me tell you this—and what I say will happen. If you lose the race, then today will be your last. The shepherd of men Nestor won't care for you, but he'll slaughter you both with the sharp bronze if we win an inferior prize thanks to your carelessness. But come on! Race as fast as you can, and I'll think of a way to pass them in the narrow part of the track. The plan won't fail!"

That's what Antilochus said. And the horses feared their master's threat. They raced forward for a short time until staunch Antilochus suddenly saw a section in the path where the track narrowed and dipped. [420] The ground was broken there where the winter's rain had puddled, causing it to erode and deepen. Ahead of Antilochus, Menelaus was trying to reach the narrow part first. He feared that the other man's horses would crash into him. Seeing this, Antilochus turned his horses aside to race next to him just outside the track.

The son of Atreus was afraid and shouted out, "Antilochus, you're driving recklessly! Rein in your horses, for the road is too narrow here! It'll be wider soon, and you can pass me then! But if you hit my chariot, you'll hurt both of us!"

That's what he said. But Antilochus whipped his horses [430] and drove all the faster as though he hadn't heard him. They raced side by side for about as far as a young man can hurl a discus when he's testing his strength. Finally, however, Menelaus let his horses fall behind since he was afraid they would become entangled and the chariots would crash. If that happened, they would fall to the ground while pressing on for victory.

Then from behind, yellow-haired Menelaus schooled Antilochus and said, "There's no one more destructive among all other mortals than you are! [440] So go! But know we Achaeans were wrong to consider you wise! And whatever happens, you won't get a prize without swearing an oath!"

442-542 *As Menelaus and Antilochus race on, the Argives strain to watch and see who is in first place. Idomeneus believes it is Diomedes. Ajax, the son of Oileus, angrily differs with him, saying he can't possibly see very well because he is older and his eyes are not the sharpest. He believes he sees Eumelus. Idomeneus offers to wager a tripod or cauldron to prove him wrong and so that the lesser Ajax might learn not to be so witless. What?! The son of Oileus can't let this fly. So he stands to trade taunts with Idomeneus.*

But Achilles stops him—he stops them both by telling them it is not the time to wage a word battle. He orders them to keep quiet and wait for the horses to pass the finish line.

Diomedes races through, and his comrade Sthenelus receives the prize from Achilles on his behalf. Next comes Antilochus, outstripping Menelaus by means of tricks rather than speed. Still, Menelaus was just behind. Homer asserts that if the course had been longer, the son of Atreus would have overtaken Antilochus. Meriones is a cast of the spear behind Menelaus, and Eumelus drags himself in last.

Achilles stands to offer prizes. Since Diomedes has already taken his, he moves to grant the next prize to Eumelus since, of the remaining men, Achilles believes he is the best. The Achaeans all agree to this—all but for Antilochus, who stands to protest.

543-562 "Achilles," he said, "I'll be very angry if you take my prize just because you think Eumelus' chariot and horses were somehow hindered, and he himself too, brave man that he is. But look, he should have prayed to the immortals, then he would not have come in last. Even so, if you feel sorry for him and choose to, there are piles of gold to give him in your shelter, along with bronze, [550] sheep, cattle, women, and horses. Take something from this store of goods and give him an even better prize if you want the Achaeans to approve you. As for the mare, I won't give her up. And if any man wants to fight me for her, well, let him step forward to do battle with his hands."

That's what Antilochus said. And swift-footed godlike Achilles smiled as he heard this and delighted in Antilochus, who was one of his dearest comrades in arms. And in reply, he addressed him with winged words, "Antilochus, if you want me to find Eumelus another prize, [560] I'll give him the bronze breastplate with a trim of tin running all around it—the one I took from Asteropaeus. It'll be worth much to him."

563-565 *Automedon fetches the prize for Eumelus, who is delighted to receive it.*

566-595 But Menelaus stood up in a rage—he was furiously angry with Antilochus. A herald placed the scepter in his hands and called upon the Achaeans to be silent. Then the godlike man addressed them.

[570] "Antilochus," he said, "what have you done—you who have been so sensible and wise before now? You dishonored my racing skill when you hindered my horses by darting yours ahead, even though yours are not as good as mine are. But come all you rulers and counselors of the Argives and judge between the two of us in the middle of the assembly. Yet consider the matter without favoring me. I don't want one of the bronze-clad Achaeans saying, 'Menelaus falsely beat Antilochus just because he's the stronger and better man—not because his horses were any better.' No, I will judge the matter myself. [580] And no Danaan man will blame me

since what I do will be straightforward. Come here, god-nourished Antilochus, and stand before your horses and chariot according to custom. Lay your hand on your horses and swear by the Earth-shaker that you didn't unfairly restrain my chariot."

Sensible and wise Antilochus turned to Menelaus and answered him. "Bear with me now, lord Menelaus. The truth is I am much younger than you, and you are the older and better man. You know the kind of inappropriate things young men do—[590] how their thoughts form quickly but their counsel remains undeveloped. So let your heart endure it. I myself will walk the horse over and give it to you. And if you claim more from my household, then I would rather give it to you here and at once, god-nourished man, than do wrong in the sight of the gods and be cast away from you all my days."

596-599 *Antilochus walks the horses over to Menelaus, who is delighted.*

600-611 Heart-warmed, Menelaus spoke to him with winged words. "Antilochus, I now withdraw my anger from you since you have not been witless like this or reckless before. Even so, recognize that your youth conquered your judgement this time. And more— you shouldn't try to outwit or cheat men who are better than you. Still, since you and your father and brother have done so much for me, I will give in to your entreaty and [610] give you the horse even though she is mine. That way everyone will come to know that I am not arrogant and harsh."

612-646 *Menelaus gives the mare to Antilochus and takes the cauldron for himself. Next Meriones is awarded, and since no one won last prize, Achilles gives it to Nestor, who is too old to compete in the games. Nestor rejoices to receive the prize and recalls the time he was the best of the Epeians and Pylians in boxing, wrestling, foot racing, spear throwing, and chariot racing. Now, however, he must surrender to sad old age. Nestor finishes by blessing Achilles.*

647-650 "I gladly receive this gift into my hands, and my heart re-joices that you are always kind and remember me and do not forget the honor by which it is fitting that I am honored among the Achaeans. [650] And in return for these things, may the gods give you happiness suitable to your desires."

651-894 *Next Achilles sets out the prizes for boxing. Epeius, the son of Panopeus, stands and challenges everyone to fight, declaring he will be the victor because he is the best man at boxing. He admits he's not the best in battle—but no one will beat him boxing, he declares. On the contrary, his opponent's kinsmen will have to carry him off. Euryalus stands assisted by Diomedes. Epeius strikes Euryalus on the cheek, and the boxing is over as the latter sinks to the ground.*

After the boxing, Odysseus and Telamonian Ajax wrestle. They fight to a draw after experiencing great pain. Achilles declares victory for both.

The footrace comes next. Ajax, the son of Oileus, Odysseus, and Antilochus race. They sprint out, turn, and come back. On the return, Odysseus prays to Athena, and she makes him fast and causes little Ajax to slip in cow dung, which ends up filling his mouth and nose. When he protests that the goddess helped Odysseus and hampered him, spitting out all the manure as he does so, everyone laughs at him. Taking third prize, Antilochus smiles and declares that the gods honor older men such as Odysseus. For this word, Achilles adds some gold to Antilochus' prize.

When Achilles calls upon the best for the armed combat, Diomedes and Telamonian Ajax stand. The first one to pierce the other man's skin and draw dark blood will win Sarpedon's stripped battle gear. They approach each other, eagerly desiring battle. Finally, though, fearing for Ajax, the Achaeans suggest they stop and take equal prizes.

After their duel, four men rise to throw a mass of iron that the winner will be able to use for a plow and the like back home on his farm. Polypoetes hurls it a much greater distance than do Epeius, Leonteus, and Telamonian Ajax.

When Meriones and Teucer next compete in the archery contest, Meriones wins because he vows a hecatomb to Apollo, the archer god, while Teucer does not. Therefore, Meriones hits the flying dove and takes away ten axes, sharp on both sides, whereas Teucer takes a single half axe.

Lastly, the spear throwers stand. Achilles pulls out a spear and an enormous cauldron for the prizes. When Achilles sees Agamemnon and

Meriones stand, he stops the contest and claims that there is no reason for them to throw because everyone knows Agamemnon is superior to all the men, has more power, and is the best at throwing spears. He urges Agamemnon, therefore, to take the cauldron and let Meriones have the spear.

895-897 That's what Achilles said, and the lord of men Agamemnon did not disobey. So he gave the bronze spear to Meriones, and to Agamemnon's herald, Talthybius, the hero gave the very beautiful prize.

BOOK 24

PRIAM MEETS ACHILLES
HECTOR'S BODY

IN BRIEF: *Achilles can't sleep. He abuses Hector's body by dragging it in honor of Patroclus. Although Apollo protects the body, many of the gods are upset about Achilles' behavior. They pity Hector. They want Hermes to get his body by stealing it. Zeus, however, through Thetis, arranges it so that Achilles will give up the body to Priam for a ransom. Iris informs Priam of the plan, and he, contrary to Hecuba's wishes, goes to fetch the corpse of his dead son. He is escorted by Hermes in the form of a young prince. Achilles and Priam mourn together; they admire each other. After he agrees to return him, the Achaean hero promises enough time to bury Hector before the two sides fight again. Once Priam returns to Troy, the Trojans mourn Hector, burn his corpse, and make for him a funeral mound with stones.*

THE ASSEMBLY NOW broke up, the men dispersed, and each man made his way to his swift ship. While the rest of the men thought about eating and delighting in sweet sleep, Achilles continued to think about his dear comrade and weep for him. He couldn't sleep. Instead, he turned this way and that longing for the manhood and might of Patroclus. He thought of all they had done together, and all the pain they had suffered—all they had gone through in the battles of men and on the pain-causing waves of the sea. While he remembered these things, large tears dropped from his eyes [10] as he lay now on his side, now on his back, and now face downward to the ground. Finally, he stood straight up, whirled around, and out of his mind with grief, he went to wander along the seashore.

Then, when he saw Dawn breaking over the waters of the sea and the sand of the shore, he yoked his swift horses to his chariot and tied Hector's corpse behind it to drag it around. When he had circled the burial mound of the dead son of Menoetius three times, dragging Hector behind, he stopped and went back to his shelter again, leaving the body alone in the dust, all stretched out and face downward to the ground.

19-32 Apollo protects Hector's body during this time. Many of the blessed gods pity Hector—all but Poseidon, Hera, and Athena. They're still ag-grieved with Paris, who favored Aphrodite's beauty, and with Aphrodite, who inflamed his pain-causing lust. The majority of the gods want Hermes to steal Hector's body to rescue it from Achilles' abuse. After twelve days of this abuse, Apollo rebukes the gods.

33-38 "You gods are cruel, a nuisance to men! Are you telling me that Hector never burned you the thighbones of great cattle and of un-blemished goats? And now you don't even have the courage to save his body so that his wife may look at him—and yes, his mother too, and father, child, and all the Trojan people. After seeing him, they would quickly burn him in the fire and offer him gifts and burial."

39-132 But this Achilles, he goes on, the one some of you gods want to help, he is stubborn and off in his mind; he's wild, without pity or proper shame and respect for others. Achilles has exacted the penalty of Hector's life, and still, he rages on.

Hera responds in anger. What you say is true, she admits. But Achilles is the son of an immortal goddess, and all the gods attended her marriage to Peleus. Zeus interrupts, agreeing that Achilles' honor must be greater. Still, Hector was the dearest of all the Trojans to the gods. He never failed to give Zeus gifts, the gods' rightful honor-prizes. Zeus calls upon Iris to go fetch Thetis.

When Iris comes to Thetis' cave under the sea, Thetis speaks of her great depression, her unceasing grief and sorrow. She's ashamed to be seen among the gods like this. All the same, veiled in black, she returns to Olym-pus where Zeus is with all the blessed gods who are forever. Zeus gives her orders to go talk to Achilles while Iris will go tell Priam to venture to the Achaean ships to ask for Hector's body in return for ransom.

Thetis zips down to the ships and sits by Achilles' side. She strokes him, telling him that he ought to sleep with a woman in love or do something to get over his sorrow. She reminds him that he does not have long to live, that his fate presses upon him.

133-140 "But quickly, obey me and give me your consent—for I come as Zeus' messenger. He says that the gods are angry with you, and he is angrier than all the immortals together since you keep Hector at the curved ships and will not give him up. Therefore, let him go and accept a ransom for his corpse."

In reply, swift-footed Achilles said, "So be it. The man who brings a ransom for Hector can take his corpse away—[140] if that's exactly what the Olympian Zeus himself orders."

141-223 *Zeus commands Iris to go to Priam to instruct him to enter the Achaean camp and ransom Hector. He must bring gifts to warm and cheer Achilles' heart. He declares that Priam will not be harmed. Zeus finishes by judging that Achilles is not without sense or heedless, and that he will respect a suppliant such as Priam.*

When Iris comes to the Trojans in Priam's halls, they are weeping for Hector and for the many other battle dead. She informs Priam of Zeus' great pity for him, and the plan for him to go with an older herald to Achilles' shelter in the Achaean camp. He'll be able to retrieve Hector and bring him to the City of the Dead, she says. She lastly tells Priam that Hermes will guide him to Achilles' shelter, and that Achilles will treat him well, as a suppliant.

Upon receiving these orders from Zeus, Priam has his sons prepare a wagon to carry their brother's body while he himself gathers gifts for Achilles. His wife Hecuba wonders where Priam's mind has gone. He must be iron-hearted, she insists. She predicts that Achilles will neither pity nor respect him. Therefore, she argues, they should mourn their son from afar and let Fate conclude his future—though she wishes to feed on Achilles' heart as recompense for taking her brave son's life. Despite Hecuba's impassioned plea, Priam says he must go anyway because Iris herself has commanded him to go. He accepts his fate.

224-227 "And if it is my fate to die by the ships of the bronze-clad Achaeans, then I willingly wish it for myself. Let Achilles slay me at once—if only I may first embrace my son and rid myself of this desire to weep."

228-484 *After gathering the gifts, Priam orders the Trojans to go home and lament elsewhere. He has lost the best of his sons, a fact they will soon know when the Achaeans slay the Trojans with greater ease. They will now easily sack Troy. But may he descend to Hades before this happens! Then he informs nine of his sons, including Paris, that he wishes they had died instead of Hector. Only his cowardly and base children remain, he explains, the ones who cause grief. Not one of his best sons remain—not Mestor, Troilus, or Hector, who was a god among men. They were all killed by Ares. Only the dancers, liars, and feasters remain.*

Fearful of Priam, they prepare and load the wagon. Before he goes, Hecuba asks Priam to pour out a libation of wine to Zeus and ask for an omen with outstretched hands. He does, and Zeus sends an eagle on his right-hand side flying over the city. They all rejoice at this, their spirits warmed and cheered.

As Priam and his herald Idaeus make their way from the city to the Achaean camp, Zeus calls upon Hermes to meet the two Trojans and guide them to Achilles' shelter. The god obeys and meets them by the river past Ilios' mound.

In the form of a young prince, Hermes offers to defend Priam. The old man reminds him of his own father, he says. Priam praises him and declares that his parents must surely be happy. The god asks if Priam is escaping Troy to another land with his treasure since Hector, the best of all Trojans, has died. Upon hearing this, Priam asks Hermes to identify himself. Hermes declares he is one of the Myrmidons, the seventh son of wealthy Polyctor, and that he has seen Hector fight many times in battle that confers glory on men. He is Achilles' attendant, he finishes. Priam asks how Hector fares. Has Achilles given him to the dogs? No, says the god. His flesh hasn't yet decayed; worms don't eat him. He's by Achilles' ship. And even though Achilles daily drags him behind his chariot, his body is still marvelously intact. His many wounds have closed, and blood doesn't stain his body since the blessed gods care for him. Priam assumes they take care of him because

Hector was ever mindful of the gods. He gives the god a gift and asks him to take him to Achilles' shelter. Hermes refuses the gift but takes him.

Causing the guardsmen to sleep, they pass over the trench and through the wall and to Achilles' shelter, the one the Myrmidons built for their lord, made of fir and soft thatch. Finally, once they pass through the massive door of Achilles' shelter, and once inside, Hermes reveals he is an immortal god sent by Zeus. He goes on to say that he must leave—it would be shameful to receive face-to-face affection and gifts from mortal men.

Priam enters and grasps Achilles by the knees in supplication, kissing the hands that slaughtered his own son. The young hero marvels as he beholds the old man.

485-551 Priam entreated Achilles and spoke a word to him. "Remember your own father, godlike Achilles, who must be about my age and therefore crossing the threshold of destructive old age. It is possible that the men who dwell nearby oppress him. And since you are gone, there is no one to ward off ruin and destruction. [490] Yet when he hears that you are still alive, I imagine he is glad and rejoices in his spirit, and his days are full of hope that he'll eventually see his dear son come home to him from the land of Troy.

"But I—an ill-fated man in every way—had the bravest sons in all of Troy. Yet now there is not one of them left. I had fifty sons when the Achaeans came here. Nineteen of them were from a single woman, and the others were born to me by the women of my household. Fierce Ares struck down most of them. And you recently killed the only one who served to guard our city and all of us—[500] you killed Hector when he was defending his homeland. Therefore, I have now come to the Achaean ships to retrieve his body with a great ransom. Respect the gods, Achilles, and have pity on me, remembering your own father. I am worthy of your pity since I have endured what no other mortal man on earth has yet endured—I have stretched out my hand in supplication to the bearded chin of the man who killed my sons."

That's what Priam said. And the heart of Achilles yearned to weep as he thought about his own father. He took the old man's hand and moved him gently away. So they both sat remembering.

While Priam sat huddled at Achilles' feet, [510] crying for man-slaying Hector, Achilles wept for his father and yet again for Patroclus. And the house was filled with their lamentation.

But when godlike Achilles was satisfied with weeping, and he felt the desire for it to leave his heart and limbs, he stood and raised the old man by the hand in pity for his gray hair and his gray beard.

Then he addressed him with winged words. "Ah, wretched man, you have endured so much evil. Tell me: how did you take it upon yourself to come alone to the Achaean ships [520] and enter the presence of the man who has killed and stripped so many of your brave sons? Your heart must be made of iron!

"But come now and sit on this seat, and let us allow the pain and mourning in our spirits to rest—because weeping will do us no good. For while the gods plan sorrow upon sorrow for wretched mortals, they live without any sorrow or grief. Their life is a life without care. On the floor of Zeus' house, there are two jars from which he gives gifts. The one is filled with evil and the other with good. To whomever Zeus, who delights in thunder, [530] mixes and gives out both, that man will meet now with good and now with evil fortune. But for the man who only receives evil gifts—ah, that man will suffer shameful treatment. Evil poverty and hunger will drive him back and forth over the earth, and neither the gods nor men will honor him.

"In a similar way the gods gave glorious gifts to Peleus from the moment of his birth. He ruled over the Myrmidons, surpassing all other men in happiness and wealth, and even though he was a mortal man, they gave him a goddess for his bride. But a god gave evil to him too, for he has no offspring in his halls [540] except for one son who is destined to an unfortunate end. Nor may I take care of him now that he is growing old since I remain encamped here, far from my father at Troy, to be a distress and trouble for you and your children.

"And you too, old man, I have heard that you were once happy. They say that in wealth and number of offspring you surpassed the rulers of all the lands surrounding your own—Lesbos, the seat of Makar, toward the sea; Phrygia, inland; and all those men who dwell upon the boundless Hellespont. But from the day when the Uranian gods unloaded this misery on you, war and slaughter have surrounded your city. Bear up and do not go on lamenting without end in your spirit. [550] You will not accomplish anything for your son by going on—you can't raise him from the dead."

552-655 *Responding to his earlier command, Priam asks Achilles not to have him sit. Rather, he wants to see Hector now and give over the ransom. The Achaean hero tells Priam not to rouse him to anger. He will return Hector in time—because Zeus through Thetis commanded him to do so. And he knows a god led Priam to his ship and shelter. Achilles is afraid he'll be angry with Priam and slay him even though the old man is a suppliant.*

Fearing the Achaean hero, Priam obeys. Accompanied by Automedon and Alcimus (that is, Alcimedon), Achilles unhitches the wagon, takes the treasure, and escorts Priam's herald, Idaeus, inside. Then he orders his women to wash and anoint Hector. When they put him on the wagon and cover him with a robe, Achilles promises Patroclus a fitting portion of the ransom.

Returning inside to Priam, he reports what has happened and offers the ruler of Troy a meal—since even Niobe, he relates, ate during her time of grief after her six sons and six daughters died thanks to her indiscretion in comparing her number of offspring to Leto's two, Apollo and Artemis. Achilles kills a sheep, and they feast on roasted lamb and bread, washing it down with shining wine. When done, Priam admires Achilles' beauty, like the gods, and the young hero gazes at him in a similar manner. Finally, the Trojan king asks his host to show him his bed. Achilles orders his comrades and female slaves to make for him a bed of soft fleece and purple throws. Then he queries Priam about his needs.

656-667 "But come and tell me this—and give me an accurate count. How many days will you need to celebrate godlike Hector's funeral? I ask to know how many days I should remain here at the ships holding back the army."

Then the old man godlike Priam answered him, [660] "If you are truly willing to let us perform the funeral rites for godlike Hector, then in doing so, Achilles, you would be doing us a favor. You know how we are pent up within our city, and how far it is for us to fetch wood from the mountain. Moreover, the people live in constant fear.

"Here's the count: we'll mourn Hector for nine days in the halls of my house. Then on the tenth day, we'll honor him with the funeral rites, and the people will feast. Finally, we'll pile a mound over him. And on the twelfth day, we'll fight if we must."

668-724 Achilles assures the old man that it will happen as he wishes, and they go to sleep, Priam in the outer shelter and Achilles in the innermost part.

As all the gods and men sleep, Hermes considers how to guide Priam safely away. In the end, he convinces Priam he must go now or face other dangers. They go. And from Mount Pergamus, beautiful Cassandra sees Priam coming to Troy with Hector's body. She cries out to the Trojans to greet them as they come through the gates.

Hecuba and Andromache meet them first, the queen mother and Hector's dear wife, along with the crowd of people. When they reach the house and set him on a bed, singers lead the threnody, the song of lamentation. The women join in the weeping, white-armed Andromache among them. She holds Hector's head as she speaks.

725-745 "Husband-man," she wept, "you have died young and leave me a widow in the halls of your house. And our own child — the one we ill-fated parents gave birth to—he's still an infant. I fear he will never reach his prime. Before then the city will be sacked — for its guardian has been destroyed, [730] you who were so diligent to keep us safe, all the wives and infant children. But now the women will be quickly carried away as captives to the hollow ships. And I—Hector—I will be among them. And you, my child, you will follow me, and you will be forced to work at shameful tasks, suffering under some ruthless master. Or it is possible some Achaean man will take you by the hand and throw you from the gated walls to a pathetic death. He'll do this out of anger, to avenge some brother, father, or son whom Hector killed—for many have fallen to the dust at his hands because your father was not gentle in this miserable war. [740] This is why the people mourn him throughout the city.

"Dear Hector! You have left unspeakable sorrow to your parents, and my own grief is greatest of all since you did not stretch out your arms and hands to embrace me as you lay dying. Nor did you speak to me any words that I might have remembered as I shed tears in the days and nights to come."

746-776 Priam's mother, Hecuba, is next to speak her sorrow. She is pleased, at least, that Hector has been returned to her as if freshly slain. Helen laments after Hecuba, revealing how dear Hector was to her, the dearest of all of Paris' brothers. She wishes she had died before coming to Troy. She remarks that it has been twenty years since their departure from her fatherland. And so many times has Hector defended her with kindness from the reproaches of other Trojans. She's unlucky to have lost Hector! Following her, the crowd of people moan in lamentation for Hector. Then Priam stands forward.

777-804 The old man Priam spoke a word to the people. "Now is the time to carry wood to the city. There's no need to fear a cunning Argive ambush, for when Achilles [780] sent me away from the dark ships, he promised me that the Achaeans would do no harm to us until after the twelfth dawn had come."

That's what Priam said. And right away they yoked their oxen and mules and gathered before the city. They brought in piles of wood for nine days. And when the tenth dawn appeared bringing light to mortals, then they carried out bold Hector with many falling tears. And coming to the great pyre, they situated his corpse on its peak and set it afire.

When the early-born rosy-fingered Dawn appeared on the eleventh day, the people gathered again around the great pyre of glorious Hector. [790] And when they had assembled, they first quenched the fire with wine, wherever it was burning with might, and then his brothers and comrades collected his white bones while shedding tears.

They wrapped the bones in soft purple robes and put them in a golden urn. Then they quickly placed the urn in an empty hole and covered it over with large stones fitted closely together. Next, they rapidly piled up a mound with watchmen stationed on every side [800] in case the well-greaved Achaeans attacked.

When they had piled up the mound, they went back again into the city. And when they were gathered in an orderly manner, the people celebrated a glorious feast in the house of Priam, the king nurtured by Zeus.

This is how the Trojans conducted the funeral rites for horse-taming Hector.

POINTS OF WISDOM
& WAYS OF PRACTICE
FROM HOMER

- Plan of Life Following Homer

- Points of Wisdom from Homer

- Ways of Practice Following Homer

PLAN OF LIFE
FOLLOWING HOMER

AS WITH ANY other plan, a plan of life is made to accomplish many goals or possibly just one significant goal. In the case of the "Plan of Life Following Homer," the goal is bare survival on the one side and happiness and thriving on the other—for we do not merely wish to live but to live well (as a later Greek philosopher would say). The following plan consists of the most significant Homeric goals and practices from both the Iliad *and* Odyssey.

1. **Act to survive.** Keep in mind that bare life is worth more than any amount of silver or gold. When life is gone, it is gone forever. Even a simple life is a good life. Cherish life. Be. Live.

2. **Be the best; act to thrive.** Strive for excellence, to be outstanding. Do your best to speak and act well in every situation. Flourish! Seek happiness, which is the satisfaction of what you truly desire. Take delight in abundance and the many good things of life. Generously request the happiness of others.

3. **Act for glory; be noble and honorable.** Flee from disgrace. Do what is necessary to build a noble reputation. Most of all, do that which is noble and honorable so that yours will be a glorious memorial. Readily acknowledge the honor and glory of others.

4. **Be home oriented.** Clearly define what home is for you—your family, your community, an ideal, a way of life. Beware of that which causes you to forget home. Yearn for home. Return home.

5. **Cooperate with others to survive and thrive.** Be loyal to your family. Be a faithful friend. Fulfill your duty as an ally. Fight alongside. Stand guard. Work together. Kindly host others. Be an amenable guest. Rule when necessary; submit to the rule of others (again, when necessary). Give advice; receive counsel. Whatever it is, play your role well and faithfully.

6. **Compete with others to survive and thrive.** Be courageous. Fight forward. Take a stand. Be angry when necessary—but quick to make amends and reconcile. Be careful when boasting. Engage in battle—but only if you must. Be fair.

7. **Cultivate your own strengths and skills.** Keep in mind human variation, that different people have different strengths and skills. Know yours. Graciously recognize those of others. Grasping the wisdom of difference, perform your own function well.

8. **Practice wisdom; deliberate well.** Pursue knowledge. Hunt for good counsel. Know in order to deliberate; deliberate in order to resolve; resolve in order to act. Think and speak in order to act.

9. **Be reconciled to the human condition.** Remember that humans are not gods, that we suffer pain and hardship and grow old and die. Choose to embrace these facts. Such a reconciliation paradoxically fosters a sense of freedom—the liberty to be human, the freedom to live the *when, how,* and *where* of one's fated role.

10. **Endure well.** Cultivate a spirit that can endure suffering, sorrow, and misfortune. Employ Odysseus' four-point endurance method: self-talk, recollection, deliberation, and command. Remember you must endure—you have no other choice.

11. **Desire well.** Learn how to deal with temptation in order to restrain your desires. Practice moderation—measure. Sail by the Island of the Sun; don't stop. Bear in mind that recklessness, which is often caused by out-of-control desires, leads to destruction. Restraint, by contrast, is liberating. Moderation will get you home.

12. **Acknowledge the divine.** Recognize the power that is behind all things. Strong and wise, it is how all things have come into existence. Dynamic, it is at peace. Concerned, it remains aloof. The divine cares for justice. Look to the divine for guidance, for the divine knows all things. Pray with hands outstretched to heaven.

POINTS OF WISDOM
FROM HOMER

The following points of wisdom come from Homer's Iliad *and* Odyssey. *Each begins in italics with a single word or more indicating the point's topic. For more points of wisdom from Homer organized by topic, read The Classics Cave's* The Wisdom & Way of Homer.

Happiness. Odysseus said, "Lord Zeus, may Telemachus be happy among men, and may everything happen as he desires in his heart."

The happiness of marriage. Odysseus said to Nausicaa, "May the gods grant you as much as your heart eagerly desires—a man for a husband, and a house. And may a noble unity of mind and feeling accompany these. For nothing is greater and nothing better than when a man and woman dwell in their household with the same feelings, thoughts, and mind—a huge pain to their enemies and joy to their friends. Their glory is very well known."

Human delight. "Different men delight in different things."

True delight. Odysseus said, "There is nothing sweeter to a man than his own homeland and his parents. . . . I declare that there is nothing better or more delightful than when a whole people join in merry festivity, with the guests sitting side by side listening to the singer, while before them the table is loaded with bread and meats, and the cupbearer draws wine from the mixing bowl and pours it into all the goblets. In my mind, this seems to be the most beautiful thing."

Fulfilment. Menelaus said, "I declare that all things find satisfaction—sleep, love, sweet song, and the stately dance. With these things a man hopes to find fulfilment."

The excellence imperative. Nestor said, "Old Peleus insistently ordered his son Achilles to always be the best and to stand out among other men."

The glory imperative. Hector said, "I have learned always to be brave and to fight in the front ranks among the Trojans, winning great glory for my father and myself. . . . Let me not then die ingloriously and without a struggle, but let me first do some great thing that men to come will hear about!"

True glory. Laodamas said, "There is no greater glory than that which a man has from the accomplishments of his own hands and feet."

The human condition. Glaucus said, "Men come and go as the leaves do year after year upon the trees. The wind sheds the autumn leaves upon the ground, but when the spring returns, the forest buds again with fresh ones. The generations of mankind are like this. The new generation springs up as the old is passing away."

The human condition. Apollo said, "Miserable mortals flourish now like green leaves in springtime, eating whatever the earth provides, but soon waste away and decay, falling lifeless to the ground."

Human variety. Polydamas said to Hector, "Some god has granted you skill in war, but . . . you can't win in everything. The gods have given to one man skill in war and to another skill in the dance. To others they've given the ability to play the lyre or sing. To still others far-seeing Zeus gives a noble mind."

Death. Athena said to Telemachus, "Death that is common to all men is certain. Not even the gods have the power to defend a loved man against it when the destructive fate of death finally drops a man to the dust."

The gods. Menelaus said, "The gods know all things. . . . Father Zeus— you are, they say, above all the other gods and men in wisdom, and by whom all these things have come into existence."

The human need for the divine. Peisistratus said, "All men need the gods."

God-dependent life. Hector said, "Everything rests with the gods."

God-dependent delight. Eumaeus said, "Eat and enjoy the food we have. The god gives on the one hand and withholds on the other depending on his spirit's wish, for the god is able to do all things."

God-dependent happiness and wealth. Odysseus said, "As for the happiness of wealth, it's up to the gods to give it or not."

Inescapable fate. Hector said, "No man has gone down to Hades beyond what Fate had decreed. But I declare that from the moment of his birth, no man has ever been able to run away from his own fate, neither the coward nor the brave man."

Zeus' two jars of fortune. Achilles said to Priam, the king of Troy, "On the floor of Zeus' house, there are two jars from which he gives gifts. The one is filled with evil and the other with good. To whomever Zeus, who delights in thunder, mixes and gives out both, that man will meet now with good and now with evil fortune. But for the man who only receives evil gifts—ah, that man will suffer shameful treatment. Evil poverty and hunger will drive him back and forth over the earth, and neither the gods nor men will honor him."

Life's great value. Achilles said, "My life is worth more to me than all the wealth of Ilium, the riches it had before the Achaeans attacked it, when there was yet peace. It is worth more than all the treasure that lies on the stone floor of Apollo's temple beneath the cliffs of Pytho. Cattle and fat sheep may be carried off as booty, and tripods and yellow-headed horses may be acquired, but when a man's life has once left him, it cannot be brought back again or won by force."

The high price of excessive riches. Menelaus said, "I have wandered and suffered much over eight years to bring these riches home in my ships. . . . If only I had stayed home! I wish that I had only a third of my possessions and that all those who perished on the plain of Troy, far from horse-nourishing Argos, were still safe and alive."

Simple life is better than death. Achilles said, "Do not speak to me lightly about death, glorious Odysseus. If only I could, I would choose to live upon the earth, working as a day laborer for some other man, some landless man who doesn't have much of what it takes to live. I'd rather be that man, Odysseus, than rule over all the rotting dead."

Hunger. Odysseus said, "There is nothing more shameful and dog-like than one's hateful belly. It calls upon a man to remember it by absolute necessity, even if he is very oppressed and is bearing much grief and misfortune in his heart and mind, as I am now carrying all the sorrow in mine. My belly always insists that I eat and drink, and bids me lay aside all memory of my sorrows and dwell on re-plenishing itself. . . . There is no hiding a hungry belly. It is an ac-cursed, destructive thing, which introduces many evils to all men. It is because of hunger that well-benched ships are made ready to sail the barren sea and carry misery and sorrow to hostile men."

Human responsibility. Zeus said to the gods, "How shameful it is that the mortals even now blame the gods! From us, they say, come all sorts of bad things. But it is through their own recklessness that they have sorrows beyond those which are fated."

The need to restrain desire. Tiresias said to Odysseus, "You may still reach home, though suffering misfortune, if you will choose to restrain your own desires and curb those of your comrades when you reach the island of Thrinacia. . . . There you will find the grazing cattle and fat sheep of Helios the Sun . . . . If you leave these alone, . . . then you may still reach Ithaca, though suffering hardship and misfortune. But if you hurt them, then I predict ruin—destruction—for your ship and death for your comrades."

The endurance rule. Odysseus said, "But pity me . . . I have come upon you first after much suffering and toil." In reply, Nausicaa said, "Stranger, . . . since Olympian Zeus himself dispenses fortune and happiness to men, to both the good and the bad as he wills, whether he be brave or a coward, noble or base—so I believe that surely he has given misfortune to you. Regardless, you must endure it either way."

The need to endure. Athena said to Odysseus, "You must endure the trouble and pain—you have no choice. . . . In silence suffer all the pain and distress, and patiently bear the violent abuse of men."

Being weak, humans must endure. Odysseus said to Amphinomus, "Of all things that breathe and move along the earth, there's nothing weaker than a human being—I tell you, the earth nurtures no frailer thing. For as long as the gods give him excellence, and as long as his knees stand strong, he thinks he'll never suffer misfortune in the days to come. But when the blessed gods send him misery, he must bear it with an enduring spirit even though it is against his will."

Craft over strength. The gods . . . beheld the artful skill of inventive Hephaestus. And glancing at the other one would say, "Bad deeds do not thrive. The slow overtakes the swift—just as now Hephaestus, slow as he is, has seized Ares, even though he is the swiftest of the gods who hold Olympus. Lame, he has seized him by cunning craft. Ares must pay the fine for adultery."

Wisdom and cunning. Nestor said to Antilochus, "The horses making up the other teams are swifter than yours are, but the other men do not know how to plan a race better than you do. Therefore, dear son, fill your mind with wisdom and cunning of every sort so that you don't lose out on winning a prize. The woodcutter is far better because of wisdom and cunning than he is because of strength. And by wisdom and cunning, too, does a steersman rightly guide a swift ship that is buffeted by the winds on the wine-faced sea. And by wisdom and cunning does one charioteer prevail over another."

Act! Patroclus said to Meriones, "Why do you . . . speak in this way? The Trojans will not fall back from the corpse just because you speak words of reproach to them. . . . Rather, in our hands is the battle's outcome. . . . So, we must not multiply words, but we must fight."

Act! Nestor said to the Achaeans, "Talking will get us nowhere. Stand, therefore, son of Atreus, and lead the Argives into battle."

Strife. Strife, who causes much sorrow, rejoiced as she beheld the two armies. . . . Strife is man-slaying Ares' sister and comrade. She starts small and grows bigger and taller until her head is sky-high and her feet drag along the earth. Strife lobbed distressful contention between them, and when it came among them, it increased their lamentation.

May strife perish! Achilles said to Thetis, "May strife utterly perish from among both the gods and men, and anger that incites a wise man to be savagely upset—an anger that drips like very sweet honey and expands like smoke in the breast of a man, growing ever larger. Even so has the lord of men Agamemnon now provoked me to anger."

Conquering anger. Phoenix said to Achilles, "You must conquer your great and angry temper, Achilles. It is not fitting to have a ruthless heart. No, even the gods are able to bend, the gods who are better."

Courage. "The bold and courageous man does better in all things."

Be brave! The son of Atreus, Agamemnon, ranged among the throng of men and called out, "Be men, friends! Have a brave heart! And feel shame before one another when you are fighting. More men live when there's such shame. But when men shamelessly flee, there's neither glory nor strength to avert danger."

Cooperate for strength "Remember, battle excellence comes even for very weak and cowardly men when they band together."

Two is better than one. Diomedes said "If some other man were to go along with me, there would be greater hope and confidence. When two go together, one apprehends before the other whatever advantage there may be. On the other hand, if one is alone, even when he discerns something, his mind is slow, and his cunning is inadequate."

WAYS OF PRACTICE
FOLLOWING HOMER

The following ways of practice, inspired by Homer's Iliad, *are offered with the goal of practice in mind, the application of ancient wisdom to our contemporary ways and lives. We hope they will serve, in some small measure, as a source of inspiration and motivation. Use them to contemplate your life—where you are now, where you are going, and how you can better get there. For these exercises and practices and other similar ones, pick up The Classics Cave's* Homer Workbook & Journal. *One last note. You will likely find that the space given for responses is not enough. If so, jot your thoughts and practices down in a separate place.*

PRACTICE 1: THE EXCELLENCE IMPERATIVE—BEING THE (MY) BEST

The ancient Greeks competed with one another to be the best, striving for excellence or virtue (*aretē*), to be outstanding in all they did—whether in running a long race or crafting lively poetry or building beautiful buildings or giving wise counsel. What about myself? How do I strive for excellence?—relative to myself or to others?

"Old Peleus enjoined his child Achilles to always be the best and to stand out among other men."—Nestor, the wise son of Neleus

Speaking to Diomedes, Glaucus, the son of Hippolochus, said, "My father sent me to Troy and insistently ordered me to always be the best and to stand out among other men and not to dishonor or shame the family of my fathers, who were the best in Ephyre and in wide Lycia."

Shooting for my best • Describe what it would be like to seek excellence in two areas of your life (for example, your home or work life; your life as a friend or family member; your extracurricular life; etc.).

Life area 1: _____

Life area 2: _____

Practice It • Identify *concrete, specific, realistic* ways you can practice excellence (being the best or outstanding) in these two areas of your life—today, this week, throughout the month. Then practice!

Practice (life area 1): _____

_____

_____

Practice (life area 2): _____

_____

_____

Evaluate It • Now that you have identified two areas and practiced for a set period of time, evaluate your progress. How did things go?

Evaluation (life area 1): _____

_____

_____

Evaluation (life area 1): _____

_____

_____

PRACTICE 2: LETTING GO OF ANGER

As mentioned in the Introduction, Homer's *Iliad* is all about anger. Wrath or anger itself is an expression of desire—*against* something (I don't want that!—to be a nobody!) or *for* something (I want that!—to be somebody!). As such, it is useful in defending what we have or who we are, as well as getting for us what we want to have or securing who we want to be. The problem is that anger often comes at a high cost to us and others.

"Wrath! Sing, goddess about the destructive wrath of Achilles, the son of Peleus—the anger that caused so much pain and suffering among the Achaeans."—Homer

We know from reading the *Iliad* that we must let go of our anger. We must somehow conquer it. If we don't, harm is sure to follow.

Phoenix said to Achilles, "You must conquer your great and angry temper, Achilles. It is not fitting to have a ruthless heart. No, even the gods are able to bend, the gods who are better."

Turning to Agamemnon, Nestor said, "And you, son of Atreus, check your wrath. I implore you to let go of your anger against this man, who is a towering wall for the Achaeans against all the evils of war."

But letting go is hard. *Really* hard. So how can we do it?

Counting the Cost · To conquer anger, we must first be convinced of its negative effects. Describe how anger can be destructive (generally speaking). Specifically, how has *my* anger been destructive?

_____

_____

_____

_____

Analyze It · If anger is really all about desire (as it was for Achilles), then it would be helpful to see our anger in terms of what desire(s) it is expressing. Think of a recent time you were angry or irritated (no matter how little or great). What did you want?—wish to avoid?

_____

_____

_____

Replace It ▪ As we learn from Odysseus, we can conquer anger by replacing it with positives, with friendliness, kindness, and the like.

Odysseus said to Achilles, "Good friend, on the day when your father Peleus sent you to Agamemnon, he gave this command, saying, 'My son, . . . restrain the proud temper in your chest, for friendliness, kindness, and gentle-mindedness are better. And let go of mischief-plotting strife so that the Argives . . . may honor you all the more.' . . . Even now I call on you to put away from you your bitter wrath. Agamemnon is offering many worthy gifts, so let go of your anger." (See also *Iliad* 16.73)

Notice how Odysseus explains that replacing anger with positives will also get for Achilles the honor he wants (to be somebody). Anger is not the only strategy we can employ to defend what is ours and get what we want. Rather, there are for more positive ways to go about it, positive in the sense that they cause benefit rather than harm. We see the same in Hephaestus' words to Hera: "If you lay hold of Zeus with soft and conciliatory words, then the Olympian will be appeased, and at once he will be gracious to us."

WRITE A POSTCARD ▪ Remember a time you were angry. Recall the harm it caused. Explain the desire that was lurking behind the anger. What could have you felt, thought, or done to replace the anger?

Dear _____

Sincerely,

MY CONQUERING ANGER PLAN

In the future, I will conquer anger by . . .

(Be sure to consider the cost of anger, the desire behind anger, and what positives can replace anger—among other points of consideration)

PRACTICE 3: COOPERATION—JOINING WITH OTHERS FOR SUCCESS

It is a cliché to say that "two are better than one." But clichés often reveal essential truths. Two *are* better than one—wiser, stronger, braver. We see this truth in the following lines from the *Iliad*:

Diomedes said to the Achaean men, "Nestor, my heart and proud spirit urge me to enter the nearby enemy camp of the Trojan men. Still, if some other man were to go along with me, there would be greater hope and confidence. When two go together, one apprehends before the other whatever advantage there may be. On the other hand, if one is alone, even when he discerns something, his mind is slow, and his cunning is inadequate."

Poseidon (disguised as Thoas) said to Idomeneus, "Take up your weapons and come here. We must go with all haste in the hope that we may profit the others, though we are only two. But remember, battle excellence comes even for very weak and cowardly men when they band together."

Agamemnon said to Nestor, "If we can join together in counsel and be united, then the Trojans won't be able to delay their evil demise for even the smallest amount of time."

The Past • Recall two times in the past when you joined with some-
one or a group and thereby you (along with the others) became bet-
ter in some sense. How were you stronger? Wiser? Better?

Time 1: _____

_____

_____

Time 2: _____

_____

_____

The Present or the Future (Practice) • List and describe how you
can cooperate with others now or in the future *to be better*.

_____

_____

_____

_____

_____

Cooperation and Dealing with Anger • Returning to the last prac-
tice for a moment, anger is something that pits us against others.
Consider how you can join with others rather than pitting yourself
against them in anger—that is, how you can *replace anger* with co-
operation. Be specific.

_____

_____

_____

_____

OTHER MATTERS OF INTEREST
RELATED TO HOMER AND THE *ILIAD*

THE CAST OF GODS AND MEN
A QUICK REFERENCE

GENERAL CATEGORIES OF BEINGS

GODS are human-like beings that are immortal and ageless because of their consumption of wine-like nectar and bread-like ambrosia. In general, the gods are more powerful than humans. They are glorious beings who live an easy and blessed life without care.

HUMAN BEINGS are mortals (their defining attribute). They age and die (in part at least) because they drink wine and eat bread. Although some humans live a relatively easy life, human existence is generally marked by toil and struggle, misfortune and wretchedness.

IMMORTAL GODS AND GODDESSES

Achaean-favoring gods and goddesses

ATHENA: daughter of Zeus (and Metis), Athena was born from her father's head. She appears as a wise warrior goddess in the *Iliad*, assisting and fighting on behalf of Diomedes, Odysseus, and Achilles, among others. She defeats Ares and Aphrodite during the battle of the gods. Finally, disguised as the Trojan Deiphobus, Athena convinces Hector to stand and fight against Achilles.

HEPHAESTUS: son of Zeus and Hera, husband of Charis in the *Iliad*. (Aphrodite shows up as his wife in the *Odyssey*.) The smith god and consummate craftsman, Hephaestus skillfully makes Achilles' shield and armor at Thetis' request. Limited by various bodily disabilities, including disabled legs and feet, Hephaestus is a wise god, who gives advice and outsmarts other gods. As fire, he fights against and defeats the divine river Xanthus during the battle of the gods.

HERA: daughter of Cronus and Rhea, sister-wife of Zeus. Of all the immortals in the *Iliad*, Hera most demands the ruin of Troy. She does thanks to Paris' judgment against her and Athena—and in favor of Aphrodite—in the beauty pageant held at Thetis and Peleus' wedding. To secure Troy's utter destruction, Hera jealously follows the course of the Trojan war and even deceives Zeus with love and sleep to get her way. Hera thrashes Artemis in the battle of the gods.

HERMES: son of Zeus and Maia. In the guise of a young nobleman, the cunning god Hermes guides Priam and his herald, Idaeus, to Achilles' shelter to retrieve Hector's corpse. During the battle of the gods, he backs out of a fight with Leto.

POSEIDON: son of Cronus and Rhea, brother of Zeus. God of the sea, Poseidon is the Earth-shaker. He fights against the Trojans because of a long-held grudge against Priam's father, Laomedon. He claims equality with his brothers Zeus and Hades on account of the prior three-fold division of the world—accomplished by lot—when Zeus won the sky, Poseidon the sea, and Hades the underworld. Poseidon lines up against Apollo in the battle of the gods, though they never actually fight.

Trojan-favoring gods and goddesses

ARES: son of Zeus and Hera. As the handsome though terrible god of war, Ares is surprisingly and even comically weak and foolish, defeated by Athena and Diomedes twice. (In the *Odyssey*, Ares, strong and quick, is outplayed by the intelligence and craft of the slow and disabled Hephaestus, when he has an affair with Hephaestus' wife, Aphrodite.) Ares is hated by his own father as well as his father's daughter, Athena, who bowls him over in the battle of the gods.

APOLLO: son of Zeus and Leto, twin brother of Artemis. The archer god, "far-shooting" and furious Apollo is responsible for the disease that plagues the Achaeans at the opening of the *Iliad*. He's the chief male divinity in favor of the Trojans. During the battle of the gods, Apollo suggests to Poseidon that they should not fight over miserable mortals who come and go like the leaves, alive one moment and dead the next.

APHRODITE: daughter of Zeus and Dione. (In Homer's *Odyssey*, she appears as the wife of Hephaestus and lover of Ares.) Goddess of marriage and love, Aphrodite plays many roles in the *Iliad*. She defends her favorites Paris, who judged her most beautiful, and Aeneas, her son, by spiriting them away from the battle at different times. She also provides a love charm to Hera, who uses it to seduce Zeus. After being wounded by Diomedes while helping Aeneas, her mother tells Aphrodite to endure, and her father says that her work is love not war. Athena defeats Aphrodite in the battle of the gods.

ARTEMIS: daughter of Zeus and Leto. Like her twin brother, Apollo, Artemis is an archer goddess. After Diomedes wounds Aeneas with a great stone, she assists her mother in healing him. In the great and comic battle between the gods, Hera challenges Artemis and thrashes her, dashing her weapons to the ground.

LETO: daughter of the Titans Coeus and Phoebe, mother of Apollo and Artemis by Zeus. With the help of Artemis, Leto heals Aeneas after Diomedes wounds him with a stone. In the battle of the gods, she faces Hermes, who backs down from her without a fight.

XANTHUS: the divine river flowing nearby Troy that is called the Scamander by mortals. Xanthus nearly drowns Achilles when the latter stops up his flow with Trojan corpses. As fire, the smith god Hephaestus defeats watery Xanthus during the battle of the gods.

Other gods and goddesses in brief

ATĒ OR BEWILDERMENT: Bewilderment personified; she is the blindness sent by the gods.

CHARIS: wife of Hephaestus (in the *Iliad*). She is one of the Graces or *Charites*. Charis hosts Thetis when the latter goddess comes to Olympus to obtain new armor for Achilles.

ERINYES (Furies): goddesses of retribution, the Erinyes make the gods and men pay for wrongdoing.

ERIS (STRIFE): sister and comrade of Ares, she is the goddess of strife. Eris loves nothing more than any kind of competition—particularly war—fueled by anger or jealousy. She "starts small and grows bigger and taller until her head is sky-high and her feet drag along the earth."

IRIS: messenger of the gods, particularly of Zeus and Hera.

OCEANUS (Okeanos): Titan son of Gaia and Ouranos, brother-husband of Tethys. He is the great river that surrounds the world.

THETIS: daughter of Nereus, the so-called "old man of the sea," mother of Achilles by Peleus. She asks Zeus to honor Achilles by helping the Trojans. The goal is to harm Agamemnon, who insulted Achilles' honor. Going to Olympus, she fetches Achilles' newly-crafted armor from the smith god Hephaestus.

ZEUS: son of Cronus and Rhea, brother-husband of Hera. Zeus is the "father of men and gods" and claims to be the most powerful and best of the gods. Although neutral in many ways, Zeus nevertheless helps the Trojans due to Thetis' request to honor Achilles. It is Zeus who dispenses good and bad fortune to humans from the two jars that sit on the floor of his house on Olympus.

HUMAN BEINGS

The Achaeans

ACHILLES: son of the mortal man Peleus and the immortal goddess

Thetis, father of Neoptolemus. Achilles leads the Myrmidons. The *Iliad* is largely about Achilles' anger. When Agamemnon takes his honor-prize Briseis and thereby dishonors him, Achilles begs his mother to help him get revenge. This revenge leads to much Achaean suffering, and, ultimately, to his friend Patroclus' death. Achilles slays Hector because he killed Patroclus. After abusing Hector's corpse, Achilles returns his body to his father, Priam.

AGAMEMNON: son of Atreus, brother of Menelaus, husband of Clytemnestra, father of Orestes and other children. Agamemnon is the leader of the Mycenaeans and the chief leader of the Achaean army at Troy. It is his refusal to return the girl Chryseis to her father that leads an angry Apollo to cast a plague down on the Achaeans. When the seer Calchas blames him for the plague, and when Achilles suggests he return Chryseis to her father, Agamemnon angrily demands another girl to take her place. Consequently, he seizes Briseis from Achilles. He later regrets his "reckless blindness" and makes amends.

AJAX (THE LESSER OR LITTLE): son of Oileus. The lesser Ajax leads the Locrians. Fast on his feet and a great warrior, Ajax argues with Idomeneus over who is in first place in the chariot race during Patroclus' funeral games.

AJAX (TELAMONIAN): son of Telamon, half-brother of Teucer the archer. One of the Achaeans' best warriors, Telamonian Ajax is the leader of the men from Salamis. Early on, he duels with Hector to a draw. He later drops him in battle with a great stone. Ajax's signature defense is a tall shield. Alongside Odysseus and Phoenix, he serves as part of the embassy to Achilles.

DIOMEDES: son of Tydeus. Along with Sthenelus and Euryalus, Diomedes leads the men from Argos, Tiryns, and the surrounding cities and land. Among the greatest of the Achaean warriors, Diomedes is sometimes paired up with Odysseus. Diomedes fights both men and the gods in Book 5 of the *Iliad*. During battle he discovers that he is the guest-friend of the Trojan ally Glaucus of Lycia.

IDOMENEUS: son of Deucalion. Eager for battle, Idomeneus leads the men from the island of Crete. He disputes with the Lesser Ajax during Patroclus' funeral games. His best friend is Meriones.

MENELAUS: son of Atreus, brother of Agamemnon, former husband of Helen. He leads the Spartans or Lacedaemonians. The Achaeans venture to Troy to retake Helen and restore Menelaus' pride. Early in the *Iliad*, he fights Paris in single combat.

MERIONES: son of Molus. Meriones is Idomeneus' dear friend and comrade in arms. Next to Idomeneus, he is second in command over the Cretan contingent of men.

NESTOR: son of Neleus, father of Antilochus and Thrasymedes. Wise Nestor leads the men from Pylos. The oldest of the Achaean leaders, he frequently gives counsel during assemblies and at other times to the Achaeans as a whole and to specific individuals. He is enormously proud of his past athletic and military achievements.

ODYSSEUS: son of Laertes, father of Telemachus, husband of Penelope. Odysseus leads the Cephallenians, the men from Ithaca and its neighboring islands. He often serves to spur on the Achaeans throughout the *Iliad*. He is part of the embassy to Achilles and later goes with Diomedes on a recognizance mission to observe the Trojan camp. Odysseus is the chief hero of Homer's *Odyssey*.

PATROCLUS: son of Menoetius. Patroclus ventures to Troy with Achilles, his dear friend and comrade in arms. Fighting in Achilles' original armor, Patroclus battles all the way to the walls of Troy before Apollo, Euphorbus, and Hector kill him.

The Trojans and Trojan Allies

AENEAS: son of the mortal man Anchises and the goddess Aphrodite. He leads the Dardanians and is destined to be the future king of the Trojans. As a result, he is not fated to die in the Trojan War but is saved several times. Virgil, the Roman author of the first century BC epic poem the *Aeneid*, makes Aeneas the forefather of Rome.

ANTENOR: counselor of king Priam. He is in some ways parallel to Nestor of Pylos.

DEIPHOBUS: son of Priam, brother of Hector. The goddess Athena chooses to appear as Deiphobus when she tricks Hector into fighting Achilles.

GLAUCUS: son of Hippolochus. Glaucus is Sarpedon's dear friend and co-leads the Lycians with him. During battle he learns that he is the Achaean Diomedes' guest-friend.

HECTOR: son of Priam and Hecuba, brother of Paris, father of Astyanax (Scamandrius), husband of Andromache. The best of the Trojans, Hector is their chief leader in battle. In addition to many other Achaeans, Hector slays Patroclus (with the help of others). Because of this death, his final act is to fight Achilles, who kills him.

PANDARUS: son of Lycaon. Pandarus leads the Trojans from Zeleia. He fires the arrow that hits Menelaus and breaks the truce between the Achaeans and Trojans. Diomedes eventually kills him.

PARIS (ALEXANDER): son of Priam and Hecuba, brother of Hector, present husband of Helen. After Aphrodite rewards him with Helen, the most beautiful woman in the world, Paris takes Helen from Menelaus and thereby causes the Trojan War. He duels with Menelaus early in the *Iliad*.

POLYDAMAS: son of Panthous. With Hector, Polydamas is second in command over the Trojans. When he advises Hector to retreat behind the walls of Troy, Hector does not listen.

PRIAM: son of Laomedon, father of Hector, Paris, and many others, husband of Hecuba. Priam is the ruler of Troy. Before the Achaean attack some nine years before, Priam and his kingdom were very wealthy and happy. Now, in the tenth year of the war, his kingdom is much reduced. At the end of the *Iliad*, and by command of the gods, Priam goes to retrieve Hector's body from Achilles.

SARPEDON: son of the god Zeus and the mortal woman Laodamia. Sarpedon is the chief leader of the Lycians and friend of Glaucus. He is killed by Patroclus.

Other Men

CHRYSES: priest of Apollo, father of Chryseis. Agamemnon refuses to return his daughter Chryseis to him. Consequently, Chryses prays to Apollo to send a plague on the Achaeans. He ultimately wins Chryseis' return.

Achaean and Trojan Women

ANDROMACHE: wife of Hector, mother of Astyanax. She leads the mourning for Hector when Priam returns with his corpse to Troy.

BRISEIS: woman given to Achilles as an honor-prize. Agamemnon takes her to replace his own lost honor-prize, Chryseis. In the end, he returns her to Achilles. She mourns for Patroclus.

CHRYSEIS: daughter of the priest of Apollo, Chryses. Though she was given to Agamemnon as his honor-prize, her father demands and eventually wins her return.

HECUBA: wife of Priam, mother of Hector. She is the queen of the Trojans.

HELEN: daughter of Zeus (or the mortal man Tyndareus) and Leda, former wife of Menelaus, and present wife of Paris. Her abduction by the Trojan Paris leads to the Achaean invasion of Troy and therefore the Trojan War.

HOMER'S *ILIAD* IN BRIEF
BOOK SUMMARIES

BOOK 1 ▪ ANGER AND FRUSTRATION—ACHILLES & AGAMEMNON, ZEUS & HERA Wrath! Agamemnon refuses to return the battle captive Chryseis to her father Chryses, the priest of Apollo. His refusal causes Apollo, now angry, to cast a plague upon the Achaeans. When Achilles calls on Agamemnon to return the girl in order to appease the god's wrath, Agamemnon agrees. Yet in recompense for his loss, and fuming, he demands Achilles' own honor-prize, Briseis, for himself. In response, Achilles moves to slay him in anger. Although Athena prevents the murder, the goddess doesn't stop Achilles from calling on his divine mother, Thetis, for revenge. Thetis talks to Zeus, who promises to restore her son's honor. To this end the god will help the Trojans against the Achaeans—all contrary to his wife Hera's ardent war objectives. And now Hera is troubled—frustrated! Nevertheless, she can do nothing about it, nothing against Zeus' power and plans. Knowing this, her wise son Hephaestus advises Hera to be gentle with her husband and obey him. And that's what happens. And so it is that the divine feast goes on.

BOOK 2 ▪ TO BATTLE MEN!—THE CATALOGUE OF THE BEST Carrying out his plan to honor Achilles, Zeus sends a dream to Agamemnon. Waking up, Agamemnon calls the men together to test them. Do you want to go home? he asks. We do! they respond—all but for Odysseus and Nestor. They shouldn't go home until each has a Trojan wife to avenge Helen! After feasting, the multitudes assemble by the ships like—as Homer has it—flies around a pail of milk. The poet catalogues the Achaean ships and leaders, offering an extended glory report. He lists various Achaean bests before panning over to the Trojans to do the same.

BOOK 3 ▪ THE BATTLE FOR HELEN—PARIS, MENELAUS & THE CHIEF ACHAEANS The armies line up. Hector schools Paris (Alexander) for shrinking back before Menelaus. In response, Paris suggests single combat with Menelaus. The winner will take Helen and all her wealth. Both sides agree to the proposal, performing pre-combat rites and swearing oaths. Meanwhile, from atop the walls of Troy, Helen introduces Priam to the big actors of the Achaean cast, including Agamemnon, Odysseus, Telamonian Ajax, and Idomeneus. Finally, the two step forward to fight. After throwing spears, Menelaus dashes forward to take hold of Paris. But just as he's dragging him off, Aphrodite spirits Paris away to make love with Helen. Agamemnon assumes the Achaeans have won and will therefore recover Helen, her possessions, and a revenge-penalty to top it off. How wrong he is!

BOOK 4 ▪ THE GODS IN COUNCIL—AGAMEMNON & THE ARMY The gods in council on Mount Olympus consider what to do with the Achaeans and Trojans. Athena is furious with Zeus. Hera and Zeus are at odds. They eventually agree that Troy will fall. This means the Trojans must break the oath they swore before Menelaus and Paris battled. At the prompting of Athena, therefore, Pandarus shoots Menelaus with an arrow. Agamemnon is angry at this, and so he stirs his men to action. The armies clash and many men die.

BOOK 5 ▪ THE RAGING RIVER DIOMEDES—AGAINST MEN & GODS Before withdrawing with Ares from the fight to sit on the banks of the Scamander, Athena assists Diomedes in order to give him glory. The Achaean leaders dominate the Trojans. Diomedes slaughters many and rages over the Trojan army like a swollen winter river. After Pandarus shoots Diomedes with an arrow, and Athena heals him, he fights like a lion. Pandarus wonders if he is a god or a man. Diomedes goes on fighting, slaughtering numerous men, including, eventually, Pandarus himself, who fights from Aeneas' chariot. Next, he slams Aeneas to the ground with a giant stone. Near to death, Aeneas is saved by his mother, Aphrodite. Diomedes' comrade Sthenelus rides away with Aeneas' horses. Finally, Diomedes goes up against the gods Aphrodite, Apollo, and Ares. He wounds Aphrodite, who zips off to her loving mother and the gentle reproach of Zeus. Apollo warns him off. And with the help of Athena, he drives a spear into Ares's stomach. Meanwhile, led on by Hector, the Trojans face the Achaeans, and Agamemnon inspires his men to fight. Zeus scolds his son Ares, who whines to him after being wounded. Paieon heals him.

BOOK 6 ▪ HECTOR RETURNS TO THE CITY—DIOMEDES & GLAUCUS, HECTOR & ANDROMACHE The battle continues. The Trojan warrior Helenus encourages Hector to return to Troy in order to propitiate Athena. While Hector is making his way inside the city walls, Diomedes encounters Glaucus, and they realize they are guest-friends. Within Troy, Hector commands his mother, Hecuba, to offer Athena a gift. She does, but the goddess refuses to be appeased. Otherwise, Hector rebukes Paris for lounging around with Helen. He must fight! he admonishes. Thereafter, he meets up with Andromache and Astyanax atop the Scaean gates. His wife tearfully begs him not to go out again. He must fight, he counters. He holds his son and prays for him. Finally, Hector returns to the battle with Paris.

BOOK 7 ▪ HECTOR FIGHTS TELAMONIAN AJAX—THE TRUCE TO BURY THE DEAD After Hector and Paris go out to fight, the battling finishes for the day with single combat matching Hector and Telamonian Ajax. Night falls and both sides join in assembly. The Trojans ask for a truce to gather and burn the dead. The Achaeans agree, using the opportunity to build a wall and trench around their ships.

BOOK 8 ▪ ZEUS' GREAT MIGHT—THE BACK AND FORTH OF BATTLE Zeus forbids divine participation in the struggle for Troy. The gods are astonished but obey. There are various battles back and forth. The scales of fate favor the Trojans. Many Achaean leaders flee. Hector pursues Nestor and Diomedes. Hera arouses Agamemnon. The Achaean Teucer shoots many Trojan men, and nearly Hector, but Hector first hits him with a stone. The Achaeans fall back once again. Hera and Athena want to help but are not allowed to—Zeus sends Iris to prevent their riding out to battle. When Zeus returns to Olympus, they sulk as he exults in his own strength. He explains what must happen before Achilles returns to battle. As night falls, Hector calls together a Trojan assembly. Their fires burn as stars in the dark sky.

BOOK 9 ▪ THE EMBASSY TO ACHILLES—ODYSSEUS, PHOENIX & TEL-AMONIAN AJAX Nestor reprimands Agamemnon for taking Briseis. Agamemnon admits his foolish behavior and agrees to make things right with Achilles by sending an embassy made up of Odysseus, Phoenix, and Telamonian Ajax, with the offer of many gifts, Briseis, and the hand of one of his own daughters in marriage. Despite the offer of generous compensation, and the speeches of the three ambassadors, Achilles rejects the proposal. He's still angry! Agamemnon treated him like a dishonored homeless man, he explains. The ambassadors return without success.

BOOK 10 ▪ AGAMEMNON'S WORRY—DIOMEDES' MISSION WITH ODYSSEUS Held in the vice-grip of anxiety, Agamemnon cannot sleep. He therefore assembles the chief men. Nestor suggests a reconnaissance mission. Diomedes volunteers, and Odysseus goes along with him. The two capture and slay Dolon who has likewise responded to Hector's request for a spy. They later kill king Rhesus and many other Thracians before racing back to camp.

BOOK 11 ▪ AGAMEMNON'S GLORY—THE ACHAEANS FALL BACK The goddess Strife (Eris) stirs up the Achaeans to fight. Agamemnon fights out front and Homer gives him a glory report. Zeus orders Iris to tell Hector to wait until Agamemnon is wounded. Then it will be his turn to triumph. Finally, Coōn hits Agamemnon, and the Achaean leader retreats, but not before slaying and decapitating Coōn. Now Hector fires up his own men. Homer gives him a glory report as he slaughters many Achaeans. The Trojans wound many others—Diomedes, Eurypylus, Machaon, and Odysseus (who, at one point, is left all alone, though he stands his ground and kills Socus). Menelaus and Telamonian Ajax fly to help Odysseus. Ajax fights and kills many Trojans. Seeing his work of slaughter,

Cebriones and Hector speed over to help them. Achilles sends Patroclus to find out what is happening. Nestor gives him a report. Given the fact that many of the Achaean leaders have been wounded, things are not looking well. He counsels Patroclus to ask Achilles for his consent to fight at the head of the Myrmidons in Achilles' battle gear. Patroclus agrees to this—but first he works to heal Eurypylus.

BOOK 12 • THE TROJANS ATTACK THE WALL—ASIUS & HECTOR, SARPEDON & GLAUCUS Like a whirlwind, Hector and the Trojans work to cross the trench and break through the enemy's wall into the Achaean camp—and this after Polydamas advises Hector to retreat. As for the Achaeans, the two Ajaxes cheer on their fellow warriors. Be men! On the other side, Sarpedon tells Glaucus they must fight. Hector throws a massive stone that bursts the Achaean wall. They're in!

BOOK 13 • THE ACHAEANS FIGHT BACK—IDOMENEUS' GLORY When Zeus glances away from the battle for a moment, Poseidon fires up the Achaeans under various guises. There's fighting back and forth, and Homer sings the Cretan leader, Idomeneus, a glory report. Menelaus prays that the Trojans will be punished. Polydamas advises momentary retreat in order to plan with the other Trojan leaders. But most of them are dead. Ajax taunts Hector. Nevertheless, Hector and his men rush the ships as the Achaeans stand firmly against the onslaught.

BOOK 14 • HERA TRICKS ZEUS—HECTOR FALLS AND THE ACHAEANS ATTACK Nestor ventures out to see what is going on. On the Achaean side, there is word of slipping away at night. Odysseus can't believe Agamemnon's word! Wounded as we are, we must return to the battle! he says. Diomedes advises the wounded leaders to go out and urge everyone on. Poseidon reassures Agamemnon. His superhuman shout rouses the Achaeans. Hera considers how to turn Zeus' attention away from the war. With the help of Aphrodite, she seduces him atop Mount Ida, with the goal of tricking him into falling asleep. He does. Now her side, the Achaeans, can fight. Hector is taken out when Telamonian Ajax hurls a huge anchor stone at him. Now the Trojans are winning! Now the Achaeans! The battle and revenge rages back and forth. Given his speed, Ajax, the son of Oileus, kills the most.

BOOK 15 • THE BATTLE AT THE SHIPS—ZEUS & POSEIDON The Trojans retreat. Zeus wakes up angry, and Hera swears she didn't mean to trick him. He relents and smiles before foretelling what will happen—including Patroclus' and Hector's deaths and the sack of Troy. Hera is afraid. Through the messenger Iris, Zeus orders Poseidon to stop fighting for the Achaeans. Poseidon balks, citing the three equal portions of each brother—the sky, the sea, and the underworld. Apollo heals Hector. The fight goes on, the Trojans advancing. Hector battle rages. He commands his men to set the Achaean ships afire. Ajax urges on the Achaeans.

BOOK 16 • PATROCLUS FIGHTS—TWO HEROES DIE Patroclus chastises Achilles for his anger and asks permission to go out and fight in Achilles' armor. Achilles agrees, but only after he recounts Agamemnon's offensive behavior once more. As they speak, the Trojans finally cast fire upon the Achaean ships. Observing this, Achilles knows it is time to act. He sends Patroclus with the Myrmidons out to fight. Achilles prays to Zeus, but Zeus fulfills only half the prayer—that Patroclus and the rest will push back the Trojans. During the fight, Sarpedon perishes. There's an epic fight for his body before Apollo zips him off to Lycia. As for the other half of the prayer, that Patroclus would return safely, Patroclus dies after scrumming before the city walls. He foretells Hector's death before perishing.

BOOK 17 • THE BATTLE FOR PATROCLUS' BODY—MENELAUS' DILEMMA AND COURAGE Now the struggle is over Patroclus' body. Menelaus stands over it in defense. When he moves off to get help, Hector strips it of Achilles' armor. Ajax arrives to defend it. Apollo spurs on the Trojans and many die. There's a great battle around Patroclus' corpse. The Trojans nearly retreat but for the encouragement of Aeneas. The fight rages on. The attempt is made to capture Achilles' immortal horses. Antilochus is sent to report Patroclus' death to Achilles. The action ends with some of the Achaeans retreating with Patroclus' body in tow, the others battling the Trojans.

BOOK 18 ▪ **ACHILLES' GREAT SORROW AND SHOUT—HEPHAESTUS, THE SHIELD AND ARMOR OF ACHILLES** Achilles learns of Patroclus' death and mourns. Out of his mind with grief, and near to suicide, he vows revenge. But he needs new armor. Thetis speeds off to Olympus to ask Hephaestus to make it. The Trojans nearly retake Patroclus. Hector's goal: his head on a stake! Achilles comes out, and with a goddess-supplemented shout, he drives off the Trojans. Ahhh! The sun sinks and the battle ends for the day. In the Trojan assembly, Polydamas advises retreat. Hector refuses. He'll fight Achilles tomorrow! The Achaeans wash and mourn Patroclus. Achilles promises a hero-sized sendoff, including a great fire, Hector's head, and twelve young Trojan males. Meanwhile, Thetis is sipping nectar with Charis, asking Hephaestus for new armor. He makes it, including Achilles' famous shield.

BOOK 19 ▪ **THE GREAT RECONCILIATION—ACHILLES & AGAMEMNON** Thetis gives Achilles his new shield and the rest of the armor. Achilles "unsays" his anger against Agamemnon. The latter man accepts, declaring that it was not his—Agamemnon's—fault. He claims that divine Bewilderment and other gods made him do it. Nevertheless, he offers Achilles gifts to make up for the wrong done. After admonishing Agamemnon, Odysseus suggests they should feast. Achilles counters, saying they should fight instead. The Achaeans move ahead with Odysseus' plan. They feast and drag in Agamemnon's compensatory gifts, including Briseis, who weeps for Patroclus. When Achilles refuses food, Athena gives him ambrosia and nectar. He likes his new arms. When the immortal horse Xanthus prophesizes his death, he is disturbed. Still, they ride off to fight.

BOOK 20 ▪ **THE GODS FIGHT—ACHILLES FIGHTS AENEAS & HECTOR** The gods assemble, and Zeus gives them permission to fight as they wish. As for Zeus, he will stay and watch the battle from Olympus. Hera, Athena, Poseidon, Hermes, and Hephaestus aid the Achaeans. The Trojans have Ares, Apollo, Artemis, Aphrodite, Leto, and the divine river Xanthus. Achilles encounters Aeneas and fights him until Aeneas is spirited away. Achilles goes on a slaughtering rampage, killing Polydorus, among others. He fights Hector, who is saved by Apollo.

BOOK 21 • ACHILLES AND THE RIVER XANTHUS—AGENOR FACES ACHILLES
Achilles kills so many that the river Xanthus (known to mortals as the Scamander) fills up with corpses, those of Lycaon and Asteropaeus included. The river commands him to stop, but Achilles refuses. Xanthus thus begins to drown Achilles. When he voices concern, Poseidon and Athena assure him that he will not be conquered by the river. Finally, Hera sends Hephaestus to fight and defeat the river—fire against water! He does. The gods battle one another. Priam calls for the gates of Troy to be opened wide. The Trojans flee into the city as Agenor debates whether to stand his ground or flee. He faces Achilles and Apollo saves him.

BOOK 22 • HECTOR BATTLES ACHILLES—ATHENA'S DECEPTION
Priam and Hecuba beg Hector to fight from a safe distance. The Trojan hero debates back and forth in his own mind. Achilles chases him. Disguised as Deiphobus, Athena fools Hector into fighting Achilles. They finally face each other. And after trading taunts, bargaining for and refusing deals, and throwing spears, the Achaean hero kills him by means of a spear through his throat. He strips Hector, glory-boasts over him, and drags him behind his chariot. Witnessing all this from atop Troy's walls, the Trojans mourn their hero—Priam, Hecuba, and Andromache most of all.

BOOK 23 • THE FUNERAL GAMES—THE ACHAEANS MOURN PATROCLUS
Patroclus appears to Achilles while he is sleeping. Though his friend speaks to him, Achilles cannot touch him. The Myrmidons mourn the loss of Patroclus, honoring him, sending him off with a great funeral pyre. Achilles holds funeral games in honor of

him: a chariot race, boxing, wrestling, a footrace, single armed combat, the iron-weight throw, archery, and a spear throw. Prizes are distributed after each contest. Antilochus reconciles with Menelaus after wronging him.

BOOK 24 ▪ PRIAM MEETS ACHILLES—HECTOR'S BODY Achilles can't sleep. He abuses Hector's body by dragging it in honor of Patroclus. Although Apollo protects the body, many of the gods are upset about Achilles' behavior. They pity Hector. They want Hermes to get his body by stealing it. Zeus, however, through Thetis, arranges it so that Achilles will give up the body to Priam for a ransom. Iris informs Priam of the plan, and he, contrary to Hecuba's wishes, goes to fetch the corpse of his dead son. He is escorted by Hermes in the form of a young prince. Achilles and Priam mourn together; they admire each other. After he agrees to return him, the Achaean hero promises enough time to bury Hector before the two sides fight again. Once Priam returns to Troy, the Trojans mourn Hector, burn his corpse, and make for him a funeral mound with stones.

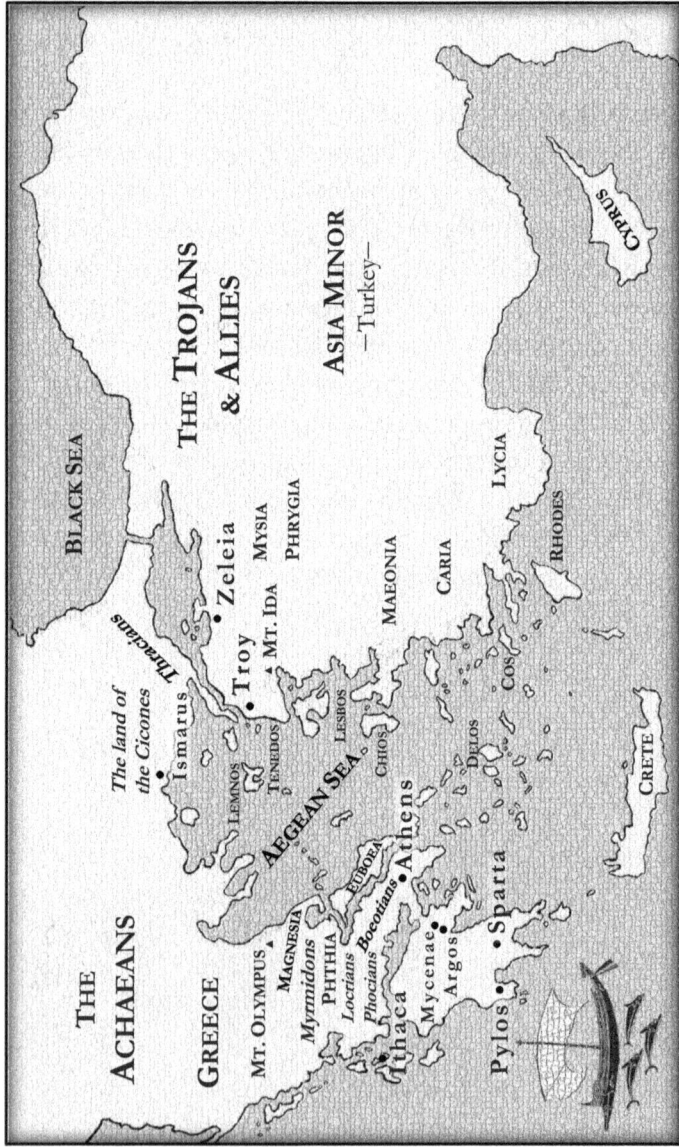

The Warring Sides of the Trojan War (Map 1)

The Achaeans were generally from what we call Greece today and the western portion of the Aegean Sea. Exceptions include those contingents from Crete, Rhodes, and Cos. The Trojans and their allies were mostly from what we call Turkey (Asia Minor).

A (Possible[1]) Timeline

OF THE *ILIAD*

DAY 1 (BOOK 1): Apollo's priest, Chryses, asks Agamemnon to return his daughter and Agamemnon's honor-prize, Chryseis, for a ransom. When the Achaean leader refuses, Chryses asks Apollo to cast a plague upon the Achaeans. The god does.

DAYS 2-9 (BOOK 1 continued): The plague persists, killing many of the Achaean men and animals.

DAY 9 (BOOK 1 continued): Zeus and the other gods journey to the far land of the Ethiopians to feast with them.

DAY 10 (BOOK 1 continued): After nine days of Apollo's plague, Agamemnon and Achilles quarrel. The occasion: Achilles calls for the Achaean assembly during which the seer Calchas ties Apollo's anger and subsequent plague to Agamemnon's refusal to return Chryseis.

Upon hearing Calchas, Agamemnon is angry! Still, he agrees to return Chryseis back to her father. To make up for his loss, though, he threatens to take the honor-prize of another Achaean and settles on Achilles' Briseis.

The threat enrages Achilles! Nevertheless, Agamemnon eventually commands two henchmen to take her.

While Agamemnon sends a mission off to Chryse to return Chryseis and appease Apollo with sacrifice, Achilles complains to his mother Thetis and requests that she ask Zeus to do something to honor him. She agrees to go but says the gods will be gone feasting with the Ethiopians for another eleven days.

DAY 11 (BOOK 1 continued): The men on mission to give back Chryseis and offer a holocaust offering to placate Apollo return.

DAYS 12-20 (BOOK 1 continued): Achilles stokes his anger, refusing to participate in the Achaean assembly or any of the fighting.

DAY 21 (BOOK 1 continued): Thetis goes to visit Zeus after he and the other gods return from feasting with the Ethiopians.[2] She asks him to honor Achilles. Led by Hera, the gods nearly quarrel with

Zeus. But in the end, thanks to Hephaestus' counsel, they feast and go off to sleep.

DAY 22 (BOOK 2): Agamemnon cannot sleep (during the night prior to and early morning of Day 22). Zeus sends him the Nestor-dream. He wakes up, and after meeting with the chief Achaean leaders, he gathers all the army together.

(BOOK 3) The Achaean army marches out to battle the Trojan army. Under the conditions of a sworn truce, Paris fights Menelaus in single combat. Nearly defeated, Paris is spirited away by Aphrodite. Agamemnon claims victory for the Achaeans.

(BOOK 4) Thanks to the decision of the gods in council, Pandarus shoots Menelaus with an arrow, thereby breaking the sworn truce. The Achaeans and Trojans fight.

(BOOK 5) Diomedes ferociously battles against men and gods, giving Homer the opportunity to sing him a glory report (*aristeia*). He wounds Aphrodite after the goddess rescues Aeneas.

(BOOK 6) Hector returns to Troy. He briefly visits his mother and Helen before saying goodbye to his son, Astyanax (Scamandrius), and his wife, Andromache. Diomedes and Glaucus nearly fight before they realize they are guest-friends.

(BOOK 7) The battle continues. After challenging him, Hector duels with Telamonian Ajax. They finally break off with no victor, bringing an end to the day of battle in obedience to night. The Achaeans and the Trojans gather in their respective assemblies, and the Achaeans accept the Trojan request for a truce in order to gather and bury the dead.

DAY 23 (BOOK 7 continued): Early in the morning, the Achaeans and Trojans gather and wash the dead. The Trojans burn their dead and return to Troy. The Achaeans do the same, piling up a mound over the dead. Afterwards, they build the wall and dig the trench that surrounds their camp. Poseidon is not happy with this because they failed to honor the gods. The Achaeans and Trojans feast and sleep.

DAY 24 (BOOK 8): Zeus forbids divine participation in the on-going struggle for Troy. Many of the gods are not pleased with this command. The Achaeans and Trojans battle back and forth.

Teucer shoots many Trojans. As night falls, Hector calls for a Trojan assembly.

(BOOK 9) Meanwhile, in the Achaean camp, Nestor admonishes Agamemnon, who readily admits his blindness and agrees to send men to Achilles in the attempt to make things right. Odysseus, Telamonian Ajax, and Phoenix go but fail to convince Achilles to give up his anger.

(BOOK 10) When Agamemnon cannot sleep due to anxiety over the proximity of the Trojan camp, he assembles the leaders and asks for a volunteer to go spy on the Trojans. Diomedes volunteers and chooses Odysseus to go with him. While out, they apprehend Dolon, who similarly has been sent out by Hector to spy on the Achaeans, and kill him. Using information given by Dolon, the two Achaeans move on to kill the Thracian king, Rhesus, and many of Rhesus' men, before returning to camp early the morning of day 25.

DAY 25 (BOOK 11): The battle goes on. Agamemnon slaughters many Trojans, earning a glory report. He finds success until the Trojan warrior Coōn wounds him; then, after killing Coōn, and experiencing great pain, he retreats. Now, many of the chief Achaeans are wounded—Diomedes, Odysseus, Eurypylus, and Machaon. Achilles sends Patroclus to find out what is happening. He learns from Nestor that the Trojans are advancing.

(BOOK 12) Sarpedon tells Glaucus they must fight. The two Ajaxes cheer their side on. Finally, Hector and the Trojans venture across the trench and break into the Achaean camp.

(BOOK 13) When Zeus glances away from the battle for a moment, Poseidon fires up the Achaeans under different guises. There's fighting back and forth. Cretan Idomeneus earns a glory report. Polydamas advises retreat—again.

(BOOK 14): Despite the desire of many to slip off during the night, Odysseus challenges the Achaean leaders to return to the fight. Hera seduces Zeus, causing him to lose sight of the battle. Telamonian Ajax takes Hector out of the fight for the moment by throwing a massive stone at him. The combat rages back and forth, victory going to one side, then the other.

(BOOK 15) Zeus wakes up, rebukes Hera, orders Poseidon to stop fighting for the Achaeans, and has Apollo revive Hector. Patroclus returns to Achilles to give him a report. Hector battle rages, commanding his men to fire the Achaean ships.

(BOOK 16) The ships burning, Achilles sends his men, the Myrmidons, out to fight alongside his dear friend Patroclus. The latter earns a glory report, slaying Sarpedon among many others. Finally, Patroclus dies before the walls of Troy.

(Book 17) The Trojans and Achaeans fight over Patroclus' body. Hector strips Patroclus of Achilles' armor and takes it for himself.

(Book 18) Achilles learns of Patroclus' death. He vows revenge but cannot fight without armor. Thetis consequently journeys to Olympus to ask the smith god Hephaestus for new armor. With the aid of Athena, Achilles shouts out loud, bringing an end to the day's battle. This end allows the Achaeans to retrieve Patroclus' body, wash it, and mourn him. Polydamas advises retreat. But for a third time, Hector declines, bragging that he will fight Achilles in the morning. While all this is happening on the plain before Troy, Hephaestus is making Achilles' new armor.

DAY 26 (BOOK 19): Thetis gives Achilles his new armor. Achilles and Agamemnon reconcile. After feasting, the Achaeans ride off to fight.

(BOOK 20) The gods assemble, and Zeus gives them permission to join in the battle. They divide into their respective sides. Achilles fights Aeneas until the latter is spirited away. Achilles goes on a slaughtering rampage, including a fight with Hector, during which the Trojan leader is saved by Apollo.

(BOOK 21) Achilles angers Xanthus (the Scamander river) by stopping him up with corpses. The divine river nearly drowns him. Among the various gods that do battle, Hephaestus fights Xanthus, and Athena defeats Ares and Aphrodite. When Achilles drives the Trojans into Troy, a disguised Apollo draws him off so that he cannot enter the city.

(BOOK 22) Achilles slays Hector after a long chase around Troy. Achilles subsequently drags Hector behind his chariot, and the Trojans mourn him—his wife, Andromache, most of all.

(BOOK 23) The Myrmidons mourn Patroclus. That night, Patroclus appears to Achilles as a dream-apparition.

DAY 27 (BOOK 23 continued): The following day, the Myrmidons gather wood, and toward the evening, they burn Patroclus on a great funeral pyre. Thanks to the North and West Winds, the fire burns all night.

Day 28 (Book 23 continued): Achilles holds the funeral games in honor of Patroclus—a chariot race, boxing and wrestling matches, a footrace, single armed combat, the iron weight throw, archery, and a spear throw.

(BOOK 24) The Achaeans feast and sleep after the games, all but for Achilles who cannot sleep as he continues to mourn for Patroclus.

DAY 29 (BOOK 24 continued): Unable to sleep, Achilles rises to drag Hector behind his chariot around Patroclus' funeral mound. Seeing this, the gods pity Hector.

DAYS 30-39 (BOOK 24 continued): Achilles continues to abuse Hector in order to honor Patroclus. As the days go on, Apollo defends Hector's flesh with the golden aegis.

DAY 40 (BOOK 24 continued): On the twelfth day of this abuse, the gods agree to allow Priam to retrieve Hector's corpse for a ransom. Priam goes to Achilles' shelter to ask for the return of his son's body. Achilles agrees, promising to hold back the Achaean army during the time the Trojans are laying Hector to rest. Priam requests eleven days, saying they will fight again on the twelfth day "if they must."[3] After feasting together, Priam stays most of the night at Achilles' bidding.

DAY 41 (BOOK 24 continued): Early in the morning, Priam returns to Troy with Hector's corpse. The Trojans mourn him—Andromache, Hecuba, and Helen, among others. The people begin gathering wood for a funeral pyre.

DAYS 42-49 (BOOK 24 continued): The Trojans continue to mourn Hector and to gather wood for his funeral pyre.

DAY 50 (BOOK 24 continued): The Trojans burn Hector atop a great funeral pyre.

DAY 51 (BOOK 24 continued): The Trojans gather Hector's bones and place them in an urn. They stack rocks around the urn and pile a mound over his grave. After, they station lookouts to watch for an Achaean attack while they feast in Priam's halls to honor Hector. So ends the *Iliad*.

NOTES

[1] Possible because it all depends on how one reads Homer in several places, and, therefore, on how one counts the days. That admitted, the above chronology will give the reader a good idea of how the events of the *Iliad* play out even if the precise count is not exact.

[2] Homer gives the time of return as twelve dawns after leaving—so day 20 or 21 of the *Iliad* depending on how the "twelfth dawn" is counted.

[3] What would be Day 52.

GLOSSARY

OF ENGLISH WORDS AND GREEK EQUIVALENTS
THAT APPEAR IN HOMER'S *ILIAD*

Ageless: *agēraos* (ἀγήραος).

Assembly; an assembly of the people; the place of assembly: *agora* (ἀγορά).

Anger: *cholos* (χόλος).

To **be angry**: *choloō* (χολόω).

To **apportion**, divide, share, distribute: *moiraō* (μοιράω).

Bad; worthless, ignoble; evil: *kakos* (κακός).

Battle, combat, fight: *machē* (μάχη). To battle, fight: *machomai* (μάχομαι).

Best, most excellent: *aristos* (ἄριστος).

Beautiful, fair; noble: *kalos* (καλός).

Bewilderment; blindness; infatuation; the blindness sent by the gods; bewilderment personified: *atē* or *Atē* (ἄτη).

Blameless, excellent: *amumōn* (ἀμύμων).

Bravest, best: *phertatos* (φέρτατος).

Blessed, happy: *makar* (μάκαρ).

Care, trouble, sorrow: *kēdos* (κῆδος).

Comrade, friend; companion in arms: *hetairos* (ἑταῖρος).

To **conquer**: *damazō* (δαμάζω).

Courage, confidence, boldness, audacity: *tharsos* (θάρσος).

Counsel: *boulē* (βουλή).

To hold **counsel**, deliberate: *bouleuō* (βουλεύω).

Cowardly; vile, worthless; miserable, luckless, wretched: *deilos* (δειλός).

Cowardice; evil, wickedness: *kakotēs* (κακότης).

Dear (dear one), friend, beloved: *philos* (φίλος).

Death (allotted time of); fate, fate as death; that which befalls one, one's lot: *potmos* (πότμος).

To **delight**, enjoy, take pleasure in: *terpō* (τέρπω).

Desire: *eros* (ἔρος).

To **desire eagerly**: *menoinaō* (μενοινάω).

Destruction, ruin: *olethros* (ὄλεθρος).

Doom, lot, fate: *moros* (μόρος). To be doomed to a sad or dreadful end: *ainomoros* (αἰνόμορος).

Drug, medicine: *pharmakon* (φάρμακον).

To **endure**: *tlaō* (τλάω) or *tolmaō* (τολμάω).

Enemy, hostile (man): *dusmenēs* (δυσμενής).

Evil, wickedness; cowardice: *kakotēs* (κακότης).

Excellence (esp. manly excellence); valor, prowess; goodness, virtue: *aretē* (ἀρετή).

Fate (personified); fate, portion: *Moira* or *moira* (μοῖρα).

Feast: *daitē* (δαίτη).

Food; grain; bread; meat: *sitos* (σῖτος) or *eidar* (εἶδαρ).

Freedom: *eleutheros* (ἐλεύθερος).

Friend, guest-friend, stranger: *xenos* (ξένος). **Dear one**, friend: *philos* (φίλος).

Girl; maiden: *korē* (κόρη).

Glory, fame; report; reputation: *kleos* (κλέος). **Glory report**: *aristeia* (ἀριστεῖα) (though this term does not appear in Homer).

Glory: *kudos* (κῦδος).

Glory-boast, the boast: *euchos* (εὖχος).

God: *theos* (θεός).

Good; noble, brave: *agathos* (ἀγαθός) or *esthlos* (ἐσθλός).

Great-hearted, high-hearted, high-spirited: *megathumos* (μεγάθυμος).

Happiness, fortune, riches: *olbos* (ὄλβος).

Happy, blessed: *olbios* (ὄλβιος).

Homeless; wanderer: *metanastēs* (μετανάστης).

Honor: *timē* (τιμή).

Honor-prize, gift of honor; right, privilege, prerogative: *geras* (γέρας).

Honor: *timē* (τιμή); to **honor**, prize, deem worthy: *timaō* (τιμάω).

Horse: *hippos* (ἵππος).

Horseman; driver of horses: *hippotēs* (ἱππότης).

Human being; man: *anthrōpos* (ἄνθρωπος).

Illustrious, glorious: *klutos* (κλυτός).

Immortal, undying; everlasting: *athanatos* (ἀθάνατος). The immortals (the gods): *athanatoi* (ἀθάνατοι).

Inferior, worse: *cheirōn* (χείρων).

Insolence, arrogance: *hubris* (ὕβρις).

King, chief; prince: *basileus* (βασιλεύς).

Life; soul, spirit: *psychē* or *psuchē* (ψυχή).

Lord, master: *anax* (ἄναξ).

Lover of property; greedy for gain: *philokteanos* (φιλοκτέανος).

Man: *anēr* (ἀνήρ).

Meat: *kreas* (κρέας).

Mortal; liable to death: *thnētos* (θνητός).

A **mortal human being**: *brotos* (βροτός).

Necessity, constraint: *anankē* (ἀνάγκη).

Pain of body or mind: *algos* (ἄλγος).

To **plunder**: *perthō* (πέρθω).

Portion, fate: *moira* (μοῖρα).

Power, strength, ability: *dynamis* or *dunamis* (δύναμις).

Prize: *athlon* (ἄθλον).

Property or possessions: *ktēma* (κτῆμα).

To **rejoice**: *gētheō* (γηθέω).

Reputation: *kleos* (κλέος).

Return home, return homeward; travel, journey: *nostos* (νόστος).

To take **revenge** or **vengeance**; to pay a price: *tinō* (τίνω).

To **school**, upbraid: *neikeō* (νεικέω).

Shame: *aidōs* (αἰδώς).

The **shame** done one; disgrace, dishonor; ugly: *aischros* (αἰσχρός).
   To make **ugly**, disfigure; to be dishonored; to feel ashamed or
   feel shame: *aischunō* (αἰσχύνω).

Shelter; hut, cabin; a place for laying down: *klisia* (κλισία).

Shepherd (of men): *poimēn* (ποιμήν).

Shield: *aspis* (ἀσπίς).

Ship: *naus* (ναῦς).

Sleep: *hypnos* or *hupnos* (ὕπνος).

Soul; life, breath, spirit, phantom-life: *psychē* or *psuchē* (ψυχή).

Spear: *doru* (δόρυ).

Spirit, passion, desire for something: *thumos* (θυμός).

Strength, power, might: *bia* (βία).

Strength, vigor, courage: *kartos* (κάρτος).

Strife, a quarrel, contention: *eris* (ἔρις)

To **strip** (the dead): *sulaō* (συλάω).

Suffering; misery: *pēma* (πῆμα). To **suffer**, toil: *mogeō* (μογέω).

To **take**, seize, and slay: *haireō* (αἱρέω).

Unhappy, miserable: *dustēnos* (δύστηνος).

Victory: *nikē* (νίκη).

To **be victorious**: *nikaō* (νικάω).

Wealth, riches: *ploutos* (πλοῦτος).

Wine: *oinos* (οἶνος).

Wrath: *mēnis* (μῆνις).

Wretched, unhappy: *deilos* (δειλός).

SOURCES AND FURTHER READING

This Classics Cave rendition of Homer's *Iliad* was made using the critical edition of D.B. Monro and T.W. Allen (*Homeri Opera*, vols. I-II, Oxford: Oxford University Press, 1920), as well as the Greek texts and other immensely helpful tools found online at the Perseus Digital Library (www.perseus.tufts.edu), The Chicago Homer (http://homer.library.northwestern.edu/html/application.html), and elsewhere.

Otherwise, the Cave checked its own version of the *Iliad* against many other translations, new and old, including that of George Chapman (1616), Alexander Pope's early eighteenth-century version in heroic couplets, Samuel Butler's late Victorian translation (1898), and the more recent versions of Richmond Lattimore (1951), A.T. Murray and William F. Wyatt (the Loeb version, 1924), Robert Fagles (1990), and Stanley Lombardo (2000), which all have their strengths and weaknesses. Where the translations of the *Iliad* in the public domain were suitable, The Classics Cave occasionally made use of them with little to no alteration.

OTHER ANCIENT LITERATURE RELATED TO HOMER OR THE EPIC CYCLE

Greek Epic Fragments: From the Seventh to the Fifth Centuries BC. Edited and translated by Martin L. West. Cambridge: Harvard University Press, 2003.

Homeric Hymns, Homeric Apocrypha, Lives of Homer. Edited and translated by Martin L. West. Cambridge: Harvard University Press, 2003.

FURTHER READING

Adkins, A.W.H. *Moral Values and Political Behavior in Ancient Greece: From Homer to the End of the Fifth Century*. New York: W.W. Norton & Company, 1972.

Alexander, Caroline. *The War that Killed Achilles: The True Story of the Iliad*. London: Faber and Faber, 2010.

Anderson, Øivind. "Happiness in Homer." Symbolae Osloensis 85, no. 1: 2-16. *Academic Search Complete*, EBSCOhost (accessed May 25, 2015).

Boardman, John, Jasper Griffin, and Oswyn Murray. *The Oxford History of Greece and the Hellenistic World*. Oxford: Oxford University Press, 2001.

Bowra, C.M. *Homer*. London: Gerald Duckworth & Company, Ltd., 1972.

Burkert, Walter. *Greek Religion*. Translated by John Raffan. Cambridge: Harvard University Press, 1985.

Finkelberg, Margalit. *Greeks and Pre-Greeks: Aegean Prehistory and Greek Heroic Tradition*. Cambridge: Cambridge University Press, 2007.

Finley, M.I. *The World of Odysseus*. New York: New York Review of Books with Viking Penguin, 1982.

Fowler, Robert, ed. *The Cambridge Guide to Homer*. Cambridge: Cambridge University Press, 2004.

Gere, Cathy. *The Tomb of Agamemnon*. London: Profile Books, 2007.

Grant, Michael. *The Rise of the Greeks*. New York: Charles Scribner's Sons, 1988.

Greene, William Chase. *Moira: Fate, Good, and Evil in Greek Thought*. New York: Harper Torchbooks, 1963. (Originally published by Harvard University Press, 1944.)

Hall, Jonathan M. *A History of the Archaic Greek World ca. 1200-479 BCE*. Malden: Blackwell Publishing, 2007.

Jenkyns, Richard. *Classical Literature: An Epic Journey from Homer to Virgil and Beyond*. New York: Basic Books, 2016.

Kirk, G.S. *The Songs of Homer*. Cambridge: Cambridge University Press, 1962.

Lendon, J.E. *Soldiers and Ghosts: A History of Battle in Classical Antiquity*. New Haven: Yale University Press, 2005.

Lesky, Albin. *A History of Greek Literature*. Translated by Cornelis de Heer and James Willes. Indianapolis: Hackett Publishing Company, 1996.

Martin, Thomas R. *Ancient Greece: From Prehistoric to Hellenistic Times*. New Haven: Yale University Press, 1996.

McAuslan, Ian, and Peter Walcot, eds. *Homer (Greece & Rome Studies IV)*. Oxford: Oxford University Press, 1998.

Morford, P.O. Mark, and Robert J. Lenardon. *Classical Mythology*. 4th ed. New York: Longman Publishing Group, 1991.

Nagy, Gregory. *The Best of the Achaeans: Concepts of the Hero in Archaic Greek Poetry*. Rev. ed. Baltimore: The Johns Hopkins University Press, 1999.

———. *The Ancient Greek Hero in 24 Hours*. Cambridge: Harvard University Press, 2013.

Nicolson, Adam. *Why Homer Matters*. New York: Picador, 2014.

Parry, M. *The Making of Homeric Verse: The Collected Papers*. Oxford: Oxford University Press, 1971.

Redfield, James M. *Nature and Culture in the Iliad: The Tragedy of Hector*. Expanded edition. Durham: Duke University Press, 1994.

Rohde, Erwin. *Psyche: The Cult of Souls and Belief in Immortality among the Greeks*. 2 vols. Translated by W.B. Hillis. New York: Harper Torchbooks, 1966.

Schofield, Louise. *The Mycenaeans*. London: The British Museum Press, 2007.

Snodgrass, Anthony. *Homer and the Artists: Text and Picture in Early Greek Art*. Cambridge: Cambridge University Press, 1998.

Strauss, Barry. *The Trojan War: A New History*. New York: Simon and Schuster, 2006.

Weil, Simone. *The Iliad: or The Poem of Force*. Wallingford: Pendle Hill, 2003.

West, Martin L. *Indo-European Poetry and Myth*. Oxford: Oxford University Press, 2007.

———. *The East Face of Helicon: West Asiatic Elements in Greek Poetry and Myth*. Oxford: Oxford University Press, 1997.

Whitman, Cedric H. *Homer and the Heroic Tradition*. New York: W.W. Norton & Company, 1965.

Willcock, Malcolm M. *A Companion to the Iliad: Based on the Translation by Richmond Lattimore*. Chicago: The University of Chicago Press, 1976.

Young, Tim J. *A Hero's Wish: What Homer Believed about Happiness and the Good Life.* Sugar Land: EuZōn Media, 2015.

Zanker, G. *The Heart of Achilles: Characterization and Ethics in the Iliad.* Ann Arbor: University of Michigan Press, 1994.

Will you help the Cave? Here's how . . .

- **Buy** a book. **Join** a club. **Sponsor** the Cave. **Give** a donation.
- **Talk** to friends and family about Cave books and the free online Cave content at the Cave (www.theclassicscave.com).
- Leave a **positive review** online—if possible, **five stars** with a **brief remark** about what you liked. This truly helps!
- **Write us** at contact@theclassicscave.com to let us know how you've benefited from our work. This inspires us to do more!

THE CLASSICS CAVE is a small, shoestring operation, on fire to spread the wisdom and ways of ancient Greek literature. We **rely on you**, the friend of the Cave, to let people know how you liked and benefited from what we're doing. We also **depend on you** to **improve our books**. Did you see something that requires editing? Something we got wrong? Something we need to add? Despite our great effort and care to get everything right, it happens. So please **let us know** by emailing us at contact@theclassicscave.com. Otherwise, **visit** the Cave to benefit from our ever-growing collection of free online content at www.theclassicscave.com. And don't forget to **support our mission** to spread the wisdom and ways of ancient Greek literature by **buying** and **reading** Cave Books, **enjoying** Cave Gear, **joining** The BAGL Club or AAGS, or by **sponsoring** or **giving** to the Cave. **Thanks!**

Read and enjoy more from **Homer**!

If you benefited from reading *The Best of Homer's Iliad*, you may wish to pick up another Cave book related to Homer. There are many now available or in the works.

Visit the Cave at . . .

www.theclassicscave.com

www.theclassicscave.com